MOTORING THROUGH THE YEARS

MOTORING
THROUGH
THE
YEARS

National Benzole Company Ltd

PUBLISHED 1969
in Great Britain
by
National Benzole Company Ltd.
3 Savoy Place Victoria Embankment
London WC2

CONTENTS

PREFACE

The story of motoring combines a nostalgia for the past and an understanding of the present which appeals particularly to the British. This attitude embraces a respect for what has gone before — witness our tender regard for the veteran and vintage models of yesteryear — and a recognition of what the motor car offers now and will offer in the future.

This is an attitude which is shared by National Benzole, which this month marks the 50th anniversary of its foundation on February 1, 1919. Though one may have a sentimental attachment for the days of two-gallon cans and uncertain journeys, there should be appreciation of the modern car and those that serve it.

Over the past half century, the technical progress and increased use of road vehicles have been matched by the steady improvement of the fuels they require. Throughout this period National Benzole can justly claim to have been in the forefront of this advance and a leader in the development of marketing techniques.

This book shows how today's motor cars are derived from the models of 1919, though the cars at the turn of the century are scarcely recognisable as both their predecessors.

In its major evolution over only a little more than a man's lifetime, the motor car has helped to change the pattern of our lives more than any other product of our century, and National Benzole's 50th anniversary book relates the fascinating story since its tentative beginnings.

National Benzole and its dealers, who have met the needs of the motor vehicle and the car industry over the past half century, are proud of the part which they play in this story.

February 1969

National Benzole Company Ltd, London

The "Scarabeo" experimental saloon built by OSI of Turin and based on the Alfa Romeo "Giulia 1600". It has a transverse engine, four carburettors and all-round independent suspension — one of the world's present-day dream cars. In less than a century, the motor car has progressed from angular freak to a masterpiece of shape and design.

CHAPTER ONE
THE ANCIENT DREAM

The dream of the motor car, of the "horseless carriage", self-propelled and capable of extraordinary speeds, is perhaps as old as man himself. Even if this book were limited to the story of the car as we know it today, we have to go a long way back through the centuries to find the first signs of what was to become one of the greatest adventures in the history of man.

A 1915 Buick "dream car".

Some people have even identified the first hints of the history of the car in Homer's Iliad — to be precise in the section in which are described the fantastic creations built by Vulcan in preparation for the Council of the Gods, among which was a magic wheel of solid gold which obeyed the gods' commands. Others have found indications of what was in future to become the motor car in the prophecies of Nahum and Ezekiel in the Old Testament, in which are described marvellous carriages capable of self-propulsion along the roads, and fantastic mechanical monsters which were perhaps even able to fly.

Traces of legends probably originating from these prophecies are also found in Greek and Roman bas-reliefs, showing mythical chariots drawn by invisible horsemen.

Jet of steam

Ideas rather more technical and somewhat less fantastic are first encountered in the studies of Hero of Alexandria, who describes a machine of his own invention which moved under its own power by means of a device — a hollow sphere out of which was expelled a strong jet of steam — which seems in some ways to anticipate the modern jet engine.

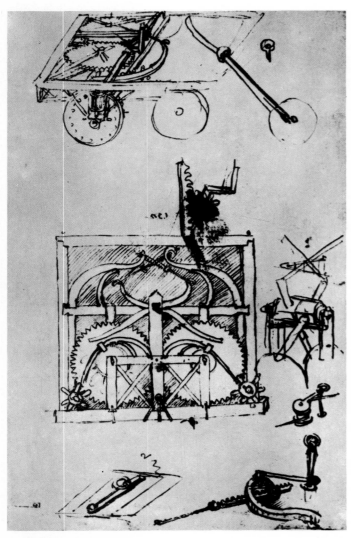

Leonardo da Vinci's self propelled cart (from the Codex Atlanticus).

The first truly self-propelled vehicles however, probably date from the time of Alexander the Great, when in man-to-man wars terrifying chariots were introduced, bristling with scythes and lances. Depending on gravity, these were hurled down steep slopes against the enemy ranks. Such weapons were to be re-invented in the Middle Ages, and used with great effect by the Swiss in their battles against the Austrian overlords.

Valturio's wind-driven machine

It has been held by some people that the motor car was invented by Roger Bacon.

Even if untrue, the unique gifts of prophecy of this great 13th century scientist and philosopher must be recognised. Bacon, in fact, wrote the following, "One day we shall construct machines capable of propelling large ships at a speed far superior to that of an entire crew of oarsmen and needing only a pilot to steer them. One day we shall endow chariots with incredible speed without the aid of any animal. One day we shall construct winged machines able to lift themselves into the air like birds". Such farsighted forecasts could only arouse

suspicion in those times, and Bacon spent ten years of his life in prison, accused of magic and of pacts with the devil. The treatise containing the above passage was not published until three hundred years after his death. In 1472 Robert Valturio described a vehicle designed for use in war which drew power for its movements from large windmill sails, transmitted through a mechanism of cranks and gears. This was no more a practical proposition than many other devices studied and described at that time, all of them characterised by a total, and understandable, lack of consideration for the effects of friction. Some of these mechanisms were intended to use the muscular power of their passengers. Leonardo da Vinci, among others, occupied himself with such a design.

All these devices, powered by other than thermal or chemical energy, constitute a chapter of their own in the story of technical development.

A clockwork vehicle

Among them figured a marvellous machine built in 1649 by the German Johannes Hautsch, of Nuremberg, a vehicle whose bodywork was in the form of a dragon. A number of men concealed in the interior constituted the "engine" and the device so aroused the enthusiasm of the Crown Prince of Sweden that he bought it.

In 1748 another strange vehicle appeared, built by

Leonardo — sketch for a vehicle powered by a falling weight.

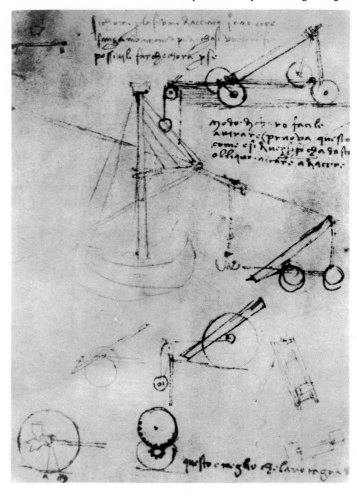

Roberto Valturio's wind-driven machine.

the Frenchman, Jacques de Vaucanson. He modified a 58-year-old design by his fellow countryman Richard, who had the idea of using a series of steel springs similar to those used in church clocks. A chronicler of the time reports "The driver was able to set the carriage in motion or to stop it without horses". The monarch congratulated the ingenious inventor and ordered a similar machine for his own use, to be added to the royal stables. The Duke of Montmar, the Baron of Avenac and the Count of Bauzum, who saw the experiment, could hardly believe their eyes. In spite of this, various members of the Académie Française issued a statement that such a vehicle would never be able to travel the roads of any city.

Mounted boiler

It cannot be said that this pessimistic opinion was wrong. The defect however was certainly not in the concept of a self-propelled vehicle, but in the means chosen to power it, as history was to demonstrate.
But the time has come to consider the first powered vehicle in which men tried to harness the hidden forces of nature. The first man to consider using steam for propelling a carriage was probably Giovanni Battista Della Porta, an Italian scientist from Pesaro, who in 1589 invented a pump capable of raising water by means of steam pressure. He actually suggested the possibility of using such a mechanism for locomotion. Later how-

ever, when his pupil, Solomon de Caous, tried to put this idea into practice, the experiment aroused such alarm among the French clergy that the man was put in a lunatic asylum.
It was to be another Italian, Giovanni Branca, who was to turn the efforts of Della Porta and Caous into reality, building the first practical steam engine. The principle of this engine was, of course, simple — steam produced by a boiler passed through a nozzle and struck holes bored around the circumference of a wheel. Thus the wheel turned, and through a train of gears caused the alternate raising of two weighted arms. In this way the ingenious inventor succeeded in replacing the manual labour necessary to use a pharmacist's mortar.
A new chapter in the long story of the predecessors of the motor car derives from the experiments of Fernando Verbiest, a Jesuit missionary in China, who succeeded in building a model vehicle which actually worked. It was powered by steam produced in a boiler mounted in the carriage. In this case, too, the principle was of a perforated wheel moved by steam pressure, which transmitted motion through a gear train to the front wheels (it was a four-wheeler).

Principle of reaction

The name of Sir Isaac Newton is often mentioned as one of the pioneers if not the outright inventor of the idea of steam jet propulsion. But this does not seem

Newton's idea — a vehicle driven by a crude reaction engine.

to survive the light of a close examination and, in fact, probably arises from a surprising misunderstanding. In one of Newton's texts, published during the author's lifetime, there is a drawing of a carriage moved by steam. In this drawing is seen a boiler installed in a crude wheeled chassis, with a nozzle connected directly to the boiler itself and directed to the rear of the vehicle. It now seems certain that this drawing was meant to be only a visual illustration of the principle of reaction and does not represent a design for steam locomotion. It is just possible that from this drawing, most likely by an unknown draughtsman, was born the idea of the steam driven vehicle which was to have such a vigorous growth particularly in Great Britain — the home of every practicable invention for the use of steam. It is necessary to say at once, however, that the inventor and constructor of the first true steam-driven vehicle was not English but French — Captain Nicolas Joseph Cugnot, builder of a tractor for towing artillery. This is rightly considered a milestone in the prehistory of the motor car.

Secret trials

A separate description of Cugnot's powerful vehicle and its characteristics and performance, somewhat laughable to-day but certainly revolutionary in its time, is alongside. It is important to note that Cugnot's studies certainly derived from the earlier invention of the Englishman Thomas Savery, who in 1698 had produced a somewhat complicated machine powered by steam energy and capable of raising a substantial quantity of water by means of what may be called a crude steel lung. The machine was actually built to pump the water which continually seeped in through the underground seams of a coal mine and it worked satisfactorily until it eventually blew up. Savery's steam engine was improved by another Englishman, Thomas Newcomen, who was the first of these

pioneers to design a version for locomotion. It concerned a simple railway for the transport of coal inside the mine, but was never actually built. It was to be the great physicist James Watt who was to apply himself, beginning in 1765, to the scientific study of the application of the steam engine (for which he had in the meantime designed important improvements) to the movement of road vehicles. Watt did not carry forward his studies to a practical conclusion.

He was heavily engaged in the large-scale production of stationary steam engines for the mechanisation of the textile industry which was in rapid development at the time.

It was one of his competitors, the London merchant Francis Moore, and one of his keen supporters, his own workshop manager, William Murdoch who were to make positive steps along the way to the steam road carriage. It was the same path that Cugnot was treading in France at the same time. Moore succeeded in building a vehicle of this kind and demonstrated it in front of the King, obtaining the royal approval. Later however he disappeared from the scene, probably due to Watt's lively protests in which he maintained that Moore had infringed his patents. As for Murdoch, he at first conducted all his experiments secretly by night, probably to keep them secret from his employer. The matter became public knowledge due to accidents during the first trials on the deserted roads. Thus, in a short time, everyone knew of his vehicle which, however, was never to become more than an interesting curiosity and was to end up in the British Museum.

Londoners' joy-rides

This chapter in the story of the ancestors of the motor car now contains a list of names, all British, of engineers responsible for an ever improving series of steam vehicles. Among the first was William Symington, who

STEAM GOES TO WAR

Nicolas Joseph Cugnot's artillery tractor is perhaps the most important vehicle in the whole history of the motor car. It is generally accepted as being the first vehicle capable of self-propulsion that man constructed, excluding all those carriages built at various times which achieved short journeys by rolling down slopes, by muscular force applied directly or stored in springs, or by means of atmospheric phenomena.

Mammoth tricycle

Its inventor, a Captain of French artillery, had unusual ability considering the small progress made with mechanisms using steam power at the time when, about 1763, he began to study the possibility of experimenting with a means of locomotion. The most credible reconstruction of his studies — there are few documents — maintains that around 1765 Cugnot had already finished a steam vehicle capable of carrying four passengers at a speed of around two miles per hour. Having the idea of using the principles of this extraordinary vehicle for towing heavy artillery pieces, he obtained permission from the then Minister of War, the Marquis of Choiseul, to conduct the necessary experiments.

No trace remains of the vehicle and it is not known if the large, heavy, self-propelled carriage which came out of these experiments and which can be seen today partially rebuilt in the Conservatoire des Arts et Métiers in Paris, was constructed like its predecessor in the engineering workshop of Brézin at Brussels. It is certain, however, that its construction was made possible by a device for machining cannon bores which the French General Gribeauval had invented and built a short time before and which made possible the construction of precision cylinders for Cugnot's carriage. This had not been previously possible.

Towards the end of 1769 or in 1770 the mammoth brainchild of the ingenious officer was ready. It consisted of a huge tricycle entirely built of wood, over the front of which was cantilevered a double-walled boiler, with the fire grate in the space between the inner and outer vessels. It was connected by a copper tube to two vertical cylinders which received steam under pressure. Inside the cylinders slid pistons connected through two conrods and two cranks to the single, powered front wheel for steering. It is not known exactly how the transmission functioned, because the reconstruction of the model preserved in Paris would not work; some component has apparently been lost.

Economic crisis

Things must have been different at the time however, for the first trials held at Vincennes in the presence of a number of high ranking officers were successful. Some time afterwards this monster, which could tow five tons and travel at three miles per hour, ran into and demolished a wall, turning itself over. This unfortunate accident discouraged the Minister who, faced with the economic crisis which preceded the French Revolution, withdrew the funds necessary for Cugnot to continue his experiments. No more was heard of the historic machine and the new regime was not favourably inclined towards the inventor, from whom it even withdrew the pension of 600 francs awarded to him by the royal government. In the end, Cugnot died unknown in Brussels in 1804.

Cugnot's artillery tractor.

built a vehicle very similar to Murdoch's. This carriage created an understandable curiosity, some enthusiasm and a considerable dose of fear among the inhabitants of 18th century England. Then followed Richard Trevithick, an enthusiastic inventor, who among the activities was to build the first vehicle to run on rails (designed to carry coal in the Pen y Darren mine in Wales), and the first steam threshing machine.

Trevithick built between 1796 and 1801 various tricycles for the transport of small goods and in 1802 the first vehicle for passenger transport. He built, in fact, a new mechanical carriage weighing all of eight tons, with which he organised public shows within a circular arena where the more spirited spectators could race the puffing monster in return for a small payment. The machine, which could do 10 m.p.h. on the level and 3½ m.p.h. up a hill, was adapted for towing horseless carriages for Londoners' joy-rides. They were however, quick to forget this great engineer when, ill and misunderstood, Trevithick was refused a grant in recognition of his ability. He died in solitude in 1833.

Era of the steam coach

Parallel with the development of the first British steam vehicles, the prehistory of the motor car records somewhat similar development in America where, however, the different state of the road network directed the inventors more towards marine applications of the steam engine. The reports of this pioneering period contain the names of Nathan Read of Brompton, who designed a particularly advanced engine with a view to road vehicle application, and of John Fitch who founded the first company to build steam engines although none went into production.

Oliver Evans, a keen scientist and Pennsylvania businessman, spent a large part of his life fighting the ignorance of his contemporaries in order to obtain the right to patent his steam engine for road propulsion and for the mechanisation of flour milling. Among other achievements, Evans succeeded in building a strange amphibious vehicle which he publicly demonstrated at Philadelphia, amidst the understandable curiosity of the crowd.

In the meantime in England there had exploded, almost without warning, what may justifiably be called the era of the steam carriage. The first name which is found in

Trevithick's three wheeler.

Trevithick's carriage.

Church's steam coach.

the history of these public vehicles, powered by much more efficient engines than those of the self-propelled vehicles of the early years of the century, is that of Julius Griffiths. He was the inventor and builder of the first real bus to be put into regular public service for passenger transport.

This bus dates from 1822, during the time Stephenson was beginning to operate the first steam railway in history. This coincidence in time and competition, in fact was to continue for some decades. The development of the two systems in Great Britain was more or less contemporaneous and gave rise to an active battle, not only on a technical basis, but also in the fields of commerce and finance due to the powerful interests which attached themselves to one side or another.

More or less contemporary to Griffiths, whose carriage had an efficient tubular boiler of a new type, were two other English manufacturers — James, inventor of four different steam buses fitted with such unheard of devices as cylinders with different pressures to give a steering effect and a gear change by means of chains, and John Scott Russell who began a regular steam coach service between Glasgow and Paisley. Another important name of the period is that of Sir Goldsworthy Gurney, builder of an improved steam coach which, beginning in 1825, supplied a regular public service between London and Bath. Before designing this vehicle, Gurney had interested himself for some time in strange projects for carriages moving on mechanical legs, inspired by the original ideas of a predecessor, David Gordon, who held that natural friction would be insufficient and that therefore designs of his type were necessary. The London-Bath steam coach could carry eighteen passengers (six inside and twelve outside) at a speed of 12½ m.p.h. It weighed two tons and had the boiler mounted at the back with the cylinders under the chassis. Coke was used as fuel. For ease of steering, Gurney had designed a front axle controlled by two steering wheels which moved the heavy tiller.

Another constructor, Walter Hancock, some years later put into service further improved vehicles on various routes which he ran in company with Francis Maceroni, a businessman of Italian origin. But parallel to this technical progress went that of the railways, whose expansion was undoubtedly due to the greater comfort and speed which they offered. Self-propelled road vehicles always suffered from boiler insufficiencies, and even improved models required frequent stops for refilling. The competition between locomotive and steam coach gradually became more bitter. Ranged against the steam coach proprietors, already targets for the owners of bridges and toll rights who demanded ever-increasing payments, were the stage coach owners who created an association specifically to combat the establishment of the steam coach.

Passing of 'Red flag Act'

The years between 1834 and 1839 saw numerous hostile act against steam buses, particularly after the effect on the public of the first major accident in which one of these vehicles crashed into a pile of stones in the middle of the road just round a bend, causing the boiler to explode with consequent deaths and injuries. In 1839 another accident, in which a steam coach ran down two people at a cross road, killing one, created the conditions for a movement of public opinion against mechanical road vehicles. This crystallised in the passing of legislation which seems incredible today. The use of steam coaches and self-propelled road vehicles in general was limited to those that could not exceed 10 m.p.h. In 1865 these regulations were made more onerous by the conditions of the "Locomotive Act", or "Red Flag Act", which required drivers of mechanical vehicles to be preceded by a man on foot waving a red flag.

These requirements, coupled with the general inferiority of road vehicles in relation to the railway at that time, started the rapid decline of the British steam coach, which finally disappeared within a few years. A similar decline took place in France with the end of the first coach service, begun in 1835 by Charles Dietz, between

9

Wheel used at Ur in 4000 B.C.

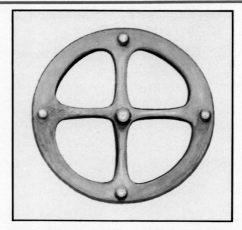

From the necessity to lighten wheels came the idea of spokes. The picture shows a Greek wheel of the 7th century B.C.

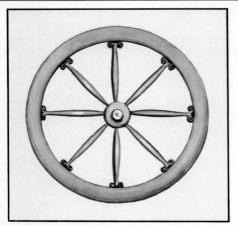

Light, elegant and modern-looking — a 4th century B.C. wheel.

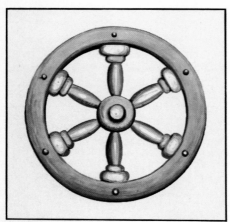

A six-spoked wheel of the 3rd century B.C.

WHEEL COMES OF AGE

The story of the wheel is either thousands of years old or very short depending upon which part of the world is considered. It is known, for example, that while the Sumerian civilisation which flourished on the banks of the Euphrates ago knew its use (as is recorded by the bas-reliefs of Ur, from which is taken the first wheel shown on this page) and while the Egyptians showed familiarity with it from 1700 B.C., the wheel was unknown in Oceania before the arrival of the first Europeans. Even the pre-Columbian American civilisations had found no practical use for it, though aware of it in principle.

First device

It is thought that the wheel was developed originally from the roller (a tree trunk) which probably represented the first device used by man to overcome sliding friction by turning it into rolling friction. After the roller became a disc, it was probably the need to get a hand to the inside to lubricate the axle which caused man to cut large holes in the disc. At some time someone thought of protecting the hub from shocks by means of a cap, and this was the forerunner of modern car hubcaps which have a more or less functional purpose. The evolution of the motor car wheel, as was the case also with bodywork, developed directly from that of the horse-drawn carriage with which it was at first identical. Almost from the beginning, car wheels had rims shod with rubber — solid and therefore long-wearing but also too hard. In the second half of the 19th century, John Boyd Dunlop, a Scottish veterinary surgeon, made his son's tricycle more comfortable by

inventing the pneumatic tyre — a cover for the rim which consisted of a rubber tube containing air under pressure. In 1888 the invention was patented in Great Britain, but Dunlop thought it unwise to abandon his profession and sold all the rights in it for a small sum. The idea proved unsuitable for motor cars, however, which continued to use solid tyres until someone thought of substituting the Dunlop tyre for another in two parts, an inner tube and a cover.

To Charles Goodyear is owed the innovation of vulcanising by which rubber acquires durability and elasticity. Until 1920, tyres were made by fixing rubber under pressure on to a body of cotton. The whole was then shaped and the exterior vulcanised. The tyres so built had a high-pressure inner tube and on average lasted about 4500 miles.

Return to past

In 1923 low-pressure, or balloon, tyres were introduced, and many of these had more than five times the life of the high-pressure tyres.

Beginning in 1955, tubeless tyres became common, particularly in the United States. These are tyres without an inner tube and are a return to the past in a sense, except that they are largely resistant to punctures or self-sealing. The tyre must fit the rim perfectly, in order to be air-tight.

a) A wheel built with wooden rim and spokes. It was with wheels of this type that Prince Scipione Borghese won the Pekin-Paris race in 1907. It is true that one of the wheels broke when the car turned over as a bridge collapsed b). But it is also true that a simple Siberian craftsman could build a replacement that took the car all the way to Paris c).

b

a

c

A wheel with metal spokes and rubber-lined rim.

A special electron tyre.

A spoked wheel typical of sports and racing cars of the 1930's.

Bordino's steam carriage, built in the Arsenal in Turin in 1854.
Consuming 66 lbs. of coke an hour, the horizontal twin cylinder
engine gave it a speed of 5 m.p.h. on the level.

Paris and Versailles. The service was held to be particularly comfortable due to the coaches' "elastic"
wheels, which had a strip of felt and rubber between
the rim and the tyre.

Revival of steam

In fact the steam road vehicle was to show various
revivals in France after this major decline, first of all
with the interesting enterprise of Lotz and Albaret,
respectively in 1860 and 1865, designers of somewhat
advanced vehicles, and later Amedée Bollée's original
vehicle, "L'Obéissante". Bollée, a bell founder in Le
Mans, designed and built a vehicle capable of 25 m.p.h.
fitted with new devices such as a gear change and
independent front wheel suspension. Later he built
even more advanced vehicles, "La Mancelle" and the
"Rapide" in which it is even possible to see certain
concepts of the modern car, such as a front engine,
rear driving wheels connected to the engine by a propeller shaft and a differential. The Bollée family made a
small fortune with these machines, which were accepted
with enthusiasm in Germany and Austria. But it was
all a flash in the pan, as was the only Italian excursion
into the field. This was a steam coach, built by Virgilio
Bordino, an engineering officer in the Sardinian army

and constructor of three such vehicles inspired by the
English models.

So closes the glorious era of the steam coach, glorious
above all for the passion with which certain far-sighted
engineers fought for the success of their inventions,
clearly too advanced for the world in which they lived.
At this point however, it is necessary to return in time
to trace the origins of what is today — as it has been
ever since the true beginnings of motoring in the last
quarter of last century — the authentic motor engine,
the internal combustion engine.

Internal combustion engine born

It is possible to see the conception of such engines in
the studies of Christian Huygens, who in 1678 described,
if only in theory, the first internal combustion engine
in history. In essence, it consisted of a piston sliding in
a cylinder, at one end of which was placed a small
quantity of gun-powder whose subsequent ignition and
explosion caused the displacement of the piston. At the
end of the 18th century a similar idea was studied, and
this time was actually built, by the Swiss De Rivaz who
succeeded in building a crude vehicle which used the
energy of exploding gas. In this case, ignition was by
means of a "Volta's pistol", or in other words, a method
relatively similar to that in use today.

Meanwhile an Englishman, Robert Street, was experimenting with the use of inflammable gas in cylinders, and in France an engineer named Le Bon was making the first experiments concerning the ignition of gases by means of an electric spark. Another enthusiastic experimenter in the early years of the 19th century was the American, Peter Cooper, whose efforts to build an efficient internal combustion engine were dramatically interrupted by an explosion which unfortunately blinded him. Cooper's experiments seem to have been very ambitious as he hoped to build also a flying machine powered by his engine.

As important step forward was made in 1825 when Michael Faraday, the author of fundamental studies in many other branches of human science, discovered benzene in tar derived from coal. It was among the first liquid fuel capable of being used successfully in i.c. engines and was quickly accepted by various scientists.

Gas replaced by liquid

At this period between 1850 and 1870, when the motor car was to appear on the distant horizon, two Italians were pioneering the building of the first true internal combustion engine: Eugenio Barsanti, a scientist and doctor of physics, and Felice Matteucci, a landowner who moved to Florence to work with him. Their experiments in the College of San Giovannino were inspired by the theoretical studies of the Milanese aristocrat De Cristoforis, who also dreamed of finally obtaining useable mechanical power from the burning of an explosive mixture.

The first engine which came out of the joint efforts of the two Italians was born in 1856, built on the basis of Italian and English patents previously taken out. It used the explosion in two cylinders of a mixture of air and inflammable gas and worked on a three-stroke cycle, without compression. From the beginning the use of petrol or benzene was foreseen in place of gas. The prototype of 1856 was followed by a second engine in 1858, and two years later a third engine was ordered from Escher and Wyss in Zurich and shown at the first National Exhibition in Florence in 1861.

In France, Etienne Lenoir's first gas engine had been patented in 1859, and the Italians secured recognition only in their own country for their work. Barsanti's sudden death from typhus in 1864 at Liege, where he had gone to arrange the series production of low-powered engines, was a deathblow also for Matteucci, who was seriously ill. A few years later their enterprise was forgotten. The gas engine designed and built by Etienne Lenoir in 1860 thus passed into history as the first, even though it was built later than that of the two Italians.

In fact this engine differed very little from that of the Italians. Both used the explosion of a mixture of air and inflammable gas inside a cylinder without compressing it. While Barsanti and Matteucci's engine had an intermittent connection between piston and crankshaft

(a sort of "freewheel" permitting the piston to be hurled freely upwards by the explosion, re-establishing connection when it was drawn backwards by gravity and the vacuum behind it), Lenoir's engine had two pistons in the same cylinder, permanently connected to the crankshaft. Introduction of the mixture was by means of a distributor and ignition was by battery and Ruhmkorff coil.

Commercial success

There has been much discussion as to the effective power developed by the two engines, and their practical value. There are those who are in favour of the Italian engine and they may be right. Certainly the French one had much greater commercial success. It was used for the mechanisation of machine tools in small workshops, but it seems that one such engine was installed in a wheeled vehicle in 1862 or 1863. This derives from a note left by Lenoir himself. According to this, the vehicle — which seems to have had sparking plugs similar to those of today and even an embryonic distributor —

Rickett's steam vehicle.

made a number of journeys between Paris and Jonville-le-Pont, a distance of 12 miles.

The doubts that exist arise from the complete absence from the press reports at the time of any news of the public appearance of such an unusual vehicle. In any case, even if Lenoir's vehicle were only an intention, the years 1854 to 1862 are of fundamental importance in the story of the motor car. It was then that the internal combustion engine, "our" engine, was born. The form in which it came into the world however, was extremely crude. It is not easy to see in that trembling, romantically simple machine, the forebear of today's descendant. It was from two Germans, Nikolaus Otto and Eugen Langen, and another Frenchman, Alphonse Beau de Rochas, that were to come the first wonderful improvements that directed technical progress along the right road.

From that day onwards, once it had received the push of the early pioneers, technical progress was almost headlong, apart from a few pauses.

THE DETERMINED EXPERIMENTERS

The official story — so to speak — of great men hides a second story, the private one, which is often dramatic, always full of interest. Their professional battles lead to ever more difficult personal decisions, often to sacrifices and poverty.

All this was true in the case of the three major figures in the development of the i.c. engine, the Germans Nikolaus August Otto, Gottlieb Daimler and Karl Benz. Otto was a twenty eight year old shop assistant when in 1860 he learned from a newspaper of the existence of Lenoir's engine. He was enthusiastic and at once conceived the idea of a similar engine but fed with liquid (petrol) fuel. He drew his brother Wilhelm into the affair, but when his request for a patent was rejected by the Prussian government — which saw no difference between his engine and Lenoir's — he was abandoned by Wilhelm. Otto passed through a critical period which would have made most people give up, but which led him to a dramatic decision — to give up his job and to concentrate entirely on experiments with his engine, notwithstanding his limited means.

In 1862 the engine was ready, though fuelled by gas. It worked for a while and then blew to pieces. Although it was impossible to repair it, Otto did not weaken but instead went to England to see Barsanti and Matteucci's model. When he returned to Cologne he built a new engine and tried to sell it and patent it, but failed in both respects.

His meeting with Eugen Langen, a businessman and engineer, another enthusiast for the work of Barsanti and Matteucci, was the piece of good fortune he needed to revive him from a series of setbacks. Langen, through his friend Franz Reuleaux, examiner for the Prussian patents commission, succeeded in getting the much desired patent for his partner Otto.

Ideas workshop

But the difficulties were not over. A year after production began, sales were down to zero because of technical weaknesses discovered by clients. Yet another effort of will was necessary to put the enterprise back on its feet and only in 1871 did the Deutz factory become possible, the future "ideas factory" for the basic progress of the i.c. engine.

Later developments in the theoretical and industrial activity of August Otto are probably even more important than these earlier ones in their influence. But his early struggles for scientific knowledge demonstrate that advances are due not only to the intelligence and creativity of a select group of people, but also to their exceptional willpower.

These considerations hold true for the other two pioneers of the time, Daimler and Benz. Both for example were men of humble origin, the first being the son of a baker in Schorndorf, and the second the son of an engine-driver in Karlsruhe, and they both had to fight hard to establish themselves. Daimler began as a mechanic in a gunmaker's and took his degree in engineering by alternately working and studying in Germany, France and England. Before settling in the Otto factory in Deutz he acquired wide experience in various German machine-tool factories. Benz, after having been a workman in a machine factory in his native city and subsequently a draughtsman in Mannheim, met with economic misfortune in his first private venture, an engineering workshop opened in partnership with August Ritter. In spite of this he found the willpower to take up his old studies on gas engines and to carry them to a successful conclusion, building his first two stroke.

There are two episodes in the story of these two great

Nikolaus August Otto (1832-1891).

Gottlieb Daimler (1834-1900).

Karl Benz (1844-1929).

"3 H.P. Velo" Benz of 1893. Rear engine single horizontal single, bore and stroke 110 × 120 mm. giving 1,140. 3 H.P. at 400 r.p.m. Ignition by coil and contact breaker. Belt clutch, 2 speed gearbox.

men that are remarkably similar and which demonstrate the atmosphere of hostility in which they had to work most of their lives. Both were subject to attacks by the press of the cities in which they worked. The "Cannstatter Zeitung" in 1855 made bitter complaints against the motor tricycle that Gottlieb Daimler was testing on the streets of Cannstatt, talking of a "repugnant, diabolical device dangerous to the life and well-being of the citizens", and it called for a drastic intervention by the local police. Confronted with this declaration of war, Daimler did not feel able to continue with his experiments with the tricycle and turned to the study of a motorboat, the "Marie", that he fitted with a 1½ H.P. i.c. engine. When the time came for trials on the waters of the Neckar he disguised the boat with wires and insulators and announced that it was electrically powered. After a successful conclusion to the trials, he revealed the truth, and the psychological battle was won.

'Useless invention'

About the same time Karl Benz was the object of a violent attack by the "Mannheimer Zeitung" which, described as "useless, ridiculous and indecent" the horseless carriage on which he was working. The newspaper asked, "Who is interested in such a contrivance so long as there were horses on sale?"

Benz was probably inclined to bow before such attacks and to withdraw from the field, but his wife Bertha decided that they had suffered enough and that it was time to counter-attack.

Thus one day, in the summer of 1888, the astounded farmers of the area saw one of Benz's snorting mechanical carriages advancing down the road, occupied by a delicate woman with her two children, one of whom was driving. It was Frau Bertha who had insisted on taking her husband's machine and refused to stop until she had reached her neighbouring birthplace and had returned without breakdowns or accidents of any serious kind. The adversaries had been dealt with and Benz too had won his battle, by proxy.

Jenatzy's "Jamais Contente" which was the first vehicle to exceed 100 k.p.h. (62 m.p.h.). It had an electric motor.

70 YEARS OF RECORDS

With the introduction of jet planes, the holder of the land speed record could no longer claim to be the fastest man in the world, even though a land vehicle can now reach over 600 m.p.h. This is a speed that an air pilot of 30 years ago might well have considered unattainable.

But the first 600 m.p.h.-plus of Craig Breedlove in 1965 was probably no more exciting than the experiences of the pioneer drivers at the end of the last century — the 40 m.p.h. in 1898 of Chasseloup-Laubat and the 65 m.p.h. of Jenantzy a year later. The table alongside is a record of courage, showing how man progressed steadily in achievements that were considered only a short time previously to be impossible — or foolhardy.

DATE	DRIVER AND VEHICLE	M.P.H.
1898	Chasseloup-Laubat in Jeantaud (Acheres, France)	39.3
1899	Jenatzy in Jenatzy (Acheres, France)	41.42
1899	Chasseloup-Laubat in Jeantaud (Acheres, France)	43.69
1899	Jenatzy in Jenatzy (Acheres, France)	49.42
1899	Chasseloup-Laubat in Jeantaud (Acheres, France)	57.6
1899	Jenatzy in Jenatzy (Acheres, France)	65.75
1902	Serpollet in Serpollet (Nice, France)	75.06
1902	Fournier in Mors (Dourdan, France)	76.60
1902	Angeres in Mors (Dourdan, France)	77.13
1903	Duray in Gobron-Brillie (Ostend, Belgium)	84.21
1903	Henry Ford in Ford "999" (Lake St. Clair, U.S.A.)	91.378
1904	W. K. Vanderbilt in Mercedes (Daytona Beach, U.S.A.)	92.307
1904	Rigolly in Gobron-Brillie (Nice, France)	93.20
1904	De Caters in Mercedes (Ostend, Belgium)	97.26
1904	Rigolly in Gobron-Brillie (Ostend, Belgium)	103.56
1904	Baras in Darracq (Mongeron, France)	104.53
1905	Arthur MacDonald in Napier (Daytona Beach, U.S.A.)	104.651
1905	Hémery in Darracq (Aries-Salon, France)	109.65
1909	Hémery in Benz (Brooklands, G.B.)	125.947
1910	Barney Oldfield in Benz (Daytona Beach, U.S.A.)	131.724
1922	K. L. Guinnes in Sunbeam (Brooklands, G.B.)	133.75
1924	René Thomas in Delage (Arpajon, France)	143.31
1924	E. A. D. Eldridge in Fiat (Arpajon, France)	145.90
1925	M. Campbell in Sunbeam (Pendine Sands, G.B.)	150.869
1926	H. O. D. Segrave in Sunbeam (Southport, G.B.)	152.336
1926	J. G. Parry-Thomas in Thomas Special (Pendine Sands, G.B.)	169.23
1926	J. G. Parry-Thomas in Thomas Special (Pendine Sands, G.B.)	171.09
1927	M. Campbell in Napier Campbell (Pendine Sands, G.B.)	174.883
1927	H. O. D. Segrave in Sunbeam (Daytona Beach, U.S.A.)	203.792
1928	M. Campbell in Napier Campbell (Daytona Beach, U.S.A.)	206.956
1928	Ray Keech in White-Triplex (Daytona Beach, U.S.A.)	207.552
1929	H. O. D. Segrave in Irving-Napier (Daytona Beach, U.S.A.)	231.446
1931	Sir Malcolm Campbell in Napier Campbell (Daytona Beach, U.S.A.)	246.09
1932	Sir Malcolm Campbell in Napier Campbell (Bonneville Salt Flats, U.S.A.)	253.97
1933	Sir Malcolm Campbell in Rolls-Royce-Campbell (Daytona Beach, U.S.A.)	272.46
1935	Sir Malcolm Campbell in Bluebird Special (Bonneville Salt Flats, U.S.A.)	276.82
1935	Sir Malcolm Campbell in Bluebird Special (Bonneville Salt Flats, U.S.A.)	301.13
1937	G. E. T. Eyston in Thunderbolt (Bonneville Salt Flats, U.S.A.)	312.0
1938	G. E. T. Eyston in Thunderbolt (Bonneville Salt Flats, U.S.A.)	345.5
1938	John Cobb in Railton (Bonneville Salt Flats, U.S.A.)	350.2
1938	G. E. T. Eyston in Thunderbolt (Bonneville Salt Flats, U.S.A.)	357.5
1939	John Cobb in Railton (Bonneville Salt Flats, U.S.A.)	369.7
1947	John Cobb in Railton (Bonneville Salt Flats, U.S.A.)	393.8
1964	Donald Campbell in Bluebird II (Lake Eyre, Australia)	403.1
1964	Art Arfons in Green Monster (Bonneville Salt Flats, U.S.A.)	434.18
1964	Craig Breedlove in Spirit of America (Bonneville Salt Flats, U.S.A.)	555.483
1965	Art Arfons in Green Monster (Bonneville Salt Flats, U.S.A.)	576.553
1965	Craig Breedlove in Spirit of America (Bonneville Salt Flats, U.S.A.)	600.841

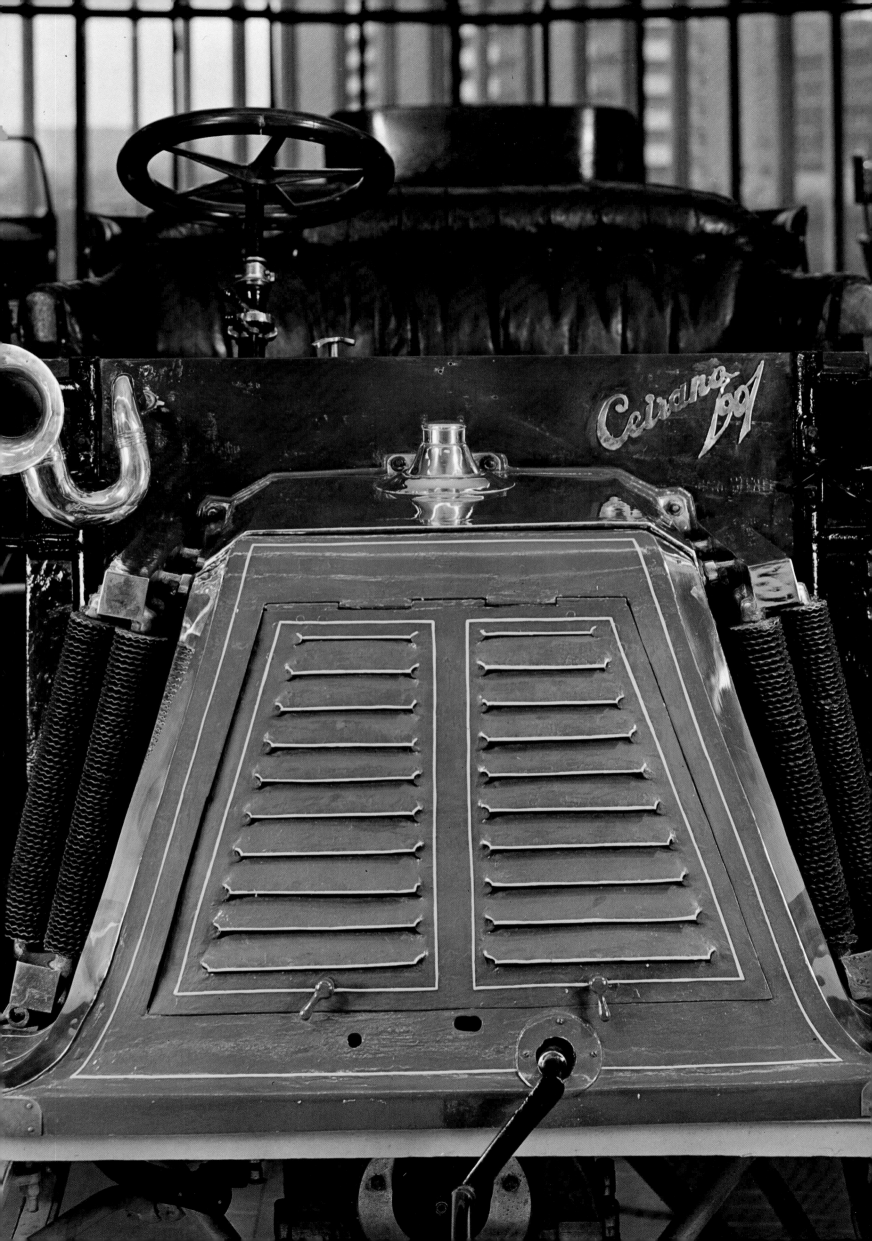

front view of a 1901 CEIRANO "5 H.P."

engine - front mounted, single vertical cylinder
bore and stroke - 86 × 110 mm.
capacity - 639 c.c.
output - 5 H.P. at 800 r.p.m.
ignition - low tension magneto
clutch - leather cone
gearchange - 3 speeds plus reverse
transmission - cardan shaft
weight - 407 lbs.

A modern high-performance car. The enormous difference in the power developed by its engines and those of the Darracq below is a measure of technological progress made by designers and manufacturers.

CHAPTER TWO
THE YEARS OF DISCOVERY

The year 1862 is an important one in the history of the motor car, for it was in that particular year that Alphonse Beau de Rochas, a Frenchman and civil engineer in retirement (notwithstanding his 45 years of age) propounded the "four stroke explosion cycle" in a memorandum. Three hundred copies were distributed to the press explaining the principle on which almost all internal combustion engines were to function to the present day. The engines of Lenoir and of Barsanti and Matteucci exploited only the kinetic effects of the explosion of the mixture and used a three stroke cycle — induction, explosion and expansion. Beau de Rochas added the fourth stroke, compression, which represented the key to the effective exploration of the potential of the i.c. engine.

About the same time, Nikolaus August Otto of Cologne began to interest himself in the problems of the i.c. engine based on Lenoir's studies. After a series of experiments conducted together with his brother Wilhelm, at the beginning of 1861 Otto sought from the Prussian government a patent for the exploitation of a "mixture of gas contained in the cylinder of an engine, ignited by an electric spark", explaining that by this was meant a mixture of air and vapour drawn from hydrocarbons and liquids. The patent was not granted however, because no fundamental difference was re-

cognised between this system and Lenoir's, although the latter foresaw the use of a gas mixture only. In spite of this, Otto continued his experiments. Following the somewhat adventurous construction of two engines based

The 1906 Darracq built at Portello, where Alfa Romeo was later to be born.

This is the world's first true motor car. It was built by Siegfried Marcus in 1865 and was driven by a 4 H.P. engine. The photograph was taken at the Stockholm International Exhibition. Note the steering.

on Barsanti and Matteucci's experiments which Otto had been able to examine during a visit to England, he went into partnership with a German businessman, Eugen Langen, who had considerable technical background and had also been interested in the Italian engines.

During the first period of his experiments, Otto became interested for a while in Beau de Rochas' cycle, patenting and building in 1866-67 a four stroke engine. This had considerable defects, and unfortunately he abandoned this line of experiment. For more than ten years, even after his partnership with Langen, his experiments and his industrial activity were concentrated on the Lenoir, Barsanti - Matteucci type of "atmospheric" (without compression) engine.

It should be mentioned that the first true and proper four stroke engine, using the Beau de Rochas cycle, was to be built in 1872 by a certain Reithmann, a Munich watchmaker, but it had no subsequent industrial development.

Emotion and experience

The early atmospheric engines, which arose in 1866 out of the association between Otto and Langen, though still very noisy and heavy, had many improvements compared with those of Lenoir. For instance, the fuel consumption was just a half. But a few years later the Otto-Langen engines were much improved and a regular series production (if the term can be used) was begun in the factory at Deutz near Cologne. It should be

emphasised that these engines were still gas engines and were for stationary use.

It was to be the entry into the Otto-Langen concern of Gottlieb Daimler, a capable engineer with long production experience, which would bring to the work of the two pioneers a spirit of enquiry and interest in research and discovery. Daimler had previously approached the ageing Lenoir proposing to build an improved version of his engine, but they were not able to come to an agreement. Later, reading the writings of Beau de Rochas, he was deeply impressed.

Silent and reliable

With the collaboration of Wilhelm Maybach, for some time his assistant and who had moved with him to

A 1894 Peugeot/Daimler car, built at Saronno, Italy, under licence from the Valentigney factory. It had a two-cylinder engine of 1,206 c.c. which developed 2½ H.P. at 400 r.p.m. Ignition was by burner and platinum wire; there was a leather cone clutch. The car had a gearbox with a four speeds and reverse. It weighed 880 lbs.

Drake's original oil well pictured in 1861, two years after being drilled.

OIL MATCHES THE PACE

On August 27 1859 an American prospector named Edwin Drake drilled a primitive well at Titusville, a small town in Pennsylvania, and struck oil at a depth of 69 feet. Just on a century later, in September 1959, Shell drillers at work in a beetroot field in the flatlands of northern Holland struck natural gas in the now famous Slochteren No. 1 well, uncovering what has proved to be the world's second largest gas field.

Seepages in mine

Over the 100 years separating those two events there has grown up an industry that now supplies more than half the world's total energy. It was not petrol, however, that the early pioneers were thinking about: the internal combustion engine had yet to be invented. They were looking for a better kind of lamp oil than could be manufactured from sperm or whale oil — a principal illuminant in the first half of the 19th century before the invention of the gas mantle.

As early as 1850 James Young, a Glasgow chemist, had noticed oil seepages in the coal measures of north Derbyshire from which he made a primitive paraffin: he went on to develop oil-bearing shales in the Scottish Lothians. But nobody had yet drilled a well with the object of finding oil.

This honour belongs to the otherwise bogus "Colonel" Drake, a half educated train conductor from the New York and New Haven Railroad. Long before he arrived on the scene American settlers had been skimming an oily liquid they had named petroleum (or "rock oil") from little springs along Oil Creek, in north-western Pennsylvania. Its medicinal properties were highly prized and bottles of the stuff were sold by itinerant quacks

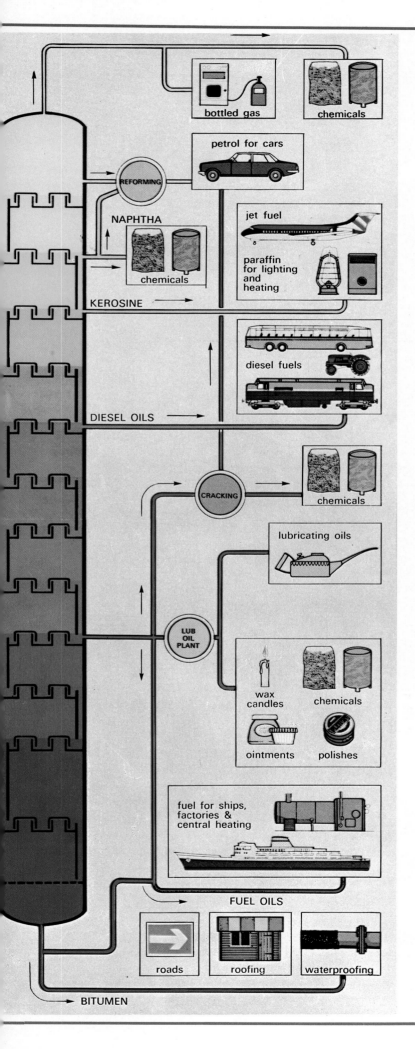

bottled gas

chemicals

petrol for cars

REFORMING

NAPHTHA

jet fuel

chemicals

paraffin
for lighting
and
heating

KEROSINE

diesel fuels

DIESEL OILS

CRACKING

chemicals

lubricating oils

LUB
OIL
PLANT

wax
candles

chemicals

ointments

polishes

fuel for ships,
factories &
central heating

FUEL OILS

roads

roofing

waterproofing

BITUMEN

who claimed it to be a cure for all ailments, human or animal. In the words of a contemporary advertisement:

> The healthful balm from Nature's secret spring,
> The bloom of health, and life, to man will bring,
> As from her depth the magic liquid flows,
> To calm our sufferings, and assuage our woes.

Ill-health compelled Drake to give up his job with the railroad and a certain James M. Townsend, President of the City Savings Bank of New Haven, Connecticut, sent him to look for oil in Pennsylvania on behalf of a company he had founded. On the site of the principal oil spring at Titusville, Drake built an engine house, set up a wooden derrick on which to swing the primitive drilling tools, and installed an engine and boiler.

Cradle of industry

His driller, a blacksmith by the name of William Smith, drove an iron pipe 32 feet through the quicksands and clay into bedrock. The drilling tools were placed inside the pipe, and about the middle of August 1859 drilling began averaging about three feet a day. On Saturday afternoon (August 27), just as Smith and his workmen were about to quit for the weekend, the drill dropped into a crevice at 69 feet and slipped down six inches. The men pulled out the tools and went home. Late on Sunday afternoon "Uncle Billy", as the bearded blacksmith was affectionately called, visited the well, peered down the pipe, and saw oil floating on top of the water within a few feet of the derrick floor.
They had struck oil with a well producing 25 barrels a day. Drake had demonstrated how oil could be secured in greater abundance. He had tapped a large reservoir of petroleum and founded a new industry of incalculable potential. The United States was thus the cradle of the oil business, although in the next 20 years oil was discovered and began to be produced in Russia and Rumania.

Bright flame

The scene moves from the United States to the Dutch East Indies (now Indonesia), where the father of the oil industry was a Dutch tobacco planter named Jans Zijlker. One day in 1880 he was caught in a storm while inspecting tobacco plantations in eastern Sumatra and had to spend the night in a shed. When darkness fell his native overseer lit a torch which Zijlker noticed burned with a particularly bright flame. The torch had been daubed with a kind of wax skimmed off the surface of small pools in the neighbourhood. Next day Zijlker was shown one of the pools, and at once recognised the smell of kerosine (or paraffin). He took a sample which on test yielded about 60 per cent of good quality lamp oil.

Zijlker bought a drilling rig, cut a track through the dense tropical forest, and in 1885 a torrent of oil gushed up his second borehole at Telaga Tunggal — a well that was still producing when the Japanese invaded Sumatra 57 years later. His discovery led to the founding in 1890 of the grandly named Royal Dutch Company for the Working of Petroleum Wells in the Netherlands Indies (Royal Dutch for short). Thus came into being the senior ancestral company of the Royal Dutch/Shell Group.

Sea shells to paraffin

On the other side of the world, half a century earlier, a young man named Marcus Samuel and his bride opened a little shop near the Tower of London, where they sold curios obtained from sailors whose ships docked in the river. Marcus enjoyed a particularly thriving trade in rare sea shells, treasured as ornaments in Victorian England, and eventually set up agents throughout the Far East to ensure supplies. His son (also named Marcus) in the 1880s conceived the idea of selling Russian paraffin in the East through the chain of agents set up by the family firm. In 1897 he founded a new company, "Shell" Transport and Trading, to handle the business.

Instead of moving oil in cases in the holds of cargo ships, as was then custom, Marcus conceived the idea of building a ship that was itself a tank capable of carrying the oil in bulk. It was vital to his plans that his vessels should be able to take the short route to the East through the recently-opened Suez Canal. Paraffin was then regarded as a highly-dangerous cargo. When the first vessel to bring kerosine from the United States to Europe — the brig *Elizabeth Watts*, loaded with barrels of Pennsylvanian oil, in 1861 — prepared to sail, the crew deserted at the last moment, fearful of

An exploration derrick in Morocco.

being burned in their bunks. Not until a scratch crew of drunken seamen had been collected from the bars along the waterfront could the voyage begin. And although the shipment of cased oil no longer struck terror, the transport of oil in bulk, with only the skin of the ship to protect its inflammable cargo, had reawakened the fear of fire. Samuel overcame all obstacles, however, and in 1892 his pioneer tanker the 4,200-ton *Murex* became the first to pass through the Canal. She was the precursor of a long line of Shell tankers all named after the sea shells upon which the firm's prosperity had originally been founded.

Samuel's invasion of the Far East brought him into conflict not only with Royal Dutch (which had had their own growing pains), but the Rockefeller's strongly entrenched Standard Oil. It soon became apparent to Royal Dutch's Henri Deterding and to Shell's Marcus Samuel that they would have to get together if they were to stand up to Rockefeller. Royal Dutch had oil, but no outlets; Shell had the outlets but not the oil, since their Russian contract was soon to expire. A full merger of the Dutch and British interests on a 60/40 basis was agreed upon in 1907.

Since then the Royal Dutch/Shell Group has developed into a community of several hundred companies engaged in more than 100 countries in every phase of the oil industry, including natural gas and chemicals based on oil and gas. The Group has become the world's second largest oil enterprise with an international spread of operations matched by few other companies.

Enter British Petroleum

British Petroleum owes its beginning to William Knox D'Arcy, who spent a fortune he had made in Australian gold exploring in Persia in the first decade of this century. After years without success his drillers struck oil at Masjid-i-Sulaiman in 1908 and the Anglo-Persian Oil Company (now British Petroleum) was founded a year later. Its development was made secure when Winston Churchill, determined to secure oil for the Royal Navy before the 1914-18 war, persuaded the British Government to take a 50 per cent interest in the company. British Petroleum has always shown an almost uncanny skill in finding oil. The trail blazed by D'Arcy more than half a century ago led to the discovery in the Middle East by various companies of two-thirds of the world's known crude reserves. British Petroleum with its oilfields concentrated mainly in that area, has grown into one of the world's largest oil enterprises, with access to greater crude oil reserves than any other international oil company.

The great paradox

The story so far told illustrates how the character of the oil industry has been shaped by the nature and location of its prime raw material. The great paradox of the business is that, ever since Col. Drake's time,

Shell Haven Refinery in Essex, near the mouth of the Thames.

oil has rarely been found in a form in which it can be immediately used. It is generally not available in the places where it is mainly wanted. And it is very difficult to find at all. (Even in the United States oil and gas have to be moved thousands of miles from the producing fields to the great industrial centres where they are consumed).

Hence very large international groups of companies, such as Shell and British Petroleum, have grown up, concerned with every phase of the business from the oil well to the customer's tank. A vast global transportation operation, by ocean tankers and pipelines, is required to move the oil from where it is found and produced to where it is needed. Oil has become the largest single commodity in international trade, and tankers carry more than half the total cargoes (by weight) sailing the seven seas.

Huge capital investment is required at each stage, and the risks involved are great, particularly in exploration. Col. Drake and his immediate successors backed their

hunches and picked out drilling sites with a pin. Science has now greatly narrowed the search for geologically promising areas, but the presence or absence of oil can still be proved only by the drill. And most holes are dry. The average odds against finding hydrocarbons on drilling are 9 to 1. And the odds against an exploration well finding a field large enough to be worth developing are 30 to 1. Moreover, production from individual wells can vary greatly — from as much as one million tons annually from one well in the Middle East Gulf to an average of 650 tons in the United States, where oil become harder and harder to find.

To give one example of the costs and risks involved: Shell and British Petroleum began a joint search for oil in Nigeria more than 30 years ago. First the country had to be surveyed and mapped: access had to be made to drilling locations in the forests and swamps of the Niger delta, and every piece of equipment and expertise brought in from the outside. More than 20 years elapsed before oil was found in large enough quantities to enable

25

exports to begin. And in 1967, when production had risen to 25 million tons a year and £200 million had been invested, civil strife brought operations to a halt. The search for oil and gas is a gamble in which the stakes are rising all the time, particularly as exploration moves from the land to the ocean bed, from which are expected to come up to half the new reserves required for the future. In the last two decades the industry has learned the know-how and perfected the technology of marine exploration. The companies have designed and built great drilling units standing on legs or able to float steadily in deeper water however strong the forces of wind and tide. They have mastered the mechanics of developing under-sea fields and of bringing the oil and gas ashore.

Searching for and developing oil or gas, with all the risks involved, is only the beginning of the story. The costs of getting oil to market are far higher than the costs of finding and producing it. Today oil is moved in tankers with a carrying capacity five times greater than ten years ago to refineries that become steadily more complex to meet the demand for more varied and sophisticated products required by the market. To ensure that the finished products reach the customer in the most efficient way, modern distribution centres, larger diameter pipe-lines, and bigger road tankers and rail tank cars are needed. All these contribute to the economies of scale made possible by the size of the industry's operations. When we think of oil we still think first of transport, for the vast majority of modern vehicles depend on petroleum for their motive power. More than 144 million cars, coaches, buses, vans and lorries carry people and goods along the roads of the world. At sea, more than 96 per cent of the world's merchant shipping uses

A floating giant — the 205,000-ton Shell tanker Megara.

BP's barge Sea Quest, which began exploration drilling in the North Sea in 1966.

fuel oil. And in the air, aircraft fuelled by highly specialised oil products fly 2,140 million miles every year on passenger routes.

In the early days of refining, petrol was burned to waste as a dangerous by-product for which there was no commercial use. Today more petrol is used than any other oil product: a world total of nearly 100,000 million gallons a year. Continuous quality research by the companies has evolved petrols that give more miles per gallon as well as higher performance in modern high compression engines.

But petrol is by no means the only product that gives transports its motive power. Paraffin, in Drake's time the No. 1 product, now plays a big part in aviation, as the principal fuel used in jet engines. Lorries, buses and coaches run on high speed diesel engines fuelled by gas oil; so do diesel locomotives on the railways. Ships are oil-fired. Paraffin, gas and fuel oil are all widely used for heating, and fuel oil for heavy industry. An immense variety of lubricants keeps the wheels of transport and industry turning smoothly, and bitumen surfaces our roads.

Natural gas will gradually take over a growing proportion of Britain's public gas supplies. Petroleum is the basic "building block" for a vast chemical industry, which has changed our daily lives by providing a host of new and useful products ranging from plastics and detergents to agricultural fertilizers and pesticides. Oil is indeed the most versatile of raw materials available to man.

Only at the point of sale to the customer is the revenue earned to finance the whole complex chain of events that keeps the industry in being. The customer has greatly benefited from the intensely competitive climate in which the industry operates. Oil companies compete fiercely with each other as well as with other fuel industries, and competition is a great spur to efficiency.

Moreover, security of supplies has never failed either in peace or war, because of the world-wide spread of the international companies' operations and the diversity of sources of crude oil available to them. The interruption of the normal flow of oil following the Israeli/Arab war in 1967 and the closing of the Suez Canal caused no hardship to the man in the street. Companies adjusted their normal pattern of operations, and supplies were maintained although at added cost.

Into the future

The prime task of the industry over the next 30 years will be to provide for the vast quantities of energy the world will need. Although nuclear power is of growing importance, oil and natural gas will still be supplying more than half of total requirements at the turn of the century. Between now and the year 2000 the industry must find nearly twice the reserves so far discovered.

These quantities (and more) are undoubtedly stored in the earth's crust and will be found and produced if there is economic incentive to do so. Despite the tremendous increase in oil consumption, discovery of new reserves has more than kept pace with demand. Between 1950 and 1966 the ratio of world proven reserves to current annual production rose from 25 to 31. And proven reserves represent only the industry's current working stocks — oil that can be produced economically by existing methods and sold at a profit. Vast unconventional deposits, such as the Athabasca tar sands in Canada and the oil shales of the United States, remain to be developed.

Enormous sums of money will have to be poured in to enable the industry to meet the challenge of the future. Only the international companies have the self-interest and hence the discipline to carry out such a huge investment programme. The bulk of the capital required will have to be earned in the market place largely by such companies as National Benzole, whose record of service to the customer ensures their continued success.

Eni's Refinery in Italy, near Milan.

Deutz, Daimler first applied himself to reorganisation in order to increase production.

By 1875 over 2000 engines had been sold in Europe and a number of manufacturers had obtained permission to build under licence. At the same time, Daimler and Maybach conducted a series of studies on the four stroke cycle, at the end of which they obtained the first-European patent of this type in 1876.

A year later the first example of this revolutionary prime mover was ready and working. It represented enormous progress over the 1867 model and was already silent and reliable. The ignition of this engine, which had a single horizontal cylinder, was by means of two jets of flame which were alternately exposed by a distributor. The Otto-Daimler engine was exhibited in 1878 at the Paris exhibition and may be considered the firm base on which all subsequent experiments were founded and improvements made, not only in Europe but also in America.

Secret vehicles

Though the progress of the i.c. engine at this period was largely associated with Otto and Daimler, that does not mean that others had not been trying in the meantime. Hugon in France and Bischop in Germany had built engines similar to Lenoir's, in some respect improved, but there was no commercial outcome.

In 1865 an original vehicle had appeared in Vienna, built by Seigfried Marcus, chemist, electrician and mechanic, who applied an i.c. engine to a hand cart. Marcus, afraid, with some reason, of prohibition by the authorities, tested it at night in a deserted street near the cemetery. Unfortunately the machine was so noisy that it attracted the attention of the police who stopped the experiment. It seems that Marcus was satisfied with this experience. His vehicle may still be admired in the Museum in Vienna. It should not be thought however, that the story of the "glorious years" of the i.c. engine was an exclusively European achievement. It could be maintained that the motor car — the vehicle powered by an i.c. engine — was an American invention. A young Boston engineer, George Brayton, before exhibiting his own i.c. engine at the Philadelphia Centennial in 1876, had already put on the streets of Providence a self-propelled vehicle powered by an earlier, cruder version of that engine. It was the encouragement he received with this vehicle, of which the technical characteristcs are unknown, that caused him to exhibit at Philadelphia. European industry was represented at the exhibition by no fewer than six Otto gas engines. Nevertheless, Brayton's sole U.S. example showed some advantages over the European engines. For example, the explosive mixture was obtained by forcing small drops of inflammable liquid along a narrow tube into an annular chamber filled with felt. Here the petrol came into contact with compressed air and was vaporised.

The exhibition at Philadelphia represented the beginning of the rapid conversion of the Americans to the i.c. engine. Up to that time, it may be said that steam powered vehicles had dominated the transatlantic scene

The 1891 Daimler with the executives of the company. To the left are Maybach and Gottlieb Daimler. On the right are Bernhard and the manager of the Esslinger factory, Gross. Note the wheel for braking.

almost without opposition. Otto's and Brayton's engines were reproduced in quantity from one shore of the continent to the other — legally, under licence, or without — and were quickly in use for the widest variety of industrial and agricultural applications. Even small fishing boats were powered — the first transport application in America.

The same exhibition caught the imagination of George Baldwin Selden, a young Rochester lawyer. Taken by the mechanical bug, Selden went home and set to work to adapt Brayton's engine to drive a land vehicle and thus obtained in 1879 a patent which, as can be seen later, was the basis for the American motor industry for many years to come.

End of a partnership

The alliance between Otto and Daimler was not destined to last for ever. Technical difference between the two became increasingly acute. In 1882 Daimler left Cologne, and on his estate at Cannstatt near Stuttgart, began a series of studies aimed at improving the Otto engine, especially as regards its weight, speed of rotation and ignition. This last represented the greatest problem. A year later the first Daimler-Maybach engine was born, with "hot-tube" ignition. This was yet another major step forward compared with the engines produced in collaboration with Otto.

Speed of rotation was raised from 200 r.p.m. to 900 r.p.m.; above all, an unusual and reasonably satisfactory system of ignition was developed, based on the continuous heating, by means of a burner mounted outside the cylinder, of a platinum tube, one end of which entered the combustion chamber.

The first tricycle

While Daimler and Maybach were busy with the first major technological problems created by the i.c. engine, in another city, Mannheim, another experimenter and designer, Karl Benz, was applying himself to similar work. In 1885 he completed the construction of a tricycle powered by a petrol engine and tested it on the streets of Mannheim just at the time when Daimler was testing an i.c. engined motorcycle. The significance of this parallel development is clearly more than the possible influence of one experimenter on the other, or the hypothetical passing of information between them. It was a measure of the progress already made in research in the field of the motor car, with the consequent nearness of success, that caused the simultaneous appearance on the still rudimentary world motoring scene of two radically new vehicles of such fundamental importance.

In identifying a common influence, the work of Otto must be considered.

Daimler's bicycle was fitted with a new version of the first "hot tube" engine of 1883. It was in fact the ancestor of the motorcycle. Benz' tricycle was driven

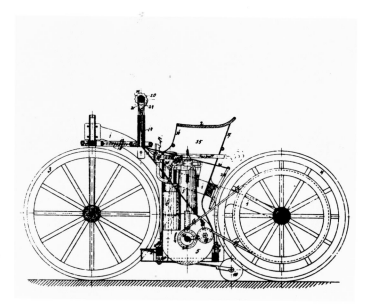

The design for a motor bicycle built by Daimler in 1885.

The 1885 Daimler motor bicycle.

The 1889 Daimler single cylinder.

Benz display. The three cars shown here were all built before 1895 but are still in working order and take part in veteran rallies.

1½ H.P. Maximum speed was 12½ m.p.h. This four wheeler was immediately put into production, because of the great interest it had inspired in technical circles.

Three to four wheels

Daimler was too involved in the manufacture of stationary engines and too dissatisfied with the state of development to begin production at once. By 1887 however, he had already made considerable improvements to his engine and began to grant licences for its construction abroad. Two years later he began commercial production in his own factory, after building a third version and now being satisfied with the solutions to the problems of ignition and carburation. As regards the former, after some attempts at an electrical system, Daimler returned to the platinum hot-tube in improved form. As far as carburation was concerned the invention of a carburettor by his colleague Maybach, which functioned by bubbling air through the fuel, made possible a more regular and richer mixture. The 1889 engine was a narrow V, two cylinder type, with single acting pistons on a common crankshaft. Inlet and exhaust were through valves, the latter being positively actuated; the inlet valve was "automatic", being opened by the vacuum created in the combustion chamber. Maximum speed of rotation was 770 r.p.m. and cooling was through the circulation of water by means of a pump, the water passing through a radiator of small bore finned tubes. Even by 1890 Daimler's engine, born out of major technical rethinking, was an immediate success due to the excellence of its technical solutions. It reached as annual production of 350. In the same year, Daimler granted about 1900 licences for manufacture abroad.

Out of the negotiations for the concession of one of

by a horizontal single cylinder engine which developed under one horsepower at 200 r.p.m. and was capable of driving the vehicle at 10 m.p.h. Some technical data: cooling was by means of the vaporisation of water, ignition was by high tension magneto and sparking plug, and transmission was by chain to spoked wheels.

In the two successive four wheeled vehicles built by the same two manufacturers, that of Benz had the mechanical components laid out in practically the same way as those of the tricycle, with a rear engine of these licences arises the romantic story of the birth of the firm of Panhard and Levassor, which was to become one of the most important concerns in the first decades of the development of the motor car. Indeed, it may be considered the most important as it was due to these two courageous Frenchmen that at the beginning of the last decade of the century, the motor car, already satisfactorily developed so far as its major mechanical elements were concerned, began to assume a shape of its own, gradually moving away from that derived directly from the horsedrawn carriage.

Courageous wife

It was the engineer Sarazin, an old friend and schoolmate of Daimler, who initiated the first contacts for the exploitation of the latter's patents in France.
As agents he chose two friends, René Panhard and Emile Levassor, both engineers with whom he had studied at the Ecole Centrale. Panhard and Levassor had been partners for some years in a business specialising in the construction of woodworking machinery, founded by a certain Périn in 1845 who had since died. When Sarazin died in the midst of the negotiations, his courageous wife took them up and carried them to a successful conclusion. From this agreement was born not only a commercial-technical collaboration of fundamental importance for the development of the motor car, but also a marriage as in 1890 Sarazin's widow married Emile Levassor. In 1889 Panhard and Levassor entered the motor car field on their own account, having first completely re-equipped their factory. From these works there first issued a "vis-à-vis" (face to face) which was little more than experimental; then, in 1894, a second vehicle with a twin cylinder engine that was to remain for many years one of the most interesting available on the European market.

1896 Bernardi. An enthusiastic pioneer, Bernardi, who had already constructed the i.c. engines "Pia" and "Lauro", in 1894 built the first Italian car with an i.c. engine. The light car shown here had the following characteristics: — single horizontal cylinder 624 c.c. engine developing 4 H.P. at 800 r.p.m. Platinum mesh ignition, spiral metal cable clutch, 3 speed gearbox, chain transmission.

The car which was born out of the early years of Panhard-Levassor production had a number of interesting features both in function and layout, and especially the controls — clutch, gearchange, differential and transverse axle. Though the transmission was by sprocket and chain, it does not detract from the substantial similarities of the layout of the basic components of that ancient vehicle and those of today. It was in fact the first true motor car. The term "automobile", used in many countries, is applied to early vehicles more for convenience of expression than for historical accuracy. It only came into use in Europe towards the end of the 19th century. There were indeed high level literary disputes in France on the matter, particularly because it was formed from words derived from two different languages — Greek and Latin. However, the word had already appeared in a French dictionary issued in 1877, and in 1895 the Académie Française gave its official approval.

Above and on the right, two 1895 Panhard-Levassors. Below an 1893 Bardon with a single-cylinder 2,000 c.c. engine. All three are still used.

FACE-TO-FACE REVOLUTION

SOCIÉTÉ ANONYME DES ANCIENS ÉTABLISSEMENTS

PANHARD & LEVASSOR

Au capital de 5.000.000 de francs

PARIS — 19, Avenue d'Ivry — PARIS

VOITURES AUTOMOBILES
ET BATEAUX

The cover and two drawings from the Panhard-Levassor catalogue published in Paris around 1895.

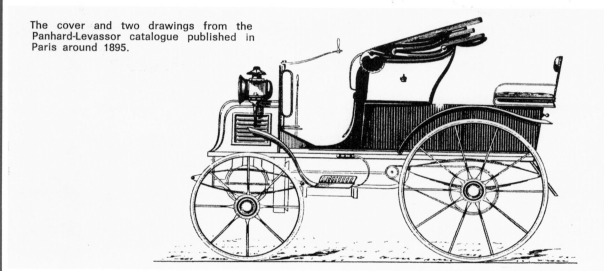

One of the reasons that the second car produced by Panhard-Levassor in 1894, five years after the formation of the company, is significant in the story of early years of motoring is that this machine represented the first serious attempt to get away from the construction methods of the horse-drawn carriage.

The new ideas which indicated this revolutionary trend consisted in the location of the engine, which in the first "vis-à-vis" of 1891 was placed not centrally but over the front wheels, thus improving roadholding; in the adoption of an enclosure for the engine itself, which could function for the first time protected from dust and atmospheric pollution; and in substituting a gearbox for belt transmission.

The second Panhard-Levassor model was to represent the ideal for many keen motorists in France and other countries, in the years immediately before the end of the century, despite being in more or less direct competition with the first cars built by Peugeot. In both cases the engine was a Daimler, or more precisely was produced under Daimler licence. Even in those days there existed the same divergence of opinion on the position of the motor that was to divide into two groups the manufacturers today. Peugeot's cars were rear-engined. The engine of the 1894 Panhard-Levassor car was no longer single cylindered like that of the "vis-à-vis", but a 15° Vee twin, of 80 mm × 120 mm bore and stroke, which developed about 3½ H.P.

Steam tricycle built in 1891 by Enrico Pecori at Caslino d'Erba in Italy. A vertical fire-tube boiler with central fire-box.

The need to present systematically the chain of events that existed from the work of first Otto, then Daimler, Benz and Panhard-Levassor, has so far prevented even a brief reference to the work in the same period of pioneers who must be considered as secondary. Their ideas were not necessarily less valid, but for one reason or another, they never produced engines or vehicles in quantity and for this reason had little influence on the development of the motor car.

Bernardi, prophet and manufacturer

Among these, a place in the foreground is occupied by Count Enrico Bernardi of Verona who, after devoting himself enthusiastically to the study of the i.c. engine even before 1880, built such an engine based on the Lenoir cycle and demonstrated it to the Royal Venetian Institute of Science in 1883. In 1884 his first experimental vehicle, powered by a third of a horsepower, appeared on the roads driven by his son Lauro.
Bernardi made his greatest contribution to motor car progress with a new engine built in 1889 exhibiting a series of impressive and farseeing technical innovations. These included a cylinder with detachable head, overhead valves actuated by camshaft and rockers, a centrifugal governer on the inlet valve, a constant level carburettor

with a float and hand control, a filter for air and petrol, automatic lubrication of all moving parts by means of a revolving distributor, cooling by water circulation and tubed radiator, and a silencer. Ignition was by a platinum mesh designed by Bernardi himself.
Bernardi built successively in 1892 and 1893 two interesting vehicles with respectively two and three wheels, and in 1894 demonstrated an improved version of his old car in which he succeeded in covering 15 miles in one hour. This vehicle had further ingenious novelties such as roller bearings for the transmission and the wheel hubs, and had properly designed steering layouts for the first time, Bernardi being an enthusiast for the exact sciences and therefore for rational mechanisms.

Engines and canals

In the following years two companies were formed, Miari and Giusti of Padova and the Società Italiana Bernardi, for the exploitation of the inventions of the ingenious aristocrat. The commercial failure of Bernardi's cars was probably due paradoxically to the fact that they were too fast. They raised too much dust and subjected their occupants to too much bumping on the roads of the time.
Another interesting Italian venture was that connected

with the name of Giuseppe Murnigotti, an engineer born at Martinengo in the province of Brescia. For a long time he lived in Milan, where he had managerial jobs in technical fields; among other things he was responsible for lining the canals. In a patent granted in 1879 at the end of some years of study, Murnigotti described an engine with two single acting cylinders, fuelled by gas and having an ignition device. The power of this engine was low as it was only intended to drive a "velocipede" and it is not known if it was ever built. But the study, whatever its value, preceded those of Daimler.

Gas tank

In the same year, 1879, Dougal Clerk designed and built in England the first two-stroke engine, little different in principle from those in use today. The name derives from the fact that the entire cycle takes place in only two strokes of the piston, which, almost at the end of the power stroke, uncovers a series of holes in the cylinder out of which most of the exhaust gases pass before the piston reaches bottom dead centre. In the meantime, a jet of gas enters through other holes and occupies the place of the burnt residual gas, both cleaning out and refilling the cylinder, which is thus ready for a new cycle. It is interesting to note that Clerk's

ideas, which were based on those expressed in 1838 by his fellow Englishman Barnett, were developed principally to avoid Otto's patents in the four-stroke cycle. Some years later it was the turn of the French mathematician, Edouard Delamare-Deboutteville who in collaboration with a certain Malandin, in 1883 built first a tricycle (which blew up) and later a car powered by an i.c. engine driven by town gas compressed to 10 atmospheres in an appropriate tank. This was yet another attempt destined to have no further development in spite of the patent granted to the inventor in 1884. The failure to develop the ideas of Delamare-Deboutteville, some of which were interesting, was partly due to his early death in 1901.

Another pioneering attempt of the time was represented by Butler's petrol-fuelled tricycle built in England in 1885, whilst Roots, Knight and Bersey were other British pioneers.

To this point the story has been of the early development of the motor car in Europe. Side by side with this, however, there was a parallel story on the other side of the Atlantic. In America, the tardiness in the years before 1860, with the almost total absence of the heavy steam vehicles that were widely distributed in Europe, was remedied by 1876, the year of the Philadelphia Centennial.

SPORT FOR ALL COMERS

"The competition is open to all types of vehicle, providing that they are not dangerous, are easily controllable by the driver and do not cost too much to run!" Probably no other motoring competition has had its regulations written so widely as those of the Paris-Rouen race, run on Sunday, 22 July, 1894.

The motoring enthusiasts of the time took advantage of this lack of restriction, turning up at the offices of the "Petit Journal", where entries were accepted, with the most dissimilar and extravagant means of locomotion. Some would-be entrants arrived simply with a design in their pockets, seeing that the eliminating trials were to be held two months later. From the records of the competition it can be seen that at the closing date for the entries, these included vehicles powered "by gravity", and in particuar "by the weight of the passengers" (Rousset, Leval and Mansart); vehicles with "hydraulic" propulsion (Berthaud, Barriquand); compressed air vehicles (V. Popp, G. Peraire, Plantard, Roge-Andrillon); vehicles propelled "by levers"; vehicles with "automatic (?)" propulsion; vehicles driven "by a system of pendulums"; pedal vehicles; vehicles propelled by "combining liquids"; electric and semi-electric vehicles; and "compressed gas" vehicles.

Naturally most of these strange mechanical vehicles did not even make their appearance at the preliminary rally on 18 July at Neuilly. The reduced numbers that did arrive (26 out of 102 entered) were further reduced to 17 when they had to perform in the eliminating trials arranged for 22 July on five different routes in the suburbs of Paris. On this occasion a further four were eliminated, but by virtue of the successive re-runs 21 presented themselves for the "off" of the race itself.

The programme of the race — this too was unique rather than rare in the history of motor racing — provided for an hour's pause for lunch at the half-way mark at Nantes. The start signal was given at 8 a.m. and at once the Marquis De Dion's huge steam tractor and carriage went ahead, powerful with the horsepower in its boiler. It was followed by Peugeot and Panhard, whose direct rivalry supplied the real interest of the race which the Parisian newspaper had organised because of the frequent

A racing Panhard-Levassor was evidently not superstitious — it carried number 13.

A De Dion-Bouton steam "Victoria" was the first vehicle to finish the race, but was disqualified.

The "type 1894" Peugeot, equal winner with the Panhard-Levassor.

arguments between keen supporters of one of other of the two new companies.

The retirements soon began, including many of the steam-driven vehicles due to overheating, which was the classic type of breakdown of this sort of vehicle, especially when pushed to the maximum.

Several retirements were due to mechanical breakages caused by the roughness of the road surface, then in a far different state from those today. Many competitors succeeded in staying in the race, however, even after early breakdowns, because of the enthusiastic assistance of the spectators.

The results of the race are relatively unimportant as the criteria of classification were very different from those used today. The significant thing about the Paris-Rouen race was the intense interest exhibited by the crowd, which reached mob proportions in the city of arrival.

Arrival in triumph

The exhausted but elated pioneers, their faces masked by dust and oil (ejection of oil in all directions and without pause being one or the characteristics of all cars of the time) were received in triumph. They were hoisted on the shoulders of their delighted supporters, after their vehicles' unsteady, banging and rattling appearance. The "equipes" of Peugeot and Panhard, equally triumphant in the great adventure, celebrated success in traditional champagne. For the record however it should be added that the official winner was a Peugeot driven by Lamaître, to whom went the attractive first prize of 5000 francs put up by the "Petit Journal".

In fact, the first to cross the finishing line was De Dion's "steamer" but the jury decided to remove him from the classification in view of the competition requirements of economy and manoeuvrability. They can hardly be blamed. This mammoth weighed two tons, consumed 16 cwts of water and fuel, and two people — driver and fireman — were necessary to keep it going!

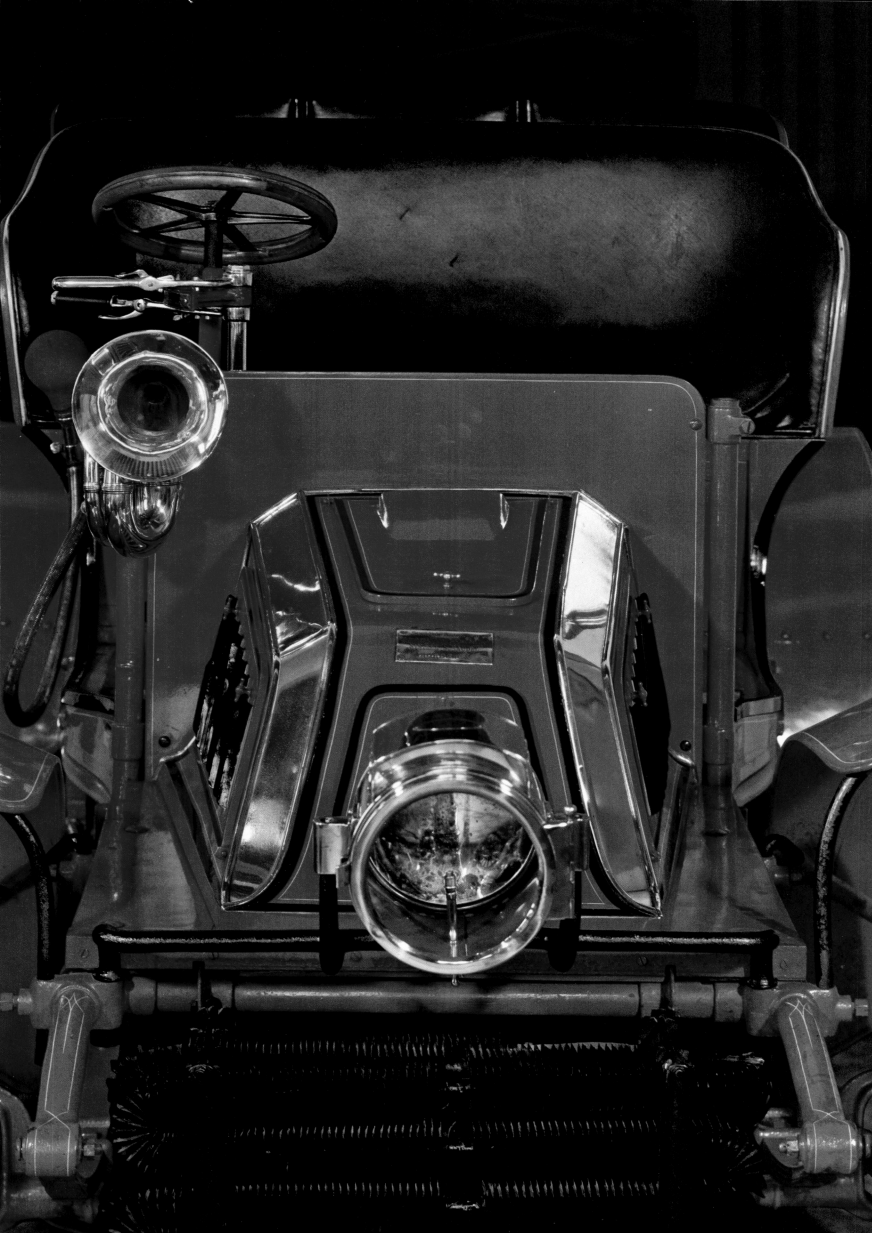

front view of a 1902 MONOBLOC "SCAUDEL SYSTEM"

engine · front mounted, two inclined cylinders
gearchange · 3 speeds plus reverse
speed · 25 m.p.h.
body · 4 seater tonneau

The elegant Ferrari 330 G.T.C. Below is an Opel 4/12 PS "Laubfrosch", which by 1924 had exceeded a production of 100,000.

CHAPTER THREE
POWER AT THE CROSSROADS

By 1879, three years after the famous exhibition at Philadelphia, George Baldwin Selden had deposited in the United States a historic patent for a "horseless carriage" driven by an internal combustion engine. This was destined to influence the development of the American motor industry for many years, right up to 1905 when Henry Ford had the courage to infringe it. The patent had no immediate results because, though Selden sensed the tremendous possibilities of the i.c. engine and the motor car, he was not particularly interested in their production.

Petrol tram

Towards the end of the century a number of interesting studies and actual cars began to make their appearance, all of American origin without any direct link with European industry, which continued to be relatively in advance.

Among these was that of Ellwood Haynes who, having exhibited his engine at Philadelphia and gained some publicity in doing so, built in 1888 a petrol engined vehicle equipped with a wick type carburettor of the kind fitted to the engine exhibited at the show. In

the same year Connolly built a petrol engined tram and gave public demonstrations in New York and Elizabeth, New Jersey.

Vehicles driven by i.c. engines were also built or designed about that time by E. Pennington, John W. Lambert, F. A. Huntingdon and W. T. Harris. Particularly worthy of mention is that of Pennington which aroused much interest for having covered, on the eve of the famous 55 mile Chicago-Evanston race, the distance of one mile in 58 seconds.

R. E. Olds, one of the American pioneers, driving his 1897 Oldsmobile. The illustration is from a woodcut of the time.

The remarkable power of Pennington's machine was due in part to his use of a system of double ignition, but this also caused the rapid death of the machine due to overheating. This explains the absence of the much talked of car from the race, which took place the following November in 1895. None of these experimental cars went into commercial production. Nor did a better fate await the technically interesting experiments of Henry Nadig, a mechanic of German extraction who, with his two sons Charles and Lawrence, built in Pennsylvania a crude vehicle powered by an engine inspired by Daimler's. His car was nearly destroyed by fire when the engine exploded, an accident due to the crude wick carburettor.

A similar vehicle was built in Milwaukee by another mechanic of German extraction, Gottfried Schloemer. In 1890 he appeared in the streets in his car which, in spite of having only two gears with no reverse, reached the respectable speed of 12 m.p.h. Charles H. Black, of Indianapolis, built a cyclecar in 1891, and J. I. Case in 1892 founded a company for the production of a tractor for commercial use.

To these should be added the name of Charles B. King, who was the first to take the rudimentary "horseless carriage" industry to Detroit, future world capital of motor production.

Probably the most interesting American car of the time was the famous petrol engined cyclecar built at Springfield in 1893 by the brothers Frank and Charles Duryea. It was driven by a single cylinder i.c. engine and was the first American car with electric ignition and spray carburation, both of which were designed by Frank.

One year later the Duryeas, who like many other pioneers came to the motor car after experience with the bicycle industry, produced a second model which among other things won the first American motor race, the Chicago-Evanston sponsored by the "Chicago Times Herald". This second car was driven by a four stroke engine in contrast to the first one, which was a two stroke. At the same time the Duryea brothers set up the first American motor company, the Duryea Wagon Company, but this was the cause of disputes between them and in 1898 Frank left the company, which went into liquidation after having built only eighteen cars.

The other interest attached to the name Duryea arises from the public controversy in 1912 between Charles and Ellwood Haynes. This arose from a meeting in 1906 of the Smithsonian Institute officially according to Haynes the position of first pioneer of the petrol engine in America. Duryea reacted six years later only when Haynes began to make use of the title. On the basis of documents submitted by Duryea, the Institute had to recognise his claims.

Ford comes on the scene

One year after the formation of the Duryea company, Henry Ford made his first appearance on the American motoring horizon, driving his first twin cylinder experimental cyclecar which developed four horsepower.

The other types of self-propelled vehicles, those not driven by i.c. engines, had by no means disappeared completely from the scene. Parallel to this first important period in the development of i.c. engined cars, a lesser story unfolded on both sides of the Atlantic relating to machines driven by steam or electricity.

So far as the former are concerned, there was a design in 1883 for a steam lorry by an Italian pioneer, Pecori, but the outcome is uncertain. In 1887 the French mechanic, Léon Serpollet, of Culoz built a revolutionary

J. Frank Duryea driving the car with which he took part in the Chicago-Evanston race. Beside him is Arthur W. White, race judge. The photo was taken on 28th November, 1895, during the race.

boiler, giving instant steam; and in a tricycle equipped with this engine he and a friend made a memorable journey two years later between Paris and Lyons in ten days (a Serpollet "steamer" was to do 75 m.p.h. at Nice in 1902, setting up an absolute speed record).

In 1891 Pecori designed another steam car, the last in Italy before the i.c. engine without question established its superiority.

In the meantime in France the younger Amédée Bollée, having succeeded his father in the management of the steam vehicle factory which bore his name, built a whole series of vehicles of interesting performance.

These included the "Mancelle" built in 1878 and capable of 26 m.p.h. with 16 people on board, and the "Marie Ann", the giant of motoring at the time (100 H.P. engine, a weight of 28 tons, and capable of carrying 100 tons). One "Marie Ann" covered over 450 miles in 74 hours at an average of 6 m.p.h. The "Nouvelle" followed, a small six-seater bus which was a steam forerunner of the modern station wagon — it weighed three tons and could reach 30 m.p.h. Then came the "Avant Courier", a 40 seater bus which was a great success due to its solidarity and reliability. In 1881 it was the turn of the "Rapide" which could exceed 37 m.p.h. Both models were built in some numbers.

World record

At this point even the famous Bollée factory had to recognise the progress made by the i.c. engine, and 1895 the production capacity was converted to meet the new demands. The following year a brother of the younger Amédée, Léon, built the first light vehicle with a tubular chassis mounted on three wheels, of which the front two steered and the rear one drove. It had a horizontal i.c. engine, air cooled and mounted on the rear wheel. This unusual vehicle, which developed 3 H.P. at 750 r.p.m. made its first appearance in the Paris - Marseilles race and in 1898 took the world 100 kilometres speed record at Étampes.

Another important changeover in production took place in the same year — that of Peugeot, an old-established steelworks whose origins lay in the 18th Century. After an inevitable period of re-organisation Peugeot

Stanley steam car built in 1898 by the Locomobile Company of America. This car was also seen in Europe. It was driven by a vertical two cylinder engine with boiler powered by petrol. Transmission was by single central chain to a crown wheel co-axial with the rear axle.

Henry Ford in his first car, built in 1897. A few years later he was to create a modern motor industry in the U.S. and to revolutionise industrial production. The car's warning bell was the forerunner of the klaxon horn.

began motor car production at the beginning of 1890. The most important French motor manufacturers in the early years of motoring were Panhard-Levassor, Peugeot, and De Dion-Bouton, a company created in 1881 by an agreement between the Marquis Albert De Dion, the mechanic Georges Bouton and the latter's brother-in-law, Trépardoux.

The 'opulent mechanic'

In 1895, De Dion-Bouton began to produce — while continuing to build the successful light steam tricycle capable of almost 40 m.p.h. — a version of the same vehicle with a single cylinder, 211 cc i.c. engine producing 1¼ H.P. The crude carburettor consisted of a receptacle holding petrol through which air was bubbled before passing down a long tube into the cylinder. By 1899, 22,000 of these tricycles had been built. It was in the same year that the circle of early French

manufacturers was completed with the birth of the first Renault.

The first Renault was created largely at the hands of Louis Renault himself, the outstanding example in the motoring field of the "wealthy mechanic". He was not a wealthy dilettante, limited to commissioning a specialist, but was entirely capable of designing and building a vehicle himself.

The car, built to a particularly advanced design, with much use of aluminium and roller bearings, had a gearbox which in top gear eliminated all intermediaries between crankshaft and drive-shaft and was virtually the first car with direct drive. Renault, a solid and reliable administrator of his affairs as one might expect from the son of a prudent Parisian button manufacturer, at once patented his invention. He quickly saw that the success of this car among his circle of friends merited series production.

Thus on 30 March, 1899, the Société Renault Frères was born with a capital of 60,000 francs on the family holding at Bilancourt, where the twenty-two-year-old Louis had devoted two years to becoming a mechanic. Louis was joined by his brother Marcel who was already familiar with industrial operations. In "Number One", of which they were about to build 25, the small 1¾ H.P. engine was substituted by a water cooled De Dion of 3½ H.P. In addition "Number Two" was being designed, which was to be the first completely enclosed car. Italy in this period was still in the stage of experiments at small craftsman level. In 1896 the Turin mechanic, Giovanni Martina, built an i.c. engined car to a design by Giuseppe Steffanini, commissioned by Michele Lanza. It was indirectly from this car that the first Italian motor factory arose. The car was bought by a Milan industrialist, Commendator Isotta, who also engaged Steffanini, thus creating in 1897 what was later to become one of the most famous European names — Isotta-Fraschini.

Silent and reliable

Before describing the circumstances in which at the turn of the century other European companies were formed — not only in France but also in the United Kingdom, Italy and elsewhere — it is necessary to look backward. Another type of mechanical transport with other than i.c. engines reached in the 1880's its peak of success in France and America, without any indication of the rapidity with which they were shortly to disappear. These were electrically propelled vehicles.

One characteristic that is immediately evident is the large number of names that figure in the list of manufactures in this chapter of the story of the car.

This is understandable when it is realised that the electric car presented far fewer problems than did those powered by steam or i.c. engines, and so their construction was relatively easy on a craftsman basis.

Nor is it difficult to imagine why so many enthusiasts were taken by the idea of building such a vehicle.

1892 Scotte steam bus. Eight seats, two cylinders, burning wood or coal. Speed — 7½ m.p.h. (Motor Museum, Rochetaillée).

The d.c. motor was already well developed, as were lead acid batteries, and thus all basic elements of an electric car were available. The intelligent exploitation of these elements permitted some of these vehicles, built between 1881 and the end of the century, to give outstanding performances in terms of speed.

Where the electric car was inherently deficient however was in its range, the distance it could cover before recharging. It was this that was to lead to its virtual extinction around 1910.

Carriage for the Sultan

In France the first to construct vehicles of this type on any appreciable scale, was Jeantaud, a carriage builder gifted with considerable ingenuity (among other things owed to him are fundamental studies on steering geometry, still accepted by engineers of today). He made his first model in 1881 and later, availing himself of the improvements recently made to batteries by his fellow countrymen, Faure and Planté, took part in the Paris-Bordeaux race. So did two other builders of electric vehicles, the Englishman Park, of Brighton, and the Frenchman Pouchain. The years 1885-1890 saw many experiments with electric vehicles and a few years later cars of this type were recording some exceptional performances. In England the Gladiator-Pingault covered the flying kilometre in one minute 46 seconds and the five miles in eight minutes 56 seconds. A few months later, at the "Velodrome de la Seine" in Paris, Edmond de Parrodil recorded 57.8 secs. for the flying kilometre, while the journalist Breyer in the same year covered

The Renault "inside drive", the first totally enclosed car in the world.

10 kilometres in nine minutes 54 seconds — nearly 40 miles per hour.

This was the era of boom for the electric vehicle. The more important manufacturers were Doré, Bouquet, Garon, Mildé, Richard and Homard. There was a final sensational record when in 1899 Camille Jenatzy covered the flying kilometre in 34 secs. at the fantastic speed of 105.904 k.p.h. (about 65 m.p.h.), in an incredible vehicle, the "Jamais Contente".

Madame and Marcel Renault in the first Renault 1 1/3 H.P.

In America the appearance of efficient electric cars dates from 1891, the year in which Doctor Orazio Lugo, of Italian origin, designed one on behalf of the Electric Road Carriage Company of Boston, the first company in the world founded to build electric vehicles for private use. About the same time another electric car appeared, built by William Morrison of Iowa which recorded an interesting record by running for 13 hours at around 15 m.p.h.

The World Exhibition of Chicago, held in 1893, gave a considerable impetus to the design of electric vehicles in America. The organisers of the show — which presented a mass of technical innovations the like of which has probably never been equalled, from the telephone to electric light, from the typewriter to the photographic camera — offered prizes for practicable projects for land vehicles with any means of propulsion other than animal. It was due to this incentive that the Chicago Perambulator Company developed an electric tricycle which, like other similar vehicles, was called a "rolling chair", for carrying visitors round the Exhibition.

Another interesting vehicle was built in the same period by David M. Parry, of Indianapolis, who received orders for one thousand immediately after the first successful trials. The death of the principal customer prevented this deal being carried through and Parry in disgust turned to the i.c. engined car, later creating two historic vehicles — the "Overland", and the "Pathfinder", each with twelve-cylinder engines. In lists of American manufacturers of electric vehicles were two more names, those of Keller and Degenhart, whose "rol-

ling chair" was used for some time as means of transport between buildings in large companies.

In England, too, there where similar efforts which in at least one case, that of the Ward Electric Car Company of London, reached industrial proportions. Among other orders, this company supplied a number of vehicles for internal transport at the Chicago Exhibition and built a sumptuous carriage for the Sultan of Turkey.

With the cyclists

By 1894, the year of the Paris-Rouen race, it was clear that the era of motor racing had been born. The competitive spirit was awakening in the hearts of enthusiasts together with the strong nerves necessary to undertake a journey in the rickety vehicles of those days.

In the same year as the Paris-Rouen race, the Austrian Von Liebig undertook a remarkable journey for those days — over 585 miles — in a "Victoria Benz" with a 5 H.P. single cylinder engine. The engine consumed

A steam delivery van, built at the time when electric vehicles were popular for use within cities.

30 gallons of petrol and 340 gallons of cooling water! Three years earlier a Peugeot had covered a much greater distance, 1280 miles, in 139 hours at an average speed of 9 m.p.h. but this had been done in short stages and for a curious reason — it was the first "suiveur" car in the history of cycle racing. Authorisation to accompany the riders in the Paris-Brest cycle race was requested by the Peugeot company which intended to use the occasion for the final development of their car.

Having obtained permission, a 2 H.P. with a Daimler engine was sent from the factory at Valentigney. After meeting 206 cyclists at the start line in Paris, the Peugeot moved off with them and in stages successfully covered the whole course.

The 1280 miles are arrive at by adding to the 750 of the race itself the journeys to and from the factory. It was this unusual exploit which suggested to the "Petit Journal", which had promoted the Paris-Brest cycle race, the idea of the Paris-Rouen race for "horseless carriages".

A Baker electric brougham built in 1912 and re-equipped in 1951 with solar batteries (in the roof), supplied by the International Rectifier Corporation.

THE AMBITIOUS MARQUIS

Albert De Dion seen in 1932 driving his 1898 "viv-à-vis".

Panhard and Levassor were both engineers. Between another pair of names famous in the early days of the motor car, Albert De Dion and Georges Bouton however, there were enormous differences not only professionally but also in social background and even physique. Tall and stout, the Marquis De Dion was the son of an ancient Belgian noble family, the house of De Dion-Le Val, although he was born in 1856 at Carquefou near Nantes in France. His partner Bouton was a wiry little man of humble Parisian origin, a very able mechanic and naturally a motor enthusiast. It is not difficult to imagine the atmosphere in which their long and happy association came to be formed.

Model-maker

The imposing Marquis alternated his social duties and frequent visits to the workshop in which the first "horseless carriage" enthusiasts bustled around their cars. As for Bouton, he was at home in that workshop and his interests led him not so much to the somewhat crude petrol vehicles but to the much more highly developed "steamer" — the steam carriage with its decades of development, but whose slow but inexorable decline was beginning even then.
Georges Bouton had in a certain sense grown up in a

more graceful tradition. His real profession was making models — toys for rich children — which he built in his shop together with his brother-in-law Trépardoux. It was probably this unusual ability to execute precision work in miniature which led to his future success. The Marquis De Dion was a frequent visitor to motor car workshops, and, with the cars that he bought from time to time, followed religiously the uncertain technical progress of the period. He did not limit himself to solemn parades down the Champs Elysées. He craved to race with other enthusiasts, to crown with a major success his position as a leading figure in that sphere. While waiting for one of the many suggestions for car racing which were discussed around 1880 to become reality, he decided to prepare for it by building for himself the vehicle which had been in his mind for some time — a steam tricycle with rapid steaming boiler, very light and therefore relatively fast. It was the first time that anyone had thought of building a vehicle exclusively for racing. Before this, and for many years afterwards, races were run with cars that were generally available.

Restless

The Marquis' ideas were good but did not progress beyond the theoretical stage. He needed a capable builder, capable enough to build something that no-one had built before, and build it in such a way that it might go on working. That man proved to be Georges Bouton.

The industrial partnership between the two men dates from 1881, and the tricycle was quickly, and well, built. But the restless Marquis had to wait until 20 April 1887, before he could finally take part in a race. On that day in fact, the first car race in history took place, the Neuilly-Versailles-Neuilly, a distance of 20 miles, organised by the journalist Fossier. De Dion and his tricycle hurled themselves into the race and completed the course in 1 hour and 14 minutes — not so fast in a vehicle that could do almost 40 m.p.h. One detail should be added — he was the only competitor!

Alone again

It was the fate of De Dion never to taste the fruits of genuine victory even though this was probably his principal aim in life. Four years after the Neuilly-Versailles, he took part in the second race in history on the racetrack at Longchamps. This time he had an opponent, who also had a steam tricycle, a Serpollet. But the latter broke down halfway through the race and De Dion had to travel the second half by himself again.

A few months later it was a 25 miles race on the track at Vincennes, and again the only entrant was a De Dion-Bouton tricycle. The Marquis, probably out of pique, did not drive himself, but sent as his driver a certain Lacaux. It was just as well; otherwise he would have tasted the bitterness of having the race stopped by a representative of the police concerned about danger to the public after one spectator had almost fallen under the wheels of the tricycle.

For the first real and important race, the Paris-Rouen of 1894, De Dion used a much more robust "steamer" than his tricycle, because of the distance involved. But the first prize was awarded by the jury to the second car to arrive, a Peugeot, because the Marquis' vehicle was held to be too expensive and too difficult to handle, and therefore not in accord with the race regulations.

Organisation

From that time onwards the Marquis was never seen again among the competitors in a motor race on French soil, although he took part in organisation. He ran the Paris-Bordeaux race in 1895 with Pierre Giffard and soon afterwards founded the Automobile Club de France with the journalist Paul Meyan.

Though he no longer took part his name continued to be carried in races by the machines which came out of the partnership with Bouton at Puteaux. De Dion always appeared among the leading places in race results, whether carried by steam cars, the last of which appeared in the Paris-Marseilles in 1897, or by a series of i.c. engined vehicles, developed from the crude but successful tricycle of 1895.

The following year a second great motor race was run, the Paris-Bordeaux and return, suggested by the enthusiastic Marquis De Dion and Pierre Giffard. This was a very different race from that of the previous year. The regulations were much more severe and the race was a clear cut victory for the i.c. engine. It marked the virtual disappearance of the steam car, notwithstanding the excellent performance of the Bollée steam bus, the "Nouvelle", so large as to have even a toilet on board. In total there were 70,000 gold francs for this race in prizes.

As usual, most of the entries failed to turn up at the start and the list of the 21 who actually took part exhibits the variety of technical solutions that still persisted. In the race were Jeantaud's electric car, six steam vehicles (including "La Nouvelle"), twelve i.c. engined cars and two motor-cycles.

One of these two-wheelers was a remarkable device built by Félix Millet. The engine had a five cylinder radial engine in the rear wheel, the movement of the conrods being transmitted to a crankshaft co-axial with the wheel hub. Another vehicle aroused the curiosity of the spectators was the "Eclair", driven by Edouard Michelin, one of the brothers, who some years before had begun to manufacture pneumatic cycle tyres and who were now trying to introduce similar products into the motor car field. The "Eclair" was a Peugeot-Daimler modified to give 4 H.P. but its particular distinction lay in the four pneumatic tyres that for the first time lined the rims. The immediate outcome was not encouraging: 50 punctures, due in part obviously to the terrible state of the roads and to the excessive fragility of the covers used.

All the same it cannot be said that the results were entirely negative for in successive races there was an ever increasing number of cars fitted with pneumatic tyres.

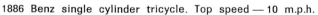

1886 Benz single cylinder tricycle. Top speed — 10 m.p.h.

1899 Renault "3½ H.P." It was the second car built by Louis Renault and had a water-cooled De Dion engine.

The passion for veteran cars knows no frontiers. This fascinating, if expensive, hobby is found all over the world. The photo shows a 1908 Léon Peugeot. Below an 1895 Benz hotel bus.

The race was won, in effect, by Emile Levassor, who drove alone in one of his own cars. Having reached Bordeaux in 24 hours he at once began the return journey, meeting his competitors coming the other way. He arrived in Paris 48 hours and 47 minutes after he left, having averaged 24.6 k.p.h. (over 15 m.p.h.). But as the rules required that the winner should be in a four seater, the official victory went to the second car home, a Peugeot-Daimler driven by Koehnin.

Flooded Roads

In the year following this enthusiastic racing season, 1896, a third great French race, the Paris-Marseilles-Paris, was organised by the first French motoring weekly, the "France Automobile". For the first time the competition was divided into stages, ten to be precise. During the pauses the machines were put into bonded parks supervised by the police. There was the usual last-minute reduction in the number of entries — 52 being reduced to 31 on the day of the race, 24 September. There were 23 cars, 3 Léon Bollée voiturettes, and 5 De Dion-Bouton tricycles.

This time even the weather was ranged against the heroic competitors. A series of violent storms burst over the course, and the weather felled trees and flooded the roads. Only 13 vehicles arrived in Marseilles, and the drivers had undergone every kind of adventure, one

48

even finding himself near naked in the middle of one of the stages.

The wind had howled into a tear in his trousers, causing the consequent, involuntary, striptease.

There were, however, more serious accidents. Léon Bollée ran off the road (he was in one of the first cars built in his factory after the conversion from steamers to i.c. engines) and hit a tree blown down by the storm. Bollée was injured but fortunately not seriously, and succeeded in continuing the race. Later on, between Montélimar and Orange, Levassor's Panhard skidded and turned over in a ditch. Levassor was injured but his co-driver, D'Ostingue, continued after giving him into the care of the spectators. The injuries the great industrialist and sportsman had received turned out to be more serious than at first seemed. He never recovered and died the following year aged 53.

The race was won by Mayade in a Panhard-Levassor which completed the course in 67 hours and 43 minutes at an average speed of 25 k.p.h. (over 15 m.p.h.). Two other Panhard-Levassors were in the first four places. A sensational fact was that a De Dion tricycle arrived only 3 hours and 19 minutes after the winner, a result which was attributed to the fact that it was fitted with pneumatics. This was due to a new idea of the Michelin brothers who, far from being discouraged by the disastrous results of the Paris-Bordeaux race, had drawn the logical conclusions and had adequately reinforced their tyres. They then bought two hundred Bollée voiturettes and one hundred De Dion tricycles, putting

Tradition died hard. The driver of this 1906 Vauxhall had to sit high in the rear just as in a horse cab.

1897 Hugot. Rear single cylinder 3½ H.P. engine. The brake was applied by a small wheel underneath the steering wheel. The body was in wickerwork.

THE ACETYLENE DAYS

The first "horseless carriage" had simple oil lamps when they had any at all. The yellowish flame rising from the wick, immersed in a small container of oil or petrol, provided just about enough light for the driver to avoid the larger holes. "Real" carriages, those with horses, travelled much faster but this light, conveniently beamed by a parabolic mirror and optical front glass, was good enough even for them. Motorists in those heroic times did not too often commit themselves to night travel, not only because it was ill-advised on the road surface but also because a meeting in the dark with any enemies of their noisy mechanical monsters might well have had unpleasant consequences.

At the turn of the century acetylene lighting began to be used on motor cars in view of the higher speeds that called for a more vivid and penetrating light. This was in spite of a certain resistance to their use due to a variety of well known defects — the danger of explosion, the necessity of frequent inspection of the carbide-water reaction, the short life of the fuel supply.

For about fifteen years acetylene lighting was the basic system in use on motor cars.

Efficient system

Contrary to popular belief, such systems attained a high level of efficiency, not only as regards the gas generator and the characteristics of the nozzle from which the vivid greenish flame issued, but also in the lamp itself. The latest models, produced just before their final disappearance 50 years ago, looked similar to those in use on modern cars.

The problem of dimming had been resolved by means of a hemispherical concave mirror which could be manually rotated through 180° until the flame itself was completely obscured. In this position, used for cruising in company with other vehicles or in the city, the headlamp sent out only a part of its light, reflected from the parabolic mirror behind. When however the dimming mirror was rotated until it was immediately behind the flame, it intensified the light.

This small mirror system, designed by Zeiss, was used for electric headlamps when they were first adopted in spite of the many deficiences of the batteries of the time. Later it was found more practical to adopt a second, less powerful bulb outside the focus of the parabola.

Double filament

The use of double filament (full and dim) bulbs dates from the second decade of this century. But as these only weakened the beam (due to the lower power of the second filament) and did not dip it, they had little success until fairly recent times. Improved manufacturing techniques have now permitted the construction of a lamp incorporating a small mirror designed to throw the light beam of the second filament upwards.

This was a big step forward. Not only was it possible to obtain a light thrown downwards (due to double reflection from the small mirror and the parabola) from the second filament, but it was also possible to eliminate the "hole" in the parabolic surface where the second lamp used to fit, thus improving the "full" beam.

This progress was for a while cancelled out by the need

to incorporate in the headlamp an auxiliary bulb — the side or parking light — as required by law in many countries. The transposition of this light to a separate housing occurred only after the second world war when headlamps were built into wings or on the front of the car. The separate mounting of the headlamps had been a legacy from the time when they were not supplied with the coachwork but were chosen by the owner according to his preference.

With the parabolic mirror returning to its unbroken form in this way, and the bulbs themselves being im-

proved by the use of inert gases which reduced "aging". headlamps showed no major progress for about a decade. Towards the end of the fifties however, an international conference accepted the so-called "European unified asymmetrical headlamp" with the lens modified to lengthen the right-hand beam. This improves visibility for vehicles approaching one another, an important safety feature.

Soon after, because of new legislation, coupled lamps began to be used. These consisted of the normal full/dip headlamps with the full beam coupled in circuit with

a separate single filament long range driving light. This development provided lighting suitable for the high level of cruising speeds which had become normal.

Another technical revolution now in progress is the increasing use of iodine vapour lamps. The advantages of this type of lighting system lie in the improvement in the quantity and quality of light produced for equal consumption, and in the absence of deterioration of the light with time ("aging" due to blackening of the bulb and consumption of the filament).

Iodine lamps require absolutely clean handling and create certain problems due to the high temperatures at which they work. Nevertheless they are now fitted as standard to certain cars and the number is rapidly increasing. Until recently their use was limited to cars with double headlamps because it had not been possible to produce a dipping type iodine lamp, but the necessary bulbs are now available.

A last-minute inspection of René de Knyff's Panhard-Levassor before the Paris-Amsterdam race run from 7 to 13 July, 1898.

them on sale after equipping them with their tyres. Another interesting point in the results of the Paris-Marseilles-Paris was the presence in the first ten places of two Delahayes. These were machines fitted with 6 H.P. engines, built by Emile Delahaye, an enthusiast and expert who had recently entered the ranks of manufacturers. He had applied an important novelty to his cars — the forced circulation of cooling water. The De Dion tricycles which took part in the race also had something new, a system of electric ignition similar to those in use today.

As an appendix to the story of these great races it can be added that the following year, 1897, was to see one of the last victories of a steam carriage, that of De Dion on the Nice circuit which included the novelty of a small hill climb. In that year competitive activity started in Italy, with the Arona-Stresa-Arona race organised by the motor club recently founded in Milan. This was a modest race of only 22 miles but it was the first step.

France was still the leading country of the world for motor vehicles but in other countries of Europe enthusiasts were beginning to lay the foundations of an industry that would make up the years lost.

1896 Peugeot coupé. (Motor Museum, Rochetaillée).

HORSEPOWER MEASUREMENT

Like people we meet often and with whom we have become familiar, even though in reality we know little about them, three motoring cyphers have come into use, although not everyone understands exactly what they mean. These cyphers are SAE, DIN and CUNA and one of these is usually found immediately after the word "horsepower" when we read information on the power characteristics of an engine.

This does not imply that different "sizes" of H.P. exist — the formula has been standardised by international convention — but that any given engine may be placed on the dynamometer, the device used for measuring horsepower, in varying degress of completeness. The engine therefore gives differing net output figures. The cyphers SAE, DIN and CUNA therefore refer to the condition of the engine when its power is measured.

These three conventions used by motor manufacturers for measuring horsepower have been established respectively by the Society of Automotive Engineers (SAE) in America, by the Deutsche Industrie-normen (DIN) in Germany and, in Italy, by the Commissione per l'Unificazione automobilistica (CUNA). The differences are given below.

SAE

The engine is placed on the dynamometer after being stripped of its fan, water pump, dynamo, silencer and air filter. It is evident that an engine cannot function in normal use in this condition.

DIN

The engine is placed on the dynamometer in the same condition in which it is fitted in a vehicle. This method gives results much closer to reality but even this does not correspond exactly to the power of an engine installed in a vehicle because, as in the other systems used, such factors as climate, pressure and humidity of the atmosphere, the type of lubricants used etc. are controlled under the test conditions in a way that is not possible with normal use in a vehicle.

CUNA

This is a compromise between SAE and DIN. Only the silencer and air cleaner are removed for testing i.e. only those accessories not strictly necessary for the functioning of the engine. Clearly even without the silencer the engine will run perfectly well. Indeed it will work better as the silencer absorbs power.

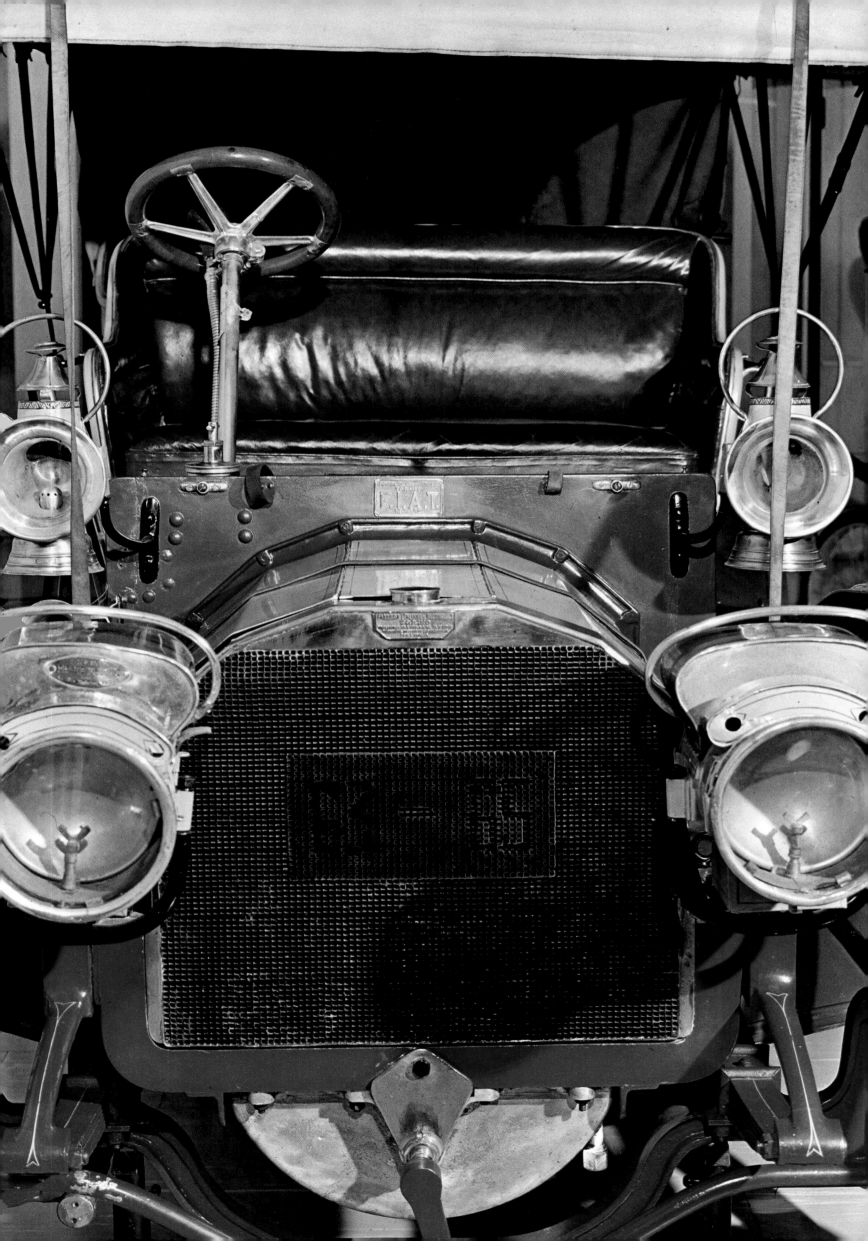

front view of a 1903 FIAT "16/24 H.P."

engine · front mounted vertical 4 cylinder in two blocks
bore and stroke · 110 × 110 mm.
capacity · 4,181 c.c.
output · 16 H.P. at 1,200 r.p.m.
ignition · low tension magneto
clutch · multiplate
gearchange · 4 speeds plus reverse
transmission · chain
weight · 2,970 lbs.

Two cars for the sporting woman. There are over sixty years between the two photographs.

CHAPTER FOUR

FASHION GOES TO THE HEAD

The last decade of the 19th century not only saw the running of the first motor races, with exciting and sometimes tragic consequences, but also marked the foundation of a large number of companies both in Europe and in America, amongst which were several of the names that were to become important in the future.

In France, a great number of new manufacturers joined the names already well-known such as Panhard-Levassor, De Dion-Bouton, Peugeot, Renault, Delahaye and Bollée. In 1895 Bertieti, Dietrich, Dewald and Mors (who built under Daimler licence) began production and the 1898 list of manufacturers worthy of mention included Chenard-Walker in Asnières, Éclipse, Minerva, Société Française d'Autos Electriques, Hurtu, Rheda, The

Société Française d'Automobile, Touraine, Créanche, Aigle, Richard (with later became "Unic") Marot Gardon et Company, Energie, David-Bourgeois, Gobron-Brillié, Vedrine-Breugniot, the Société Ancienne d'Automobiles et Traction de Paris, Sphinx, Nationale, Dumond-Saralegui of Levallois and Gaillardet in Puteaux.

Pioneers amalgamate

Others, however, are worth more than this passing mention. In 1897 Alexandre Darracq founded at Suresnes the company which bore his name and was to figure prominently in the early years of the new century. In 1904, for instance, a 100 H.P. Darracq driven by Barras took the world flying kilometre record and it was Darracq's branch in Milan which was to be indirectly the origin of Alfa Romeo in 1909.

In 1898 Emile Delahaye, the ingenious manufacturer of "sporty" vehicles in his small workshop in Tours, amalgamated with Desmarais and Morane, hydraulic machine manufacturers in Paris. He transferred his factory to the French capital, where production was recommenced on a larger scale. The moving spirit of this change was a young engineer, Charles Weissenbach, who had benefited from experience with Léon Bollée voiturettes. The workmanship of the Delahaye models was of high quality, and the company quickly became famous.

In the same year another interesting new model was introduced — the Decauville "3½ H.P." built by the Société des Voitures Automobiles Decauville, which was founded to exploit the patents of two Bordeaux engineers, Cornilleau and Guesdon. The engine was rear-mounted — a relatively new technique — a vertical twin with separate cylinders. It had a capacity of 494 c.c. and produced 3.75 H.P. at 1200 r.p.m.

Four reverse speeds

Ignition was by means of a battery, two coils and two plugs; there were two forward gears and no reverse; and the engine was air-cooled. The Decauville has become famous in the story of the motor car for its lightness — it weighed under 4½ cwt.

In the meantime improved models began to issue from

In the early days of motoring, women drivers were rare — and taking a car ride to the country was a hobby of only the rich, as this photograph shows.

the workshops of established French companies, which were showing an adventurous spirit of innovation.

This was true of the "B 1" Panhard-Levassor, a more heavily built car than its predecessors; among many improvements common to vehicles of the time it had one characteristic of its own. By using a separate lever it was possible to reverse all four forward gears, a feature which was to remain unique.

Renault in the same period built the first car with an enclosed driving position — a justly famous model though one which may have a ludicrous appearance to modern eyes. On a very short wheel base was fitted the high coachwork necessary to allow the fashionably dressed men and women of the time to enter comfortably with their imposing headgear. Surprisingly, the idea of totally enclosed coachwork was not followed for a long time by other makes, even though the car was in effect the forerunner of the modern saloon.

France at this time was the undoubted world leader in the field of motoring. The new mechanical means of transport had passed from being a curiosity, accepted or not according to taste, to being a fascinating possession. It provided the opportunity for adventure — besides

A less publicised one had been held in 1894 by "Figaro". In 1898 the first Continental motor show was held in the square in front of Les Invalides from 15 June to 3 July, almost at the same time as a similar show in Boston in the United States. It represented an act of considerable courage by which the Automobile Club de France challenged public opinion. In the previous year a few models had been shown in a corner of the Palace de L'Industrie — but in a show mainly devoted to bicycles.

Change of heart

It cannot be said that authority viewed the occasion with enthusiasm. The President of the French Republic himself, Félix Faure, as he hurriedly took his leave of the organisers, did not hesitate to say "How ugly these machines are, and how they smell!".

When the second edition of the show took place the following year, however, public interest had grown enormously. It was at this show that the tradition was born — it was to be maintained to the present day — of

An 1898 De Dion-Bouton.

This Amédée Bollée car of 1900 won the 1963 Paris-Turin rally.

A 1902 George Richard.

ostentation and eccentricity — for both sexes. In 1897 the first ladies' "world motor racing championship" was organised by a newspaper, "L'Echo de Paris", on a short road circuit at Longchamps. The name of the winning lady driver who attracted the attention of the men and not a little secret admiration from her own sex, is unknown. But it was perhaps the first tentative chapter in the still developing love story of woman and the motor car. In the Paris reports of the same year, a competition for new styles of coachwork was announced.

Two of the prize-winning designs in the 1894 competition run by the Paris newspaper "Figaro".

a profusion of flowers and lights, and even an orchestra to entertain the visitors.

French industry was now in rapid expansion. There was a waiting time of two months for a Darracq, six for a Delahaye or a Peugeot, eight for a Mors and twenty for a Panhard-Levassor. Even then the customer received only the chassis and had to make his own arrangements for the bodywork with a specialist.

The police, faced with some thousands of cars on the dusty roads of the region of the Seine, met for the first time problems which other countries were to have to deal with shortly afterwards. As early as 1892 the Paris Prefecture had established a speed limit of 12 k.p.h. (under 8 m.p.h.) within the walls of the city. Now a

By the beginning of the century the i.c. engine was revolutionising the carriage of goods. This is a 1898 Daimler motor lorry.

succession of other problems arose. What was to be the Rule of the Road? How was precedence to be given at crossroads? How were vehicle and driver to be identified?

The last of these problems was solved by giving each car a registered number incorporating the number of the Département as already used by the Ministry for Mines, to which body was given the responsibility for vehicle registration. This system is still in use in France today. Then there was the problem of the position of the steering wheel, which was beginning to replace the tiller — was it to be placed to right or left? It was not to be easily solved and was under discussion for several years to come.

Often decisions were contradictory, especially as there continued to be uncertainty on whether to drive on the right or the left. It was not until 1908 that, perhaps due to the influence of America where it had already been decided to drive on the right, it was generally decided to mount the steering wheel on the left. Even then there were many exceptions as any early British motorist on the Continent found.

The walking man

The explosion of popular interest was to be reproduced in other European countries within a few years. In Britain before the turn of the century the foundation of a small factory, Wolseley, in 1895 was exceptional, when it is remembered that the country still suffered under the notorious "Red Flag Act". This required that cars on the road should be preceded by a walking man carrying a red flag — undoubtedly not the best of encouragement for starting a car factory. Although the law was rescinded in 1896, the motorist was still severely restricted by a limit of 12 m.p.h. which was to be raised to 20 m.p.h. in 1904 and remain at that speed until the end of the first World War.

A year later the English branch of Daimler was founded in Coventry, with the intention of building for the British market cars identical to those of the German parent. Some official recognition of the motor car was given when the Prince of Wales, the future Edward VII, visited the Coventry workshop. The Prince accepted a short drive in a "Cannstatt" driven by F. R. Simms, who had invented an improved version of the hot-tube ignition fitted in all Daimlers of the time. In fact, both the

English and German companies were to remain faithful to this system for many years even after high tension systems were available and were being fitted by competitors.

The engine of the first English Daimlers was a 1500 c.c. Vee-twin with four gears. Later a 3000 c.c. four cylinder was fitted. A characteristic common to all Daimlers for many years was unequal diameter of the wheels; the front ones were smaller. The company was to produce some of the most luxurious vehicles ever to be built in the British Isles.

Also in 1896, an agreement was made between Selwyn Francis Edge and Montagu Stanley Napier. From this was to arise the company bearing the latter's name and

A 1932 Riley in a race for post-vintage cars.

which was to become famous both for the oustanding cars and aero-engines. Edge was a racing cyclist who became a motoring enthusiast. Napier, a friend of his youth, went into partnership with Edge to study French racing cars and to build similar ones in England.

Pneumatic tyres

Edge and Napier bought the Panhard-Levassor which René de Knyff had brought into second place in the Paris-Marseilles race, having borrowed the 30,000 gold francs purchase price. After various modifications, including the fitting of Dunlop pneumatic tyres in place of the original solid tyres, replacing the tiller by a steering wheel and fitting an English engine, a new Napier 9 H.P. was born in 1900.

Later that year a four-cylinder 16 H.P. was built, the first of a´ long series of fine cars which, right down to 1925, were to delight motorists on both sides of the Channel with their outstanding technical qualities.

Edge himself, having become in the meantime the United Kingdom concessionaire for De Dion-Bouton, was to figure in 1907 in fierce dispute with the Marquis when Edge created the company of De Dion-Bouton Limited.

A 1912 Chenard Walker.

A 1902 De Dion-Bouton imported into England by S. F. Edge.

A solemn example of the working in Britain of the "Red Flag Act", under which all vehicles had to be preceded by a man walking ahead. The car in the illustration is an 1895 Knight two-seater.

The same historic year of 1896 saw also the birth of Humber in Coventry by the conversion of an existing bicycle factory into one for building motor cars. The first Humbers were an immediate public success. The "Four Cylinder", designed in the opening years of the new century by a young French engineer, Louis Coatalen, received so many orders that assembly lines were set up in the streets outside the factory.

In 1898 Riley started as a company producing both cars and cycles, but production was soon concentrated exclusively on motor cars. Their second model, a 10 H.P., was to become famous, partly due to its unusual radiator shape, consisting of two eccentric circles. This car was to remain in production for ten years without change.

BRAKING BY TREE TRUNK

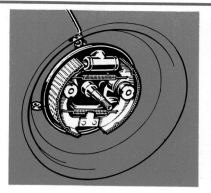

Drum brake.

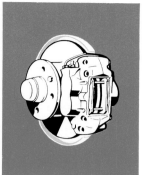

Disc brake.

The story of motor car brakes has ironical elements for a motorist of the 1960's who was driving before World War II. In the 1930's some manufacturers were still building cars without front wheel brakes. The relative slowness of designers to accept the idea that it was necessary to provide an efficient braking system is even more disconcerting when it is realised that, right from the first decade of the century, motor cars were capable of such speeds that instant braking was a necessity if an emergency arose.

The casual attitude towards braking in the early days is illustrated by the first car crossing of the St-Gothard Pass, by the French engineer Arrou in a 3½ H.P. De Dion-Bouton in 1901. The account of the trip records that "the leather-lined brakes were burned out after only a few minutes of the descent" and that, having reduced speed to almost zero to avoid going over the mountain side at every bend, it was necessary "to fasten a tree trunk to the car with a steel cable, which was then dragged behind".

Dual system

The brakes of these hurtling vehicles consisted then of shoes acting on the wheel-rims, a logical consequence of the ancestry of the horse-drawn carriage. A series of tests in New York in 1902, which was considered impressive for the time, showed that from the braking point of view the car was considerably safer than the carriage. The car could stop in a quarter of the distance required by a carriage with four horses.

Of course, this would now be considered far from a safe braking distance.

In the following years, partly because of the legal requirements operated in some countries, there was general adoption of a dual braking system, one acting on the rear wheels and the other on the transmission.

The first of these continued for some time to depend on external shoes lined with leather or camel skin, but this system was soon replaced by internal shoes and drums. The transmission brake acted on the differential when transmission was by chain or on the transmission shaft itself when these were introduced·

Although the general introduction of four-wheel brakes was slow, the first studies came quite soon. Early ex-

periments took place between 1905 and 1910 and some strange solutions were envisaged, such as the control of brakes through movement of the stub axle (Renouf) or a system which used compressed air and necessitated the carrying of an air bottle (Cavello).

The complexity of these ideas came partly from the need for braking to be independent of the position of the front wheels and partly from the need to avoid dangerous reactions by the braking on the steering itself.

Isotta-Fraschini introduced four-wheel brakes in 1909, and dropped them the following year. The credit for a successful system controlled by one action is due to the Frenchman Perrot, manager of Argyll, a Scots car manufacturer. In 1913 his brakes were first fitted to racing cars, above all due to the interest of the racing driver Boillet. Slowly, until about 1932, they were adopted by more and more companies, and extended to production cars.

Hydraulic actuation gradually came into general use, though the first users met difficulty in guaranteeing their reliable and safe functioning, because of the danger of fracture of the often exposed pipes or because the liquids then used corroded the seals or froze at low temperatures. In the meantime the friction materials themselves were being improved, first by using cast-iron shoes and later asbestos lining compounds. The design of shoes was also improving to give braking effect in proportion to the speed of rotation of the hubs, while in some cases the adoption of alloys for the body of the drums assisted heat dissipation.

Drum and disc

Recent years have seen the gradual substitution of the drum by the disc, pioneered by the British concerns Girling and Dunlop. This system — which offers intense braking especially at high speeds, resists "fade" and is unaffected by water and mud — is now used on all four wheels for high-speed cars and on many family cars' front wheels. Pads can also be substituted easily.

The types of brake-servo mechanisms — which reduce the effort required from the driver — in most general use today is that which uses the depression (vacuum) in the engine inlet manifold.

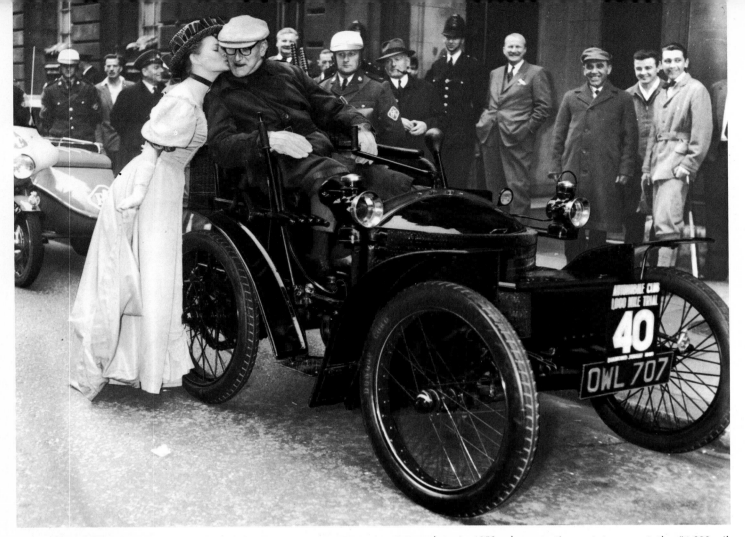

Celebrated motoring pioneer St. John C. Nixon receives an appropriate salute in 1959 when starting out to repeat the "1,000-mile trial" run round Britain in the 1899 Wolseley which he had used in the first trial. Below an 1899 Darracq.

Much later Riley was absorbed by Morris Motors; then, like Wolseley, it became part of the British Motor Corporation and subsequently of Leyland Motors.

About this time, Panhard-Levassor cars began to be imported into England. The fact is of particular interest because the man concerned was the Hon. Charles Stuart Rolls, youngest son of Lord Llangattock, who was to become famous in motor car history as the co-founder of Rolls-Royce. This young man lived for motoring and even in 1898 his "stable" consisted of a Bollée tricycle, and the ex-de Knyff Panhard-Levassor bought from Edge.

Making of a name

In Italy, where the early enthusiasts had worked in a country insensible to the lure of the motor car, a motoring industry was now at last emerging. By 1898, the year in which a small group of Piedmont pioneers started what was to become the biggest Italian manufacturer, Fiat, and is now the largest in Europe, there were already a number of small workshops devoted to the production of cars. These included those of Miari and Giusti, of Padua, builders of Bernardi's car, Prinetti and Stucchi, who assembled De Dion-Bouton tricycles under licence, and the Milan bicycle factory of Edoardo Bianchi, who built a prototype cyclecar (series production of i.c. engined vehicles began some years later). The limited success of these companies was probably due then to the Italian passion for foreign goods rather than to any intrinsic defects. A strong personalty such as the former cavalry officer, Giovanni Agnelli, was

necessary before a home-produced car could overcome this tendency of the Italians.

The agreement out of which Fiat was born was between Agnelli, Count Emanuele Cacherano di Bricherasio, Count Roberto Biscaretti di Ruffia and the banker Gustave Deslex. The first prototype was constructed for the partners in 1899 by Giovanni Ceirano, a young motoring enthusiast from Turin who, with his brothers, had built up a flourishing cycle business. As soon as the 5 H.P. prototype had been approved, the company that was to build a model was soon formed, "Fabbrica Italiana Auto-

mobili Torino" (the Italian Motor Car Company, Turin), the initials giving the brand name FIAT.

The first car built by company was similar to the prototype and had a twin-cylinder, 600 c.c. engine. The car, called the "3½ H.P.", had its engine mounted horizontally in the rear, with water cooling. The inlet valves were automatic, petrol being fed by gravity to the constant-level carburettor; ignition was by battery and coil. There were three gears. Transmission was by chain and differential and there was a leather clutch. The car had two hand brakes, one acting on the rear axle, the other on the rear wheels.

At the same time that Fiat was beginning its activities, a bicycle and sewing machine company, Orio & Marchand in Piacenza, also started production of motor cars. It was destined to be well-known for a few years both inside and outside Italy, but was to disappear in 1909. In the meantime Prinetti & Stucchi, who had also moved to cars from sewing machines, added to their assembly

An 1895 Peugeot "vis-à-vis", with a horizontal twin cylinder engine of 1,056 c.c. and three forward speeds plus reverse. Output was 8 H.P. and top speed 20 m.p.h.

An 1892 Peugeot "vis-à-vis" with a 15 H.P. twin cylinder engine.

A photograph and a drawing of the 1899 Fiat "3½ H.P.".

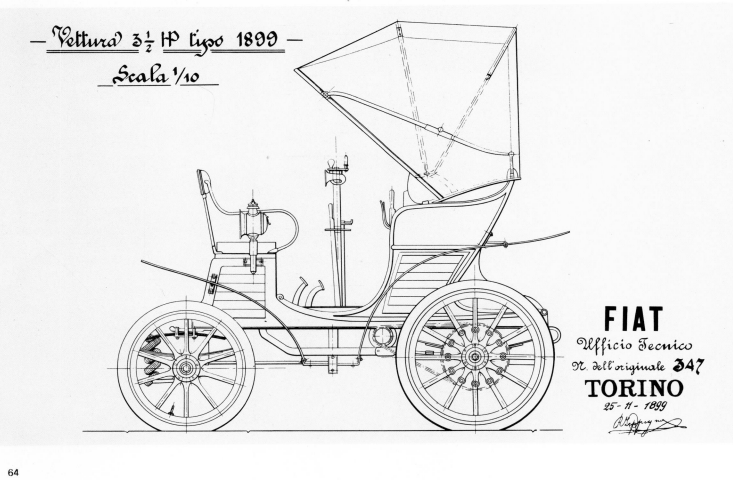

— Vettura 3½ HP tipo 1899 —
Scala ¹/₁₀

FIAT
Ufficio Tecnico
N. dell'originale **347**
TORINO
25 - 11 - 1899

of De Dion-Bouton tricycles the production of a new car designed by a certain Ettore Bugatti. It had a half-litre two-cylinder engine mounted forward, with two speeds.

Bee-hive radiator

In Germany Daimler radically modified its design in 1897, getting nearer and nearer to the motor car as known today. Among other features, the engine was mounted forward, the four wheels were given the same diameter, pneumatic tyres were fitted and the wheel replaced the tiller. The bee-hive radiator was adopted instead of the finned-tube type, and for the first time there was a starting handle.

In 1898 another motor company appeared, Adam Opel, converting to car production after many years of general engineering. The first car, a small 4 H.P., was followed by a Darracq - Opel in which a German engine was fitted to a French chassis.

In Belgium Goldschmidt founded the Compagnie Belge de Construction Automobiles, which took as its trade mark the symbol of a pipe. The Pipe was for some twenty years to be among the best cars in Europe. At the same time a number of other companies were formed — Dasse; Métallurgique; Henri Piper; Lemaire & Paillot; Vincke; De Cosmo and Minerva.

In Austria manufacture was begun in the same year, 1898, of an unusual car by an old-established coach-builder, Jacob Lohner. The vehicle had a petrol engine but electric transmission and its designer was to figure prominently in motor car history. His name was Ferdinand Porsche.

On large scale

At this time, across the Atlantic there was impressive activity in the United States. The conditions were being born for the industrial power which was to take America to the forefront of world motor car production, at least so far as quantity was concerned. Almost from the beginning, manufacture was to be by large scale production methods that Europe was to know only many years later. At the end of the century America was discovering the importance of the motor car, not only as a vehicle but also as an industrial activity.

Its enthusiastic businessmen threw large sums of money into the industry of manufacturing cars with the near-certainty, rather than the hope, of success.

This part in the story of the motor car is that of men of enormous willpower who were able, above all due to the favourable economic climate, to achieve spectacularly swift success. In these ranks of courageous, ambitious men, the outstanding figure is that of Henry Ford.

A 1911 Isotta-Fraschini Model B 28/35 H.P. Engine — front mounted 4 cylinder in two pairs. 130 × 150 mm. bore and stroke, 7,964 c.c. Ignition by high tension magneto. Output 30 H.P. at 1,000 r.p.m. Leather cone clutch, 4 speeds and reverse. Final drive by chains. Weight — 2,464 lbs.

PETROL INJECTION
GAINS GROUND

Charging an internal combustion engine by the direct injection of petrol into the cylinders (direct injection) or into the inlet manifold (indirect injection) are not new ideas. Experiments to this end were begun in 1935 and 1936, above all by Daimler-Benz who were interested in applying the system to an aero-engine to permit it to go on working indefinitely even upside down, as in aerobatics.

This was not the only advantage of petrol injection as the engineers of the time knew perfectly well. These included better charging of the cylinders, and therefore more power or more economy; better cooling by injecting the fuel at the hottest points; elimination of flat spots in the power curve and better performance at low engine speeds.

The principal difficulties met by Daimler-Benz lay in the injectors. Each of these very fine jets has to spray, in a fraction of a second, a precise quantity of petrol at a pressure from 300 to 550 lb per square inch. Above all they work at high speed and must be efficiently lubricated without the oil interfering with the fuel.

Furthermore, they must continue to work efficiently for a long time.

These technical problems have long since been solved, but remain relatively costly to overcome and for this reason mainly, the carburettor is still widely used. Injection, however, is gradually gaining ground, being used by a certain number of companies such as Triumph, Lancia, Chevrolet, Jaguar, Maserati and Ferrari, apart from all constructors of racing cars where economic factors are less important.

The choice between direct and indirect systems is above all an economic one. In racing cars the former is almost always chosen because, other things being equal, it gives a higher specific output. For touring cars however, the indirect system is usual, even though its advantages over the carburettor are less pronounced. This is because, apart from the fact that it is cheaper, the pump is smaller and much less noisy and because it can be used with engines designed for carburettors, which is not possible with direct systems. In this way it is possible to supply indirect injection as an extra or alternative to normal carburation.

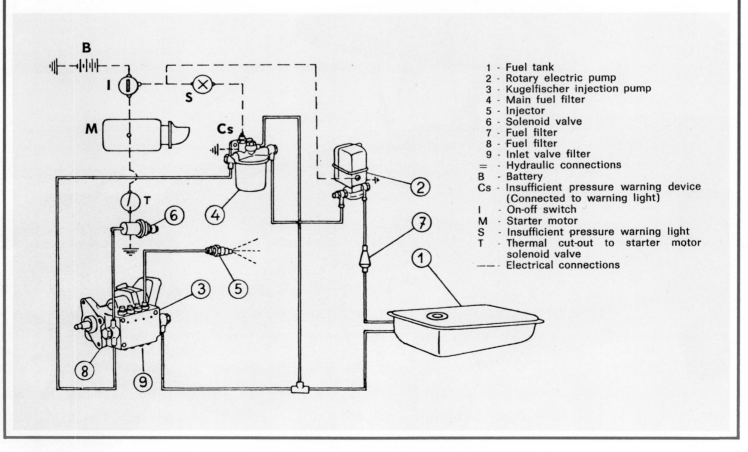

1 - Fuel tank
2 - Rotary electric pump
3 - Kugelfischer injection pump
4 - Main fuel filter
5 - Injector
6 - Solenoid valve
7 - Fuel filter
8 - Fuel filter
9 - Inlet valve filter
= - Hydraulic connections
B - Battery
Cs - Insufficient pressure warning device
(Connected to warning light)
I - On-off switch
M - Starter motor
S - Insufficient pressure warning light
T - Thermal cut-out to starter motor
solenoid valve
--- - Electrical connections

In September of the same year the first motor race on a track in America was run at Narranganset horse racing course near Providence, Rhode Island; seven cars took part, five Duryeas and two electric cars.

The rules were unique — five circuits of a mile each, to be run as separate races. In the event, due to darkness which settled early on the track, it was possible to run only three races, with the inevitable protests from the back-markers who had counted on the last two races to improve their position. All three races were won by an electric Riker Electric Stanhope at an average of 27 m.p.h.

On the other side of the Atlantic there was an epic event in England, following the repeal of the "Red Flag Act". The London-Brighton rally was run on 14th November, 1896, and was appropriately called the "Emancipation Run". Duryea did not hesitate to go to England to take part — he had also commercial reasons for going — and publicly announced that he would beat the Bollée i.c. cars, considered to be the major threat, by at least an hour.

On this occasion, too, the outcome was confused. Due to the thousands of spectators who lined the route between London and the seaside town, it was not even possible to establish an order of arrival. The compe-

titors had been forced to stop many times to avoid spectators. Duryea objected, claiming he should have been awarded the victory. His claim was not recognised, but he received gratifying publicity from the Press for his car, which aroused much interest in Europe.

Cars at the circus

The indefatigable Duryea quickly returned to America to appear with his now famous car in Barnum and Bailey's Big Top, between the Indian elephant act and the ape-man from Borneo. It was a resounding success, even though the rickety vehicle limited itself to a few circuits of the ring. The Franklin brothers, owners of a rival circus, quickly approached Charles King in Detroit, to obtain another horseless carriage with which they formed another equally successful act.

The same historic year, 1896, saw the introduction of the first i.c.-engined car in the U.S. and also the first American industrialist in the modern sense of the word — Ramsom Ely Olds, a young man from Ohio who had established himself at Lansing in Michigan. After working on stationary petrol engines, he had had some experience with steam vehicles, building first a

A typical road of the period.

A NAME
OF ITS OWN

The name "Curved Dash" given to the early Oldsmobile was obviously derived from the existence of a handsome scroll-shaped front bulkhead of the car. The continued use of the name was probably due, however, to the fact that no-one regarded it as a real car, because of the extreme simplicity of its appearance and its mechanical parts, coupled with its exceptional lightness. The car, in fact, was never given an official title by Eli Ransom Olds.

The christening of this famous car with its own name was to be repeated with the famous Ford "T" which, apart from its official designation, was known affectionately everywhere as "Lizzie".

The similarity with America's most famous car does not end here. The "Curved Dash" had all the attributes to achieve aesthetically what the model "T" Ford was to do later in terms of commercial success. It had also the necessary simplicity of construction which enabled it to

be sold at the then unheard of price of only 650 dollars. But Olds' exciting industrial adventure with the "Curved Dash" was to be limited to a five-year boom, at the end of which production ceased, with output having reached the then incredible figure of 5000 a year.

The mechanical components in this car were reduced to the minimum. There was a single horizontal cylinder engine mounted at the rear, magneto ignition, epicyclic gear change, chain drive, a rudimentary differential, leaf springing and light spoked wheels with pneumatic tyres. Steering was by tiller. Behind the two seats was a box which contained all the mechanical parts.

The "Curved Dash" could barely exceed 20 m.p.h. but because of its lightness (800 lb) it was able to climb gradients impossible for other vehicles of the time. Its abilities in this aspect can be noted in the annual Commemorative Run from London to Brighton, when several can usually be seen among the entrants.

A 1903 Mercedes with a "Tonneau" body with access to the rear seats. In the background is a Thornycroft of the same year.

tricycle and then a four-wheeler. Olds was 30 years old when, in 1896, he went along the streets of Lansing in his first single-cylinder i.c.-engined car. A year later he built a more advanced vehicle and, feeling already capable of competing with Duryea's cars, the only ones so far produced in series, he went in search of financial aid.

Capital from his friends in Lansing was soon found to be insufficient for large scale production. At this point Olds received a visit from an acquaintance from Detroit, Samuel L. Smith, a scrap merchant, who said he was prepared to put up the capital to start a company provided it was situated in Detroit. It was due to this casual circumstance that the first U.S. motor company was established in Detroit, then a virtually unknown town a few miles from the Canadian border.

Birth of Oldsmobile

The beginnings of the new company, which took the name of Oldsmobile, was anything but promising. Eight thousand dollars were spent on prototypes, some electric, before some models were finally built. Some of these were light and some heavy, and it was the latter which were placed on a reluctant market at a price of $1250. At the end of 1901 the factory caught fire due to the carelessness of a workman, who went too near a forge with a can of petrol, and in a few hours the entire plant was destroyed. Due to the courage and initiative of a young tester, J. J. Brady, the prototype of a new light vehicle that Olds had just completed was saved. It was this design in the months to come — thanks to Old's tenacity and the support of his partners the factory was rebuilt — that was to be the basis of Oldsmobile's first great commercial success.

The car, which soon acquired the famous name "Curved Dash" among American motorists due to the elegant contours of its front, was put on sale at $650, an act of commercial faith. The outcome was profitable; before the end of the year, 433 were on the roads in America. For 1902 Olds planned a production of 2,500, demonstrating both the enormous immediate potential of the

The Louis XIV interior of a 1927 Rolls-Royce Phantom, a masterpiece of elegance reminiscent of the horse-drawn era

If it were not for the plates showing the years, it would be difficult to tell which car is the earlier. Early body design was relatively slow and unadventurous. The 1905 car is a Peugeot with two seats for passengers and the driver behind. The single cylinder 7 H.P. engine was capable of nearly 20 m.p.h. Below is an 1892 Peugeot four-seater "Victoria" with a twin-cylinder engine developing 18 H.P. at 600 r.p.m. With three speeds plus reverse, it could reach nearly 20 m.p.h.

America's first motor factory, built in 1899.

American market and the initiative of its industrialists who were prepared to invest heavily in such a new product. In 1903 four thousand "Curved Dash" models were built, and in 1904 five thousand.

The next year saw the separation of Olds and his partner, Samuel Smith. More and more acute disagreements between them caused Olds to leave the company and start another, the Reo Motor Company, financed by his old friends in Lansing.

The Oldsmobile company continued its life until 1907, when it was absorbed by that of another great figure in American car history, William Crapo Durrant.

By the service entrance

A curious episode forms part of the history of Oldsmobile. It concerns one of the journeys from coast to coast, along stretches of rough country, which in the early years of this century attracted the attention of the Press all over the world. The episode was in 1902 when, for publicity purposes, a young tester, Roy D. Chapin, undertook to make the long journey from Detroit to New York to arrive in time for the motor show in the city.

The journey took 7½ days in appalling conditions. The driver, partnered by John Maxwell, a future motor manufacturer, was forced to follow canal-side roads and many times risked being bogged in the mud.

When the "Curved Dash", which had suffered no damage during its adventures on the trip, finally reached Fifth Avenue in New York one of its wheels hit the kerb — and fractured. After making an emergency repair, Chapin succeeded in travelling the few hundred yards to the entrance of the Waldorf Astoria. He forgot, however, that he was masked in mud and that his clothes were filthy; the doorman refused him entry to the hotel. Thus Chapin (who was to become Secretary for Commerce under Herbert Hoover) reached the objective of his heroic adventure via the service entrance.

The great journeys which characterised motoring history of the time almost everywhere had begun several years earlier in America, with Alexander Winton's undertakings.

Winton, an ex-mechanic from Cleveland who built cars of his own design, succeeded in covering the 800 miles from his native city to New York in ten days, though the roads of America in 1897 were even less adequate than those of Europe. Two years later Winton repeated his exploit, covering the same route in exactly half the time.

From coast to coast

After Chapin's feat in 1902, the American public looked forward to other tests of endurance, which were well publicised by the newspapers. Doctor H. N. Jackson, of Burnington in Vermont, drove a Winton, accompanied by a mechanic, from San Francisco to New York between 23 May and 26 July, 1903. A month later the exploit was repeated by Tom Fetch in a single-cylinder Packard, "Old Pacific". He did the journey in 53 days, ten less than his predecessor. A few days later yet a third team, L. L. Whitman and E. T. Hammond, made the third crossing of the continent on the same route, this time in an Oldsmobile.

It is natural at this point to refer to the great European trials, in particular the most famous and adventurous motor car competition ever held, the legendary Pekin-Paris race, and an account of the race is given later. In 1897, the year of Olds' second experimental car, the imminent industrial boom was probably best exhibited by the activities of the Studebaker brothers in Michigan. Their activities were quickly to reach large scale production. The brothers were already the largest coachbuilders in the world and they visualized production in series of several hundred vehicles at a time. It may be noted in passing that many of the existing companies which

The famous "Curved Dash" quickly gave rise to a popular song "In My Merry Oldsmobile".

An Audibert et Lavirotte with horizontal twin cylinder 16 H.P. engine.

converted to motor car production at that time did so from a field very different from that of Studebaker. In fact, many were manufacturers of bicycles, for which there was a huge market in America. The first Studebaker car, an electric one, was made in 1902.

Also in 1897 other manufacturers — most of them destined to have little success, however — were building experimental cars in America. Amongst them were Louis S. Clarke and William Morgan, who founded the Pittsburgh Motor Vehicle Company (later renamed the Autocar Company), and Gilbert Loomis, a mechanic from Westfield in Massachusetts. In addition to building his own single-cylinder car, the latter passes into history as reputedly the first holder of a motor insurance policy. The premium was 7½ dollars and the maximum cover 1000 dollars, the contract being based on those for horse-drawn carriages.

Another company, the Pope Manufacturing Co. of Hartford, Connecticut, continued to produce electric "phaetons", the term used for many years in America to indicate large open four-wheelers and derived directly from the use of horse-drawn coaches. These vehicles were

A 1905 Rolls-Royce, with familiarly elegant gauges and detailed finish. This car was found on an Australian farm and restored.

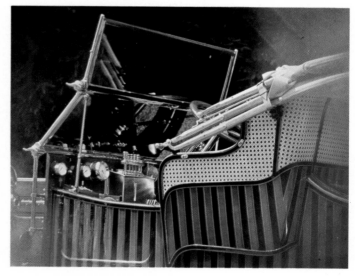

The first car to cross the American continent driven by Dr. H. N. Jackson.

probably more widespread at the time in America than the motor car.

As a vehicle, they were already doomed, though in 1898 the city of New York considered them still economic and invested heavily in them to provide a public service of such vehicles. Electric trucks continued to be used in many of the major cities and by the U.S. Army.

First American show

In 1898 the Boston motor show — the first show in America if the term can be applied to such a small exhibition — opened at almost the same time as the Paris show. Of the ten vehicles entered only four showed up on the first day. Before the close there were 12, but few American manufacturers were inclined to demonstrate their cars' inferiority to European models (many European car designers were induced to cross the Atlantic at the turn of the century and set up manufacturing on their own in America, including Albert Champion, a French motorcycle specialist who was to become one of the best-known manufacturers of sparking plugs).

A second American show was held in 1899 at Philadelphia. The publicity for the show called it the first in America, though there is some doubt whether the organisers were unaware of the Boston show or whether they ignored it for publicity purposes. Again, it was disappointing. In Paris the organisers of the second show in the French capital were trying to find a larger hall. In Philadelphia only four vehicles were exhibited. In 1900 there were too many motor shows in America — four during the year, each one still claiming to be premier in America. The first in time was held in Bedford, Connecticut, on a track where races alternated with the presentations. Most of the famous drivers of

the time, including some who had come from Europe for the occasion, took part.

Special trains were organised from nearby New Haven and one came from New York bringing the authorities of the newly-formed American Automobile Club and representatives of some of the major manufacturers. The second American motor show in 1900 was the Chicago International, which followed the pattern used at Bedford, with races as well as an exhibition.

It was much better organised. Eighty powered vehicles were present at the show, including 20 with petrol engines, 26 steam and 33 electric. The strongest representation was from Olds and Packard, the latter being the brand name of the New York and Ohio Company formed a few months earlier by James Ward Packard, his brother Warren and a partner, George L. Weiss. The two Packards had begun their motor car experiments in 1893 in Warren, Ohio, but for economic reasons could not begin production until 1899.

Spectators boom

There were thirty races at the Chicago exhibition, run in various classes over different distances. The Mobile steam car, which had just taken over the patents of two famous manufacturers, Freeman and Stanley, distinguished itself. So did Winton's car, which was specially designed for racing.

The third show held at Trenton, New Jersey, was similar and had an attendance of 95,000, against the best figure so far in America of fewer than 20,000.

A version of an action-packed accident in a crowded street of Naples by a famous Italian artist of the turn of the century, A. Beltrame.

THE FLOATING CUSHION
PAYS ITS WAY

The present-day use of the hovercraft and its exciting potential for the future bear many points of similarity with the early days of the motor car. With its commercial value established, there can be little doubt of an ever-increasing range of activities for this brainchild of the 1950s.

Inventors and designers have expended a great deal of time, effort and ingenuity during this century in an endeavour to overcome the depressing effect friction has on the speed of surface vehicles.

Increasing skin friction

The frictional drag of water on ships and boats is an acute instance of this; at low speeds water does not have a significant effect, but its effect increases rapidly with speed — to such an extent, in fact, that you would have to quadruple the installed power of a 40-knot patrol-boat to achieve only a few extra knots.

None of the experiments to solve the problem was successful until Christopher Cockerell, the inventor of the hovercraft, set to work in the middle 1950s. He is by training an engineer and, as a good engineer, he went back to first principles in his investigation of surface friction and its resulting drag.

He asked himself why boats are characteristically boat-shaped and came to the conclusion that our forefathers had clearly appreciated that drag is at a minimum if the surface area of the boat is also at a minimum. However, a circular boat — for that is what it would mean — offers great resistance to waves when it is making speed. The typical boat shape was thus a

compromise between low drag and low wave resistance. But Cockerell saw clearly that the more one designed for high speed (low wave resistance) by making the craft slimmer and slimmer, the more the area of its sides was increased. That meant that the area of craft-surface in contact with the water was increased in fact, increasing skin friction, and so largely defeating the objective.

He concluded that the best thing was to get the craft out of the water. He wondered whether it might be possible to have something between the craft and the water that would act as a lubricant, in the same way that the minute amount of water (ice melted by friction) under a skate acted as a lubricant. Air struck him as the obvious choice, but it took him many months to find a way of getting air there and keeping it there.

Eventually he devised a means of expelling pressurized air round the periphery of his research model in the form of a ring of jets, closely spaced and directed slightly inwards, towards the centre of the under-surface. The jets formed a sort of air curtain, so that they not only supplied air to the "cushion" but also tended to keep it there at a sufficient pressure to lift the craft. At that stage a natural phenomenon called the ground effect came into play. The force of the pressurized air on the ground first lifts off the craft; then the reverse thrust of the air returning from the ground to the underside of the craft adds further to the lift. As the area of the underside increases for a given weight, the effect of the reverse thrust is increased, and considerable savings in installed power are thus possible if a constant "hover-height" is desired.

Flexible extensions called "skirts" were later added to

full-size craft to improve efficiency. They "contained" the air cushion more effectively than the air curtain, and permitted appreciable obstacle-clearance without fear of damage to the hard structure.

The hovercraft industry has come to achieve a high level of sophistication in the short period between 1956 and the present. Hovercraft of a number of different designs and capabilities are in use in many different parts of the world, ranging from the Canadian Arctic to the Persian Gulf.

One hovercraft operator on the South Coast has carried well over a million fare-paying passengers across the Solent since 1965.

So far all hovercraft yet manufactured have been designed for maritime applications, though most of them have a worthwhile amphibious capability. Whether there will ever be suitable vehicles for exclusively overland operation depends, to a large extent, on whether there is a pressing need for them in that role.

Hovercraft on roads?

If so, the present problems, such as skirt wear and the ingestion of dust and sand, would quickly be overcome. Perhaps one possibility at present being explored by a potential purchaser may point the way ahead. An Australian is studying the purchase of a number of hovercraft to connect locations in the outback; he is confident that a fleet of fast hovercraft would be much less costly than the construction of many hundreds of miles of roads.

As regards the use of hovercraft on congested urban roads, little is being done at the moment. A true hovercraft (that is, one completely clear of the ground) would not be sufficiently easy to steer to permit its use on crowded roads, but a wheeled vehicle with a cushion of air to take most of the weight has many attractive features.

The next ten years of hovercraft development are likely to be as spectacular as the first decade of this century proved to be in the case of the "revolutionary" motor car.

An outstanding pilot, Prince Bernhard of the Netherlands, at the controls of a Vickers VA-2 hovercraft.

A gymkhana organized at the first National Automobile Show in New York.

The last of the four shows in 1900 was also the most important. It carried the seal of authority as it was organised by the American Automobile Club. At this Automobile Show in Madison Square Gardens, New York, 34 makes exhibited, 19 having petrol engines, seven being steam powered, and six electric, whilst there were two with mixed propulsion — i.c. engine and electricity.

Going up the ramp

Ironically, the biggest attraction was outside the show, due to the initiative of John Brisbane Walker, editor of the magazine "Cosmopolitan" and manufacturer of motor cars. Not being able to obtain space inside the show, he hired the hanging garden itself and built a ramp, up which he ran Mobile steamers 20 times a day from ground to roof.

Due to the success of the show, the Automobile Club decided to prolong a part of it and in a special pavilion they exhibited a dozen so-called "veteran" cars, including the 1890 Nadig and the 1893 Duryea. Even in the youthful days of motoring, age had its attractions!

The first Vauxhall, in 1903.

A 1903 Oldsmobile "Pirate". Below the first Chevrolet, built in 1912. Louis Chevrolet, famous as a racing driver in the early years of the century, was persuaded by W.C. Durant to design a new engine. From this partnership were born the Chevrolet car and company.

front view of a 1904 CORRE

engine - front mounted vertical 4 cylinder
gearchange - 3 speeds plus reverse
cooling - by water with two radiators
speed - 40 m.p.h.

The joys of the open car and the open road — but not only the weather must be fine. While the modern couple can relax, a testing time faces manufacturer Adolphe Clement and his passengers (Below) about to leave home for a drive in the country. Masks are functional; only the mechanic has his face unprotected against the dust.

CHAPTER SIX
MUD AND DUST BELOW ZERO

At the dawn of the century, when the first car factories were being built in Europe and the U.S., considerable technical progress had been made after the first twenty years. So far as the engines were concerned, two cylinders were most frequently used. Many solutions, differing widely one from another, were to be found with each manufacturer trying to avoid each other's patents.

Thus there were side-by-side twins such as the Gobron and Décauville, and horizontally opposed "flat twins", but many manufacturers built single cylinder engines. De Dion was a conviced adherent of this simpler form, as was the youthful Packard in America, who obstinately refused advice to build a twin (it was Packard who was to put into series production fifteen years later a 12-cylinder engine!).

In 1900 four-cylinder engines were just passing from the experimental phase to that of production. French engineers were prominent in this respect. Forest was experimenting with multi-cylinder engines for marine use, including an in-line six. Mors, noted for his racing cars, built the first practical Vee-4 in 1899, and Tent-

Passengers in a De Dion-Bouton receive an old-world greeting.

ing, an ex-Peugeot driver, was building big four cylinder engines.

Without exception, these engines adopted automatic inlet valves but positively actuated exhaust valves. Ignition was generally by hot-tube though electrical systems were gaining popularity. The magneto was invented simultaneously in this period by Frederick Simms in England and Robert Bosch in Germany, opening a new chapter in motoring. Also at this time the Frenchman Claudel invented the so-called "submerged" carburettor, in which the jet was situated below the level of the petrol in the float chamber.

Wheel differences

So far as coachwork was concerned, 1900 was the year that the early manufacturers ceased to look only backwards to the horse-drawn carriage for their layouts and styling, and started tentatively to study the layout of the motor car from first principles. Thus some of the vehicles built at that time had wheels of equal diameter, while the rest had wheels with substantial differences between front and rear. Pneumatic tyres had already almost completely replaced solid ones, but most wheels were still similar to those of carriages, with thick wooden spokes. Nevertheless, light spoked wheels were appearing on many smaller cars.

By this time the engine was nearly always at the front, hidden by the finned-tube radiator. Already there was the choice, which still exists today, of air or water cooling. The steering wheel had been adopted instead

A typical car at the turn of the century. A 1902 Gillet Forest passingan 1899 Haynes-Apperson at a standstill after breaking down.

An 1895 5 seater Peugeot V-2. The 1,645 c.c. engine developed 12 H.P. There were four speeds plus reverse and a leather cone clutch. Top speed about 20 m.p.h.

of the tiller by almost all manufacturers. There was, however, the widest variety in coachwork, every builder having his own ideas. Some did not supply a body at all, limiting themselves to producing only the mechanical chassis.

Starting handles were fitted on most cars. A fracture of the wrist was to constitute one of the occupational hazards of motoring for another quarter of a century, due to backfiring of the engine at the moment of ignition.

Furs, goggles and gauntlets

The cars of 1900 were nearly all open — the Renault enclosed driving position had remained unique, an eccentricity viewed with amusement — and this meant that the driver was exposed to all weathers. This was the reason for the fabulous bearskins, still impressive in today's yellowed photographs, and explains their function: it was the only way to keep warm. This was in spring or autumn (in the depths of winter it was better to give up the idea altogether, in view of the condition of the roads).

A 1903 Mercedes "Simplex" tourer with 4 cylinder 28/32 H.P. engine giving a top speed of nearly 40 m.p.h.

The masks, the mufflers, the goggles were all strictly practical accessories often hiding the entire face under the flat, peaked cap worn to fight another terrible enemy, dust.

In the first motoring magazines is found straightforward technical advice ("it is essential to drain the radiator water after each journey, and during pauses it should be kept warm by starting up the engine briefly every twenty minutes or so"), beside invaluable remedies for burns from the exhaust pipe, a process for waterproofing driving clothes, a prescription for "driver's eyesalve" (1 lb cocoa leaf brewed, 1 oz. cherry laurel water, ½ oz. sodium borate), a method to prevent steaming of goggles (smear the insides with glycerine) and instructions for cleaning dusty furs at the end of a journey. Fashion advised semi-opaque veiling for lady motorists, with a tiny transparent opening over the eyes.

While fashion played its part, especially for the ladies, the more serious affairs of racing held the masculine interest. It was not always an occasion for celebration. In 1898, during the Périguex-Bergerac-Périguex race, the Marquis de Montegnac lost control of his car as he waved to another competitor, Montarid, who was overtaking him. The other car locked to his own, and the marquis was killed instantly. Some months later Mayade, winner of the Paris-Marseilles two years earlier, was also killed.

In Italy in 1898 Luigi Storero won the Torino-Asti-Alessandria-Torino race, which might be considered the first real motor race in Italy, after the somewhat minor Arona-Stresa of the previous year. In fact a Torino-Asti-Torino race had been held three years before, but it was so slow that the five competitors were overtaken by a group of cyclists.

From Seine to the North Sea

The most important competition of 1898 was the Paris-Amsterdam-Paris, organised by the Automobile Club de France with detailed regulations. It comprised both

A 1901 Roy drives in with suitably accoutred occupants.

Benz "Victoria" in the 1895 Paris-Bordeaux.

The sellers of useful car accessories were quick off the mark.

Cars are losing the "motorised carriage" look and becoming more functional. Above — a 1904 FIAT "16/24 H.P." and below a 1901 FIAT "8 H.P." in which the radiator was still a finned tube. Note the gear change, brake levers and the huge single headlamp.

1892 Peugeot with 1,645 c.c. twin cylinder engine, leather cone clutch and chain drive. Below a Daimler proudly bears its age.

what is now called a rally and an out-and-out race. It was held in three stages between the 7 and 9 July over a total of 820 miles. There were 26 and 29 entrants for the "tourist competition" and the race respectively. The first competition proceeded smoothly, but the second ran into great difficulties with the police, whose first requirement was that every competitor should have a certificate of origin. Because hardly any driver had one, they ordered the race to be postponed. The drivers were so determined to proceed, however, that a detachment of hussars and a troop of artillery were sent to Champigny, where the start was to take place, and barred the road with an impressive show of armed force!

The drivers therefore discreetly moved to Villiers-sur-Marne, a town in the Département of Seine-et-Oise and therefore outside the jurisdiction of the police representative M. Bochet, who had imposed the ban. From there they expected to set out at once for Château d'Ardennes, the finish of the first stage.

Fashion and function are offered as attractions to cold weather motorists in this advertisement for an all-purpose muffler.

Certain idiosyncrasies were born early. In 1903 Lord Russell waited all night to get the first numberplate, A1.

They raced, they bounced and often they turned over. There were no road patrols in those days!

A 1906 Edwardian gets police directions in Rome.

In fact, when they arrived at Villiers they found that the drums of petrol to be used for the first stage were still at Champigny. So Amédée Bollée set off on a dangerous raid, going back to Champigny and securing the drums from under the noses of the guards. At last, the drivers set off.

One competitor, Richard, had 14 punctures between Paris and the first village, Epernay; another, Koechlin, finished in a canal near Maastricht and had to return to Paris in a schoolboy's suit, all he could find to replace his own sodden clothes.

There was a major complication on the return journey. When the 26 surviving machines reached Verdun the competitors were required to turn on to the road for Corbeil and Versailles. It was a subtle move by M. Bochet, who was already preparing for his revenge when the speeding cars finally entered his area of authority. But once again he had reckoned without the resource of the drivers. They simply refused to continue, and

TEAMWORK IN SECONDS

For many years the ingenious ideas, the experience and the hard work of the mere individual have been insufficient for success. Almost every product created is the result of the work of a team or of many teams who succeed or complement one another on the same project. This is especially true in the motor car industry. Before any car is produced on a large scale, hundreds of specialists have been at work transforming an idea, a rough sketch, into reality. The new car is born in laboratories and experimental centres of large industries where artists, engineers, physicists and chemists gradually improve the appearance and the mechanism.

Testing

When the first prototypes have been built they are subject to two kinds of tests — those in the laboratory and those in real-life conditions, both conducted under severe criteria. In the laboratory every component in the new car is tested to the limit, to reproduce the effect of wear to which they would be subject over tens of thousands of miles.

This represents at least half the work load of the laboratories in a big company. For example, an engine will be run for weeks, shock absorbers are compressed and released, doors are opened and closed for days and weeks.

In the meantime, other models are sent to regions in the hands of expert testers. Conditions of heat or dust or cold are at their extreme and the cars have to demonstrate their functional adaptability. In addition, most big companies have built special test tracks which include a wide variety of surface conditions in a limited space. If the prototypes pass these tests, during which modifications are made to improve the design, the model finally goes into production. In the meantime in the factory all kinds of machine tools have been prepared and laid out, from the large presses for the body-work to the lathes and milling machines, drills etc., usually fully automated.

Other specialists have been setting up the assembly lines, they have determined the sub-divisions and methods of assembly and have decided to a fraction of a second the time allowed for every operation.

Components

Experts have decided which components shall be made in their own factory and which bought out. In practice, little more than half of the components which comprise a modern quantity-produced car are actually made by the principal manufacturer whose name the car bears.

The importance of a close study of methods of production can be illustrated by the fact that in 1908 a highly skilled specialist took eight hours to make the upper half of a petrol tank, while today three semi-skilled men operate a machine which makes one every 20 seconds!

Last step

Motor car production took its first major step forward when assembly methods were revolutionised. At one time, operators moved round the car to work on it. Now it is the car which moves, presenting itself at the right moment in front of the right man for a particular operation. In a modern factory the various components and sub-assemblies are conveyed to the assembly lines, where the body of the car is moving already welded and painted. At various points on the line operators install the engine, the gearbox and other mechanical components. Then they fit the wheels, electrical equipment, steering, and so on. At the end of the line a tester jumps into the completed car, which nowadays is filled up with petrol, and drives away what a few minutes before was a mass of separate parts.

A 1901 Progress finishes triumphant in the London-Brighton run.

City to city trials were common in Great Britain in the early years. The photograph shows officials and members of the Automobile Club of Great Britain and Ireland (now the R.A.C.) before the start of such a race on 4 June, 1901.

the Automobile Club agreed to finish the race at Mont-géron, outside the jurisdiction of the Paris Préfecture and M. Bochet. The cars then drove slowly to Versailles, being careful to give the police not the slightest excuse for interference.

Interest in the Paris-Amsterdam-Paris was not limited to the results, but also indicated the social attitudes of the time. Racing drivers in particular, and motorists in general, found a section of the public nursed a fierce antipathy towards them. This was not entirely without cause, perhaps, in view of the manouevres by some drivers in the presence of a public who were not yet accustomed to their vehicles and who therefore considered themselves exposed to considerable danger.

The police often gave official backing to such a reaction. But the obstacles placed by authority only served to develop the spirit of motoring supporters.

First 'Round France' race

The year 1898 closed with a minor hill-climb at Gaillon in France which is memorable for one fact. It was won by Ettore Bugatti at the wheel of a car built by himself in the workshops of Prinetti and Stucchi. The same name appeared in first place in the tricycle class of the Verona-Mantova-Brescia-Verona race the following year, while the car category was won by another famous driver — Giovanni Agnelli, founder of Fiat — in a Phoenix.

The next year passes into history as the year of the first motor tour of France. The Automobile Club of that country had decided to organise a much tougher race than those of the past in view of the growing robustness of cars then being manufactured. They organised, therefore, a race to be run in seven stages over three quarters of France for a distance of 1,375 miles, including hill sections.

Two major "stables" took part in the race — Panhard-Levassor with eight 12 and 16 H.P. cars, and Bollée with four 20 H.P. models having independent front suspension. This time there were no incidents, though many competitors, including Jenatzy who was to set up the world's speed record in that year, had a fantastic number of breakdowns but still finished the race.

Mountain stages

The principal problem for all competitors was that of punctures due to the poor roads in the mountain stages. The result was a triumph for Panhard-Levassor, led by René de Knyff, who won in his 16 H.P. at an average of over 30 m.p.h. After three more Panhards, the first Bollée was in fifth position, followed by yet another Panhard and a Mors.

A success similar to Panhard's was achieved by the Renault 1¾ H.P. in two other races, the Paris-Ostend and the Paris-Rambouillet-Paris.

In all these cases the results of the race were reflected immediately in increased sales, a confirmation of the commercial as well as the technical importance of racing.

Three Edwardians in the Monte Carlo "Tour de la Principauté" in 1966. From top to bottom — a 1909 Roland Pilain, a 1908 Clément and a 1910 Lion Peugeot.

93

Above — a 1917 Ford "T" coupé. Below — a 1926 model. Built nine years apart, the two cars are almost identical.

The year 1900 marked the first Gordon Bennett Cup race. This famous race was run to regulations which seem quite usual today, but which were a major innovation of the time. For the first time vehicles were classified by their characteristics. These races were held over a number of years and are associated with the first period of "maturity" of the motor car.

James Gordon Bennett was the wealthy son of the owner of the "New York Herald" and lived in Paris, managing the European edition of that paper. An animated discussion between his fellow countryman Alexander Winton, manufacturer and racing driver, and the Frenchman Charron suggested the idea for the races. In that argument Charron maintained the superiority of French cars and Winton that of American.

Gordon Bennett decided that the only way to resolve the matter was to organise a race between the two countries' manufacturers; he thought it would be more of a test if a great number of competitors took part. A condition which was to give rise to much criticism was that requiring cars to be built entirely in their country of origin.

The Gordon Bennett Cup was formally instituted a short time later by its promoter. He invited all the existing automobile clubs in the world — there were seven, those of France founded in 1895, Belgium in 1896, England, Italy and Ireland in 1898 and Germany and America in 1899 — to nominate an official team. The regulations required that no team should consist of more than three cars, each weighing not more than a ton.

The race was first held in France over a course of just over 340 miles; it was to be held each year in future in the country which had won the cup the year before (it is a formula similar to that of today's Davis Cup in tennis). A difficulty was that few nations could enter teams because of the requirement that cars should be built entirely in the countries they represented. This restriction included accessories and even tyres.

The Automobile Club de France decided on a course on the route Paris-Chartres-Orléans-Nevers-Moulins-Roanne-Lyon, and appointed as its representatives De Knyff, Charron and Girardot. America sent a team headed by Winton. Germany decided on two Benz and a Canello-Durkopp and Belgium a team of Bolides. On this occasion for the first time national colours were given — blue for France, yellow for Belgium, white for Germany and red for America (red was later to be used also by Italy).

As usual, a much smaller number appeared at the start line — the three French, the Belgian Jenatzy in a Bolide and Winton in one of his own cars.

The race began with an unexpected complication — the unauthorised participation of a private entry, Levegh, who proposed to beat them all. In fact, he won the first stage to Orléans by half an hour but then no more was seen of him. Breakdowns made the course difficult for all competitors. Jenatzy was late and Winton went out of the race at Orléans, so there remained only the three Frenchmen, of whom Charron had a broken half-shaft, Girardot had steering trouble and De Knyff's gearchange would not work. Each of them was aware of the others' situation and each tried hard to stay in the race and be the one to win the cup for France.

Round the trees

As if mechanical troubles did not present enough problems, there soon came more from another source. Dogs seemed to be maddened by the noise of the cars and frequently threw themselves under the wheels, often killing themselves but also causing damage to the cars. Charron had already killed at least five when, leaving the village of Arbresle, an enormous St. Bernard jumped on his Panhard and damaged the steering. At over 60 m.p.h., the car jumped a ditch, circled two trees and rushed down the road in the opposite direction. Fournier, Charron's mechanic, succeeded once again in getting the car back in the race. They finally reached Lyon, after having averaged about 39 m.p.h., beating Girardot by an hour and 27 minutes, after he also had been delayed by steering troubles. Thus finished the first race for the Gordon Bennett Cup, with the exciting and eventful victory of the French representative.

The first Alfa built after the break with Darracq — the 24 H.P. built from 1910 to 1915. It had a 4,084 c.c. 4 cylinder engine which produced 42 H.P. at 2,200 r.p.m.

THE FIRST MERCEDES

The name of the 1901 Mercedes, which many enthusiasts regard as one of the first "modern" motor cars, was chosen not by the man who built it but by the one who was about to sell it. It involved the dropping of the famous name of Daimler, which to that date had been applied to all the products of the factory at Cannstatt.

Publicity

To the ears of the man concerned, Emile Jellinek, an Austrian banker, the name sounded too Germanic and ugly. So the new car designed by Wilhelm Maybach was called Mercedes, the name of Jellinek's daughter.
Jellinek was the Daimler representative for the Côte d'Azur, and the new car owed much to him as he had requested its design. The Nice week with its local motor race was a few months ahead, and Jellinek wanted to consolidate his position as a major client-salesman of the German company. He was keen to obtain useful publicity from the race.
To win, however, it was necessary to have something more powerful than the 23 H.P. Phoenix then in production at Cannstatt, and the 35 H.P. Mercedes was the result. Jellinek contracted to buy 36 of the new model — a huge figure for the time — and to undertake their distribution in France, Belgium, Austro-Hungary and the U.S.
Maybach, who had been for some time the important figure at Cannstatt though often overshadowed by the powerful personality of Daimler, met the challenge with a car full of new ideas. It was to be the inspiration for cars for many years to come.
For the first time the chassis was in pressed steel. The engine was mounted in front under a true bonnet, in front of which was one of the first honeycomb radiators which had begun to replace the fragile finned tubes. It was a four-cylinder in-line of six-litre capacity; all the valves were mechanically operated and ignition was by magneto. The gearchange was of the lever and gate type. The 35 H.P. developed was enough to give it a good chance in the Nice-Salon-Nice race and in other races yet to come.
The first models were already in production and the problem of a name, raised by Jellinek, was still unsolved.

Famed beauty

"Mercedes" was an acceptable solution. Miss Jellinek herself was a beauty famous all over the Côte d'Azur, though for Paul Daimler to give up the name when he was seriously will seemed cruel. Daimler, however, died soon after, and any possible embarrassment was avoided.
The Nice race, won by Werner, was a triumph for the Mercedes, which was much admired. So was the flesh and blood "Mercedes" who had a warm ovation from the grandstand. For many years Maybach's "white jewel" (nearly all of the models were in this colour) was synonymous with prestige among the wealthy of Europe.

front view of a 1907 SIZAIRE AND NAUDIN "8 H.P."

engine - front mounted single vertical cylinder
bore and stroke - 120 × 110 mm.
capacity - 1,244 c.c.
output - 8 H.P.
ignition - low tension magneto
clutch - single dry plate
gearchange - 3 speeds plus reverse
weight - 1,980 lbs.

Tracks as well as cars have improved over the years. An Opel racing model rounds a bend in the 1914 French Grand Prix. Above is a Formula III Lotus-Ford.

CHAPTER SEVEN
CAPITAL-TO-CAPITAL RACES

In 1901 most of the important races were again in France; and if the routes were international, these races were also organised there. The first of the latter was the Pau Grand Prix, which was held in the middle of February.

Opinion at that time was divided among manufacturers as to the ideal racing car from the point of view of weight. Race regulations varied; one race classified cars into as many as four groups according to weight.

The results of the Pau Grand Prix demonstrated a success for the protagonists of the voiturette, or light car. The heaviest category was won by Maurice Farman in a 24 H.P. Panhard, while that for medium cars was won by his brother Henri in a 12 H.P. Darracq. Louis Renault won the light car category in one of his own voiturettes. (The racing exploits of Louis and his brother Marcel were to be impressive in days when it was not unusual for an industrialist to drive his own products in races). The following month the Nice-Salon-Nice race was run, in which Emile Jellinek entered the new 35 H.P. Daimler named after his daughter Mercedes, and won with Werner at the wheel.

The second Gordon Bennett Cup race followed. It will be remembered that the regulations permitted three cars from each nation and required that these should be entirely built in the country they represented. This latter regulation was bitterly resented by those manufacturers it excluded.

For the second Gordon Bennett it was not possible to change the regulations, but it was possible to lessen their effect by running it in conjunction with a second edition of the Paris-Bordeaux-Paris to which the disputed rule did not apply.

The 1901 Paris-Bordeaux. The Renault team: Louis Renault, Marcel Renault, Oury and Griis.

Thus, though there were a considerable number of participants, only a small proportion were competing for the Gordon Bennett Cup; the distance to be covered was 525 kilometres (328 miles). Though times were changing rapidly, there were still echoes of earlier pioneering ways in the race. One of the drivers, Baras, reached the finish with his engine tied to the chassis with electrical wire.

The race was won by Fournier, who had figured in the first Gordon Bennett as Charron's mechanic. His Mors averaged more than 50 m.p.h. The technical progress made over the previous six years may be gauged from

the fact that the 1895 Paris-Bordeaux race was won by Levassor in his Panhard at only 15 m.p.h.

Behind the Mors were five 40 H.P. Panhards. The touring category was won by another Panhard, a 12 H.P. driven by Giraud, ahead of three Darracqs. The light car category was won, as usual, by Renault; Louis and Marcel, Oury and Szisz took the first four places in that order.

A short while afterwards the Paris-Toulouse-Paris race was run, in three exhausting stages, over a total of 710 miles, mostly on poor roads. In the light car category only Renaults finished the race. One of the two

The 1903 Paris-Madrid. Marcel Renault and Vauthier entering the fatal curve at Couché-Vérac at 80 m.p.h.

A 1901 Renault voiturette "type D" Single cylinder 450 c.c. engine with three speeds plus reverse. Top speed about 28 m.p.h.

famous brothers, Louis, was injured but managed to keep his badly damaged car running; though he was the last competitor to reach Paris he did so without assistance. He repeated the exploit the following year, in the legendary Paris-Vienna race.

The peak of the 1901 racing season, however, was the race from Paris to Berlin, the first of the big inter-capital races which were characteristic of the first years of the century. The last of these races was the 1903 Paris-Madrid. Accidents had taken too great a toll.

The Paris-Berlin was run over 750 miles in three stages, Paris-Aix-la-Chapelle of 285 miles, Aix-la-Chapelle-Hanover of 280 miles and Hanover-Berlin of 185 miles — a more severe test for men and machines than any race so far run. The rules were also strict. No competitor could spend more than 15 minutes on his car at the end of each stage; in this time he had to do all the repair work, greasing, tyre changing and other jobs. After the 15 minutes, the cars were bonded until the start the next morning.

There were 110 competitors in the Paris-Berlin race, divided into 40 heavy cars (weighing over one ton) 51 touring cars (from 880 lb to one ton), nine light cars and 10 motorcycles. The most important European manufacturers were represented, including Mors, Panhard and Renault from France, Mercedes from Germany and Napier from England.

Details of the race are scarce, though it is recorded that when Pinson in his Panhard 40 H.P. suddenly found the road blocked by a tram in the village of Metternich, he deliberately ran into the vehicle to avoid the crowd of spectators. The tram was knocked off the rails; the

Two typical racing cars of their period. Above is a Panhard and below a 1913/1914 four-cylinder Opel, with four valves a cylinder and 12-litre capacity.

this race had the official title of "Circuit du Nord", it was known everywhere and remembered as the "Concours du Ministre" — the "Minister's Competition". It was open to any type of i.c.-engined vehicle, provided it ran on alcohol. This stipulation was made by the Third Republic's Minister for Agriculture, Jean Dupuy. He was concerned by the superiority of foreign commercial interests in supplying petrol and wished to encourage engine designers to adopt alcohol, which was widely available in France.

Going ahead with organising the race, the minister and his permanent secretary sounded out the mayors of the towns through which it would pass. They were afraid of opposition from local public opinion, which often considered motor vehicles as extremely dangerous. When all fears had been allayed, the race went ahead. It was in two stages, from Champigny to Saint-Germain and then to Arras.

car was hardly damaged. At Rheims Brasier hit and killed a child with his Mors.

The lack of background information was not surprising. The Press showed little interest before the race, which was described as madness by most journalists. Nationally, attitudes changed in France as Fournier won all three stages. His Mors averaged 70.5 k.p.h. (about 44 m.p.h.); immediately behind him was the usual group of Panhards, this time seven in the first ten places. Again the touring category was won by Giraud in a 12 H.P. Panhard, which was also eighth in general classification. The results gave little satisfaction in Germany as the first Mercedes to arrive, driven by Werner who had won the Nice-Salon-Nice race, came in seventeenth.

An unusual race had been run earlier in 1901. Though

Welcomed

The race was almost a disaster because of persistent downpours, with much skidding in consequence, and because engines ran erratically in using alcohol instead of the petrol for which they were designed. The only exception in performance was Rigolly's Gobron-Brillié, which was modified specifically to use alcohol.

The race was won by Farman, who had won the Grand Prix du Pau the previous year. Once again all the Renaults which were entered finished at the head of their category. "Alcohol races" were later held in other European countries, including Italy, where Lancia and Storero finished first and second at an average of nearly 70 m.p.h.

At rest behind glass in the Renault museum in Paris. This sleek car performed with honour in the Paris-Vienna race of 1902.

The Paris-Vienna race of 1902 was hailed as the "race of races" by the Press, which was much more interested than in the previous year's Paris-Berlin.

The public was excited by the prospect. When 137 competitors gathered at the start line in the afternoon of 24 June, a tremendous crowd of 10,000 saw them off. Spectators arrived by special trains, carriages and bicycles.

Increase in power

This time the race was over 1060 miles through Burgundy, Switzerland, Tyrol and the Arlberg on roads where motor cars had never previously ventured.

It was by no means easy for the organisers, headed by the Automobile Club de France, to obtain official agreement. The authorities considered the cars dangerous, not least because of the spectacular increase in power of engines specially designed for the race. The Swiss government gave permission for the competitors to cross its territory but not to race, so the Belfort-Bregens stage was simply a parade.

All the big manufacturers were represented, and those who had hopes of winning had made special efforts in view of the difficulties of the race. Panhard, fresh from success in the "Concours du Ministre" and their experience with alcohol, put their faith in a 70 H.P. using that fuel. The engine was a four-cylinder of no less than

13,700 c.c. Mercedes, which carried German aspirations, had a "Simplex" model of 40 H.P. Mors had a 60 H.P. racing car.

As usual, the Renault brothers concentrated on the light car category and were present with a new 16 H.P. four-cylinder with which they had been experimenting for

Oury in the 1902 Paris-Vienna.

Veterans on show: above, a 1906 Mercedes which took part in the Paris-Geneva-Turin Rally. Left, from top to bottom, a 1908 Fiat, a 1909 Roland-Pilain tourer and a 1913 De Dion-Bouton.

months. It developed 30 to 35 H.P. at the relatively high engine speed of 2,000 r.p.m. The car weighed about 1300 lbs and was the first to be distinguished by the famous Renault "coal scuttle" bonnet which was to be one of the signs of a Renault for 20 years or more. The regulations provided for three categories, vehicles over 650 kg (about 1430 lb), for cars between 400 and 600 kg (from 880 to 1320 lb) and another for cars under 400 kg — tricycles and motorcycles.

From 3.30 a.m. the competitors began to leave at one minute intervals, beginning with the big cars. The first to start was Girardot in a C.G.V. He was followed by Edge in his Napier, René de Knyff in a Panhard "60 H.P." fuelled by alcohol and later Marcel and Louis Renault.

Over the mountain

The beginning of the race was promising, even as a spectacle. Fournier and his Mors succeeded in overtaking a special train taking motoring enthusiasts to the finish of the first stage at Belfort. All the same, Fournier had to pay a high price for over-stressing his car — he had covered the first 50 miles at an average of 70 m.p.h. — and at Chaumont, 150 miles from the start, he fell out with a broken gear-change. Girardot also dropped out. The first stage was won by de Knyff, who averaged over 60 m.p.h. for the 260 miles, followed by Farman and Jarrot, also in Panhards.

But the situation changed completely following the relatively gentle drive from Belfort to Bregens. The drivers then had to face the terrible mule tracks of the Arlberg on the third stage, finishing at Salzburg. These were very different conditions from the long straights of the first stage. The great strain on the cars was matched by the

LANGUAGE OF THE COACHBUILDER

In the story of the motor car there has never been a precise terminology to describe different kinds of bodywork, or a way of differentiating among the kinds of vehicle for transporting drivers and passengers. On the contrary, there has always been some confusion in terms particular words being employed at the same time to describe different kinds of cars and body style.

Furthermore, the same word has often meant different things to, say, an Englishman, a Frenchman, an American or an Italian. The confusion persist today. It is possible, nevertheless, to detail a simple vocabulary for the period 1895 to 1915, to identify the various types of vehicle in use in that period. In alphabetical order, the terms are:

BERLINA - *Rarely used before the first World War. In general it meant a closed luxury car, often with a small window which permitted the occupants to see but barely to be seen.*

CAB - *A term taken directly from horsedrawn carriage vocabulary and used to define a vehicle in which two passengers were enclosed while the driver was situated some distance away, usually in front and unprotected. But there were also electric cabs with the driver seated high up at the rear.*

CABRIOLET - *A word used towards the end of the period to describe a car with collapsible hood, with two or four seats.*

COUPE' - *Originally a vehicle "cut" by a glass division, fixed or moveable, behind the front seats. The driving position was only partially protected by the roof whilst the totally enclosed rear was very luxurious.*

COUPE'-CABRIOLET OR DOUBLE-CABRIOLET - *A long vehicle the front part of which was designed as a coupé, whilst the rear part had the collapsible hood of a cabriolet. There were often two supplementary seats.*

COUPE'-CHAUFFEUR - *A coupé with the driving position completely covered by a fixed roof, which was an extension of the rear roof.*

COUPE' DE VILLE - *A coupé with the driving position completely open.*

COUPE'-LIMOUSINE - *A vehicle with a totally enclosed rear and with the front part closed on the sides only.*

DOUBLE BERLINA - *A lengthened berlina with the driving position enclosed but separated from the rear part of the vehicle.*

DOUBLE LANDAULET - *A lengthened landaulet with two permanent seats plus two occasionals in the rear, and a driving position in front.*

DOUBLE PHAETON - *A phaeton with two double seats, including that of the driver.*

DOUBLE TONNEAU - *A lengthened tonneau in which the front seats were completely separate from the rear.*

LANDAU - *A cabriolet limousine in which only the roof behind the rear windows was collapsible.*

LANDAULET OR LANDAULETTE - *A small landeau with only two seats in the closed collapsible roof portion.*

LIMOUSINE - *A lengthened coupé with double lateral windows in the rear part.*

LIMOUSINE-CHAUFFEUR - *A limousine with the rear roof extended forward to cover the driving position.*

PHAETON - *A term again taken from the days of the horsedrawn carriage. In the early days of motoring it described a light car with large spoked wheels, with one double seat and generally a hood.*

RUNABOUT - *An open sporting type of vehicle, generally with only two seats and simple bodywork.*

SKIFF OR CAB-SKIFF - *An open sports car with streamlined, light bodywork.*

TONNEAU - *An open vehicle with a bench seat in front and a semi-circular seat behind. A part of the seat was built into the rear door.*

"GLASS" SALOON - *A large closed vehicle, generally similar to a double berlina but with very large windows.*

SALOON - *A vehicle with the driving seat inside the enclosed car with no separation from the rear seats.*

TORPEDO - *A long sports vehicle with hood, which was attached to the windscreen.*

VICTORIA - *Another term derived from the era of horses. The Victoria was long and luxurious with a separate driving position and a large rear seat, and was equipped with hoods and sidescreens.*

VOITURETTE - *Used to describe an early touring car with two seats only and no hood.*

WAGON-SALOON - *A particularly luxurious saloon used in America for civic and other official purposes.*

A 1909 four-cylinder Roland-Pilain which came in second in the Mont Ventoux hill climb.

demands on the nerves of the drivers, who had to climb long stony tracks flanked by sheer drops, round thousands of bends.

While climbing the pass, which rises to a height of 5950 feet, one of the drivers, Max, made a mistake on a bend and hit a bollard. The car rolled over the edge and fell 100 feet down the mountainside, but fortunately Max and his mechanic had been thrown clear on to the road. Max climbed down the mountainside to examine the car and, seeing that nothing could be done, began to climb up again.

A short while later another competitor, Baras, passed just as Max was reaching the road. At the end of the stage Baras reported that Max and his car had fallen 100 feet over a cliff and Max had then walked up on his own two feet!

Another competitor, Rigolly, finding his little Darracq would not go up a hill, turned it round and, using the reverse gear, went up backwards. To reach the top he had to leave behind anything moveable in the car, including drums of petrol and oil, tools and spare parts and even pieces of bodywork. When he had taken the car to the top, Rigolly had to walk back and carry up the most essential pieces.

A 1904 Renault followed by a Cadillac of the same year.

Edge and his Napier ended up in a ditch but he managed to man-handle the vehicle out and continue to Innsbruck. By reaching Innsbruck he won the third Gordon Bennett Cup, which was run concurrently with the Paris-Vienna race as far as Innsbruck. His competitors were Girardot and de Knyff for, respectively, America and France; de Knyff, though he succeeded in crossing the Arlberg, broke his differential 20 miles short of Innsbruck.

At this point a series of misfortunes began to afflict Louis Renault, whose car had performed well over the pass and beyond. At Innsbruck Renault accidently hit the car of another competitor, Baron de Caters. This made him and Szisz lose a great deal of time in repairing the differential by using wire, string and hemp; he added sawdust to the differential oil to thicken it and to reduce leaks.

At last Renault and Szisz set off for Salzburg, but in the

The 1902 Fiat "24 H.P." Lancia won the Sassi-Superga hill climb in such a car, beating Mercedes. The 6,370 c.c. four cylinder engine had low tension magneto ignition, leather cone clutch, chain transmission and gave a top speed of about 60 m.p.h.

The 1907 120 H.P. Itala.

dark they ran into a level-crossing barrier. Yet again they set off after having repaired the car as best they could with the help of a local smith. The most unlikely materials used this time included a chair for making improvised wheel spokes. After they got moving again they found the radiator was leaking, and Szisz had to sit on the bonnet as the car went along, continually pouring water into the radiator.

'Special technique'

The Salzburg stage was won by Baron De Forest's Mercedes and the next day the Renault brothers set off on the last stage to Vienna. The course of the race was at once influenced by Marcel Renault's remarkable driving. He left in seventh position and, risking all, he took the bends at high speed. Slowly Renault caught up on Farman until he drew level. For a long time the two cars raced along side by side until at least Renault, with what he called his "special technique" on bends, succeeded in overtaking the Panhard some 33 miles from the finish.

Still at full speed, Marcel Renault reached the trotting track at the Prater in Vienna, the finishing line, two hours sooner than forecast. It was mid-day and not even judges were waiting for him; they were at lunch. People near the line at first refused to believe he was one of the competitors in the race — and Renault's command of the German language was almost non-existent. At last every doubt was cleared and the spectators, though they

had hoped for a Mercedes victory, sportingly carried him off in triumph.

The performance of the little Renault, small in comparison with the giants in the race, was interesting from the technical point of view. The average speed — almost 40 m.p.h. — was high.

Above all the Paris-Vienna race demonstrated that sheer power was not everything and that many other factors, from robustness of the chassis to the courage and initiative of the drivers, could be vital in a race.

A little time after the Paris-Vienna race there was another outstanding car achievement, almost incredibly by a steam car. Serpollet, inventor of the famous flash steam boiler, took his aerodynamic "Oeuf de Pâques" (Easter Egg) on the Promenades des Anglais at Nice, and put up the flying kilometre record to 120.761 k.p.h. (about 75 m.p.h.). His unofficial mile record was about one m.p.h. higher. The record was to be taken back by an i.c.-engined car shortly afterwards, still in this memorable year, 1902, when Farman in a Mors raised the record first to 123.249 k.p.h. and immediately afterwards to 124.102 k.p.h. at Dordan.

In France these were triumphs of speed, but in England there was still a speed limit of 20 m.p.h. and, indeed, until a few months earlier it had been 12 m.p.h. This caused some embarassment to the organisers of the fourth Gordon Bennett Cup race. As the third race had been won by Edge, it was England's turn to organise the fourth.

The impact of races elsewhere was strictly national. So far as Italy was concerned, one race of some interest

arose out of a challenge by the Duke of Abruzzi to
Garibaldi Coltelletti, the Panhard representative in Italy,
concerning the merits of the respective cars, a "24 H.P."
Fiat and the "24 H.P." of the French company. Giovanni Agnelli had the foresight to add Felice Nazzaro
as an unofficial competitor. The race, run between Turin
and Bologna, had two winners. Coltelletti won the stake
of 5000 Lire when he arrived in triumph at Bologna, the
Duke having literally fallen by the wayside at Alessandria
when he hit the parapet of a bridge. Nazzaro, nevertheless, covered the course in his 12 H.P. in four minutes
less than Coltelletti, at an average speed of 22 m.p.h.

Round the world

In the meantime the passion for long-distance trials had
crossed the Atlantic from the U.S. In 1902 two Engl-
ishmen, Dr. Lehwess and Mr. Cudell, left London at the
end of April in a kind of bus, built by Panhard-Levassor,
the "Passe Partout", to drive round the world. A little
more than six weeks later the "Passe Partout" reached
Paris — evidently speed was not their greatest concern
— and then took another four months to reach Warsaw.
They called at St Petersburg and reached Nijni-Novgorod

The proud owner climbs aboard his 1904 Rolls-Royce, which he
found abandoned in a shed and restored.

The Italian racing driver Cagno in the 100 H.P. Fiat in which he won the Mont Ventoux hill climb.

THE DETERMINED INNOVATOR - HENRY FORD

Henry Ford, perhaps the most important figure of all in the story of the motor car, would have become a farmer if his parents had had their way. He was born in 1863 of a father who was an immigrant from Ireland and a mother of Dutch origin. From a very early age however, he had little interest in his father's plans for him, being fascinated by all things mechanical, particularly clocks, spending all his time taking them to pieces and putting them together again.

Years of experiment

He was young when he left his native town of Greenfield in Michigan and went to Detroit, a much more attractive place to Ford's mind. His first job was with Flower Brothers, manufacturers of machine tools. Then he passed to a marine engine company, the Dry Dock Engine Company, and finally to a small firm which installed Westinghouse steam engines. All these companies represented useful experience for him and formed the basis of his mechanical knowledge.
When his father died he was left 40 acres of land, but this was not enough to draw him back to his home town.

A little later, in 1888, Henry married Clara Bryant and took a small isolated house where he set up a workshop. It was from this time that he began ten years of experimenting and building protoytpes in his spare time. In the meantime the Detroit Edison Company had offered him a reasonably well paid job — 135 dollars a month — firstly in charge of fire precautions and then as an engineer. Then came the moment when his first "quadricycle" was ready and the town coucil, in spite of some opposition, had given him permission to use it on the public roads. He saw the great Edison himself who advised him to follow his inclinations, and so Henry resigned to devote all of his time to the motor car.

Powerful friends

Thus began a hard, wearing period of experiment and unsuccessful tests which caused him disillusionment and the loss of a lot of money. With a partner, Tom Cooper, an ex-racing cyclist, he built a few racing cars. One of these won the challenge against Winton and served as a springboard for further activity, thanks to the publicity received.
A little while later, scraping up everything he possessed, Henry formed the Detroit Automobile Company with 5,000 dollars. The beginning was difficult and the help of some powerful friends, such as the mayor of Detroit himself, proved to be of little use. The company got into serious difficulty even though Ford himself drew only 100 dollars a month. It was necessary to sell the company to Leland and Faulconer in 1900 (and this was later to become Cadillac).
But at last the worst was behind him. On the wave of popularity generated by his Grosse Pointe victory against Winton, Ford was able to found the Ford Motor Company, once again risking everything he had, using a capital 28,000 dollars provided by 12 fortunate subscribers — fortunate because, to give an example, Senator Couzen's investment of 2,500 dollars increased to 30 million!

Lowest possible price

The reasons for this immediate success were many, including the victories of Ford's racing car "999", and the technical characteristics of his cars, but above all it was due to the startling ideas of Henry Ford himself who right from the beginning thought of the motor car in terms of an instrument for mass consumption, to that end cutting every unnecessary cost, building in series and selling at the lowest possible price.

He is best described by the things he did, such as the theory in which he first laid down a modern law of economic production, or the seven months of inactivity he imposed on the company in 1927 after the finish of the model "T" and before the introduction of the new model. There was his "Peace ship" which he sent to Europe in 1915 to try to stop the war; his unsuccessful attempts to enter politics, first in 1918 as Democratic candidate for the Senate and then for the Presidency in 1924; and the huge industry he set up when already old, to ensure his company an important position in the tyre business.

His only son, Edsel, to whom the old Henry Ford had given control of a good part of his huge industrial empire, died young, but before he himself died, Henry was able to pass his job to his grandson who bore the same name. Henry Ford died aged 84 in 1947, leaving behind him a substantial number of books in which he had expressed his social and economic ideas, often original and always enlivened by understanding.

The cabin in the oak tree where Ford worked.

Henry Ford in one of his first cars. Edsel Ford is behind in the 25,000,000th.

where they stopped, their vehicle being unable to travel further.

In the same year an American, Charles Glidden, began a fantastic journey of over 50,000 miles in one of the first Napiers. Having crossed Europe, Glidden went into Scandinavia as far as the Arctic Circle, and in the years that followed he went round the world twice.

A 1902 Renault shows its paces.

A view of the Ford factory at Dearborn in 1912 — an early assembly line. Below the Oldsmobile machine shop in 1901.

In 1901, however, a race took place which was to leave rather more lasting traces in motoring history. It was held on 10 October on a track at Grosse Pointe, near Michigan, arising out of a challenge between manufacturers.

One was Alexander Winton and the other was Henry Ford, who had recently left his job with the Edison Illuminating Company to devote himself entirely to building motor cars in partnership with a racing cyclist, Tom Cooper. This was Ford's second adventure into motoring, after his famous light car had noisily attracted the attention of his fellow-citizens some years before.

The great challenge

Ford was not a racing driver but he had noted the tremendous publicity value of racing and decided that he too must make use of it. He therefore sent a formal challenge to Winton, suggesting a 10-mile race. This challenge had a more positive outcome than the one which, two years before, Winton himself had sent to all American manufacturers, challenging them to a race between Chicago and New York. In the end, this challenge came to nothing because each competitor insisted on the race being held in his own area.

This time things were different. The Grosse Pointe race, well publicised by the local Press, drew a large crowd of spectators. The prize at stake was a glass of punch, but in effect the stake was much higher. At Ford's instigation, a third competitor took part in the race, William N. Murray, a millionaire owner of one of the fastest cars in Pittsburgh. He withdrew, however, at the last moment owing to an oil leak.

Winton took the lead in the race at once, and gained an advantage of half a mile. At the end of the seventh lap, his engine began to smoke and the car gradually slowed to a halt. Ford could then just coast to victory. His time was good, his car covering the course in 13 minutes 23 seconds at an average of 45 m.p.h. In their enthusiasm for the young and as yet unknown winner, the public forgot Winton's brilliant performance in setting up a new one-mile record of one minute 6 seconds. Ford's industrial fortune sprang indirectly from this race.

8547 CH75

front view of a 1907 DE DION-BOUTON MODEL "BG"

engine - front mounted single vertical cylinder
bore and stroke - 100 × 120 mm.
capacity - 942 c.c.
output - 8 H.P. at 1,400 r.p.m.
ignition - high tension magneto
clutch - a bronze disc between two steel discs
gearchange - 3 speeds plus reverse
transmission - cardan shaft
weight - 1,320 lbs.

For many years most of the world has driven on the right with the steering wheel on the left. In Great Britain and in many countries of the Commonwealth, however, the reverse is true. Above is a Vauxhall Viva in Sydney, and below a Prince Henry Vauxhall of 1911.

CHAPTER EIGHT
THE GREAT NAMES EMERGE

After his victory of Grosse Point, Ford prepared a second machine, the "Arrow", in which he reached a speed of 97.37 m.p.h. — a record which was broken by a narrow margin two weeks later by William K. Vanderbilt, Jr. An Oldsmobile, the "Pirate", then raised it again; and finally in 1901 a Baker electric car, the "Torpedo", achieved 105 m.p.h.

Not long afterwards the powerful figure of Barney Oldfield impressed itself on American racing when he held a meeting at Yonkers, near New York, called "Mile-a-minute Racing", which attracted a large crowd for the time, 5,000. Oldfield set up a new mile record of 61 seconds.

Later the "999", a new Ford car, astounded the public

A 1906 Cadillac.

first run in 1902 did not produce any exceptional results, and it was not until 1906 that spectacular records were set up, including the prodigious 127 m.p.h. of Marriott in his Stanley Steamer.

Cadillac is born

At the beginning of this century a new name was added to the list of American motor manufacturers, that of Cadillac. Its origins lay in the dramatic events at Oldsmobile. The fire in 1901 had set Olds on a desperate search for capital with which to re-equip and start production of the famous "Curved Dash". Among those who helped him was Henry Martin Leland, a 58-year-old industrialist, who since 1890 had owned, with his partner Faulconer, a machine tool factory which also built i.c. engines for boats.

Leland helped Olds in two ways: he gave him financial assistance and he provided him with parts for the new car. (Among others who helped Olds at this time were the Dodge brothers, who were to help Ford and later still to set up their own company, which was to play a part in the creation of Chrysler).

Leland's relationship with Olds in 1901 created an interest in motor cars that led him to decide on a direct involvement. At that time the affairs of the Detroit Automobile Company, set up by Henry Ford, were faring badly and Ford had to give up his company and his workshop. It was Leland and Faulconer who bought it up and started production of a light car with a single-

because it consisted only of essentials — chassis, engine, wheels and controls — and in this Oldfield covered the mile in 56.25 seconds at Columbus. Then, in the same vehicle, he returned the spectacular time of 55.8 seconds on a circular track at Yonkers.

The year 1902 was also when a series of races began on the famous beach at Ormonde Beach, Daytona, in Florida. The promoter was W. J. Morgan, an ex-sports writer who had specialized in cycling and motoring and had passed to organising races. He organised a number of "special carnivals", including a race across Florida called "Climb to the Clouds" and various "beach runs" across the 20 miles from Daytona to Ormonde. The

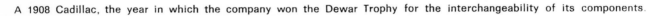

A 1908 Cadillac, the year in which the company won the Dewar Trophy for the interchangeability of its components.

A 1903 White Steamer, with a 10 H.P. twin cylinder engine.

taken to Brooklands and run for 500 miles. They emerged in perfect condition.

This proof of the interchangeability of Cadillac parts impressed technical experts, and the company was awarded the coveted Dewar Trophy for the most significant demonstration of motor car technical progress in the year. (In 1913 Cadillac won the Dewar Trophy for the second time, the only occasion it has ever happened, for having equipped their cars with an automobile starting device and electric ignition).

In Europe, too, the early years of the new century marked the creation of new companies. In Great Britain Sunbeamland began series production; later the name was abbreviated to Sunbeam. The vehicle was decidedly unusual in that the four wheels were arranged in a rhomboid, i.e. one forward, two at the middle sides and one at the rear.

Working abroad

The idea was due to an engineer who had non-conformist ideas, Mabberley Smith. He persuaded the company to build this car even though, since their foundation in 1887, they had specialised in bicycles. The engine of this strange vehicle — it is impossible to say now whether it was a two-seater or a three-seater — had a water-cooled single-cylinder engine of 327 c.c. and developed 2¾ H.P. Ignition was by coil and contact breaker. The vehicle had two speeds; transmission was by chain and belt; and suspension was by semi-elliptics for the front and rear wheels, while the centre axle was rigid.

The French engineer, Louis Coatalen, also worked with Sunbeam in the early years of the century, after having designed one of the early Humbers built in Coventry. At about the same time he worked with a third new

cylinder engine designed by an acquaintance, A. P. Brush. One year later the car was given its name — it was the first Cadillac, named after the French gentleman who was credited by legend as having founded Detroit.

The Cadillac Automobile Company changed its name in 1904 to the Cadillac Motor Car Company. From the start its cars had a standard, then unknown for American manufacture, in the precise nature of design and the high class of finish. Leland always insisted on this, as did Royce in England, and the prestige which their names still have is a continuing demonstration of the importance which the public has always given to quality.

Interchangeable

A proof of the value of quality was given by a series of tests to which three Cadillacs were subjected in 1908. The cars were shipped across the Atlantic and completely dismantled in Britain. All the parts were mixed and, under the supervision of the Royal Automobile Club, the cars were rebuilt under the supervision of judges. They chose at random so that each of the three cars was rebuilt with components and parts that could have originally been on the others.

The mechanics could use only four types of tools for the assembly — screwdrivers, spanners, hammers and pincers. As soon as the cars were re-assembled they were

Jack Brabham at the wheel of a 1904 Sunbeam 12 H.P. in the 1960 London-Brighton Run. On this occasion he was last!

Displayed like works of art — a room of the Renault museum in Paris.

company, Hillman. It is strange that these three then independent companies should be united 50 years later in one complex, the Rootes Group.

Another name that is repeatedly found in the history of British motoring is that of Thomas Charles Pullinger, an English engineer who had spent many years in France working with Teste, Moret and Cie., a well-known motor manufacturer in Lyons. Pullinger also took part in the birth of Humber and Sunbeam and was also to design one of the most successful Scottish cars, the famed Arrol-Johnson.

Another interesting name in British motoring at the time is that of Clément-Talbot, founded by D. M. Weigel, representative of the French company Clément, and the Marquis of Shrewsbury, whose family name is Talbot.

The first Sunbeamland, built in 1899.

The ubitiquous Coatalen was to arrive there, too, though much later.

In 1901 and 1902 no French car companies of lasting interest were formed, though there were to be many in the following years. In the former year the Paris Salon de l'Automobile finally found a worthy home in the Grand Palais, and attracted an impressive number of visitors, 170,000.

Among the large manufacturers, Panhard launched the new "16 H.P.", directly derived from the "24 H.P." which had won the first Gordon Bennett, and from its more powerful version, the "28 H.P.". On the 16 H.P., the engine was again mounted in front but the car was a four-seater. The radiator was still a finned tube.

Renault in 1902 recruited M. Viet, a brother-in-law of Georges Bouton. Viet was the author of a technical revolution in the expanding Billancourt factory. He was an excellent engineer and had designed a four-cylinder engine with many new features. He had first turned to the Marquis De Dion to produce it, but the latter was still wedded to the single-cylinder (he was soon to give it up with a vengeance for a V8) and refused.

When Renault met Viet he was at once impressed by his abilities and added him to his team of designers. The engine of the 16 H.P. with which Marcel Renault won the Paris-Vienna was, in fact, the work of Viet. It was this victory which convinced Renault of the merits of the four-cylinder engine. At once he put one into production that was more suitable for general use; thus was born the "20 H.P.", which, though subjected to many improvements and changes, was to be the backbone of Renault production to 1928.

In the meantime, in 1901, the first light cars built by

Darracq at the famous Suresnes works were born. It was the "9½ H.P." which had a "coal scuttle" bonnet similar to the Renault. Underneath, the engine and its accessories were arranged in a sensible way to allow easy separation from the chassis.

Darracq was also preparing cars for record attempts, such as that in which Baras was to set up a world land speed record three years later at 105 m.p.h. on the track at Montgeron.

Bicycles to cars

In contrast to France, there were a number of new manufacturers who entered the field in Italy in the early years of the century. Many of them were to last only a short while, such as the Adani and the Bugatti-Gulinelli of 1900, the Devecchi-Strada, the Dobelli and the Florentia of 1903 and the Aquila Italiana of 1905. Other companies, however, were more important.

In 1901 the Società Fratelli Ceirano was formed in Turin. Giovanni Battista had come from Cuneo to Turin, where he spent his early years first selling and then making bicycles. In 1898 he formed a company, Ceirano G. B. & C., to produce a light car, the "Welleyes" designed by Faccioli. Lancia and Nazzaro also worked in the company as mechanics. A year later Ceirano G. B. & C., with all the prototype Welleyes so far built, was bought by Fiat. The prototype was to become the first Fiat. The restless Ceirano and his nephew created a number of other companies — the Società Fratelli Ceirano in 1901, the STAR (Giovanni, in 1904), the Italia (Matteo, 1904), the Junior (Giovanni, 1905), the SCAT in 1906 and, much later, Ceirano S. A. in 1919. The first of these companies lasted only a year but produced some models of a "5 H.P." with a rear-mounted single-cylinder engine of 640 c.c.

In Fiat, in the meantime, only two years had passed since the first "3½ H.P." and only one since it had been replaced by the "6 H.P.", the racing car with which it was hoped to gain useful publicity. Already a third car was ready; this was an "8 H.P." with a vertical twin engine that went into production in 1901. It was the first Fiat with the engine mounted in front.

This four-seat, four-door saloon "X" was designed built by Pininfarina for Fiat in 1960. The four wheels were in rhomboid layout with the front one steering and the rear one driving. All-rubber suspension and 1098 c.c. engine.

1911 Vauxhall.

1903-1904 Fiat 16-24 H.P. with four vertical cylinders in two pairs and 4,181 c.c. Multiplate clutch and chain drive. Top speed — 45 m.p.h.

1907 Dupressoir.

A 1908 Oakland. This car was famous in its day for its ability to climb hills.

It was this car which caused the break, in 1901, between Agnelli and his chief engineer, Faccioli. The former had returned from the Paris Salon, where he had been impressed by the honeycomb radiator which could replace the fragile finned-tube type used till then. Agnelli wanted to fit one of these new radiators on the "8 H.P." but Faccioli preferred to wait until it had been tested by other companies. Faccioli left.

The new chief engineer, Enrico, then designed a four-cylinder engine which was fitted to the next model, the 1902 "12 H.P.". This was a new car from back to front. It had a wooden chassis reinforced with metal, pneumatic tyres, automatic lubrication and an inclined steering column.

The three pedals were placed in what was to be the standard position for many years in Europe — clutch to the left of the steering column, brake immediately to the right of the column and the accelerator further

The vogue of the "torpedo". A 1908 Peugeot "116" with 4 cylinders, 16 H.P., 2,211 c.c. engine, four speeds plus reverse, a leather cone clutch.

FROM TILLER
TO TWIST
OF THE WRIST

Early motor cars were not controlled by a steering wheel but by a different and much less convenient system. It is surprising, however, that a system so natural and effective as the steering wheel took so long to be adopted. The reason, however, is not altogether inexplicable. It should not be forgotten that in the first 15 years of their life motor vehicles were called "horseless carriages", not as a colourful metaphor but because they really were considered only as a slight deviation from the horse-drawn carriage, as may be seen by the coachwork adopted.

When manufacturers of the new motor car had to design a method of steering — because steering devices did not exist on the horse-drawn carriages — they stayed as close to the cart shafts as they could.

This explains the origin of the "queue de vache", "cow's tail", or tiller — a bar of metal or wood, usually suitably curved in two directions, which, through a simple linkage, varied the angle of the front axle to the centre line of the chassis.

It was obviously a system practical only for low speeds, as it was impossible to have precise control of steering due to "whip" in the bar.

The tiller continued to have its supporters even after it had been rejected by most manufacturers; then at the end of the 19th century a considerably less crude system was introduced. It was mechanically much more complicated, and generally known as the "two handle" system.

Vertical handle

It consisted of a vertical steering column connected at the bottom to steering linkages similar to those in use today, so that instead of the whole axle pivoting, only the wheels turned on kingpins.

The upper end of the steering column was rigidly attached to a horizontal bar some 20 to 30 inches long, with a vertical handle at each end held in the hands. This system was a vast improvement on the tiller, but could not cope with sharp angles.

It was but a short step to the steering wheel, which was itself used at first with a vertical column. It was quickly adopted almost everywhere, partly because its convenience was apparent to everyone and partly because it was not protected by patents.

At first these wheels were smaller than those in use today. With the introduction of inclined columns, wheels grew considerably larger, reaching enormous sizes on sports cars in the first decade of the century.

There was, however, a practical reason for the large wheel. The poor road surfaces of the time transmitted heavy shocks through the steering linkages to the steering wheel (research to eliminate these was to come much later). The only remedy then was to reduce the effect of the shocks, which were extremely tiring at speed on drivers' wrists, by increasing the diameter of the wheel. Early wheels usually had five spokes but these were soon reduced first to four, then to three. If the wheel

rim was made of metal tube, it was usually thick, because of the technical difficulties in those days in making small-diameter tube. Some rims were made of wood. At first they were covered in leather, if covered at all, Celluloid being used later to cover metal rims and spokes.

Fitting on wheels

A familiar fitting on steering wheels for 40 years was the manual ignition advance/retard lever, usually mounted in the centre. This lever was used every time the load on the engine varied, such as going up a hill or when there were wide variations in engine speed. This is now done automatically.

The horn button at the centre of the wheel came much later, and for many years other acoustic warning devices were used. These included not only the well-known bulb horn but also much more complicated devices; one was actuated by exhaust gas and operated by a foot pedal. Secondary controls have been fitted by manufacturers to the steering column from 1930 onwards. There has been a wide variety, and the reasons were not always rational.

There has always been considerable variety in the design and number of the spokes. The number seemed recently to have been stabilised at two, but now appears to be returning to three again.

These is, however, one famous steering wheel with only one spoke — that of the Citroën DS 19 and models derived from it. Even this, though, had a worthy but little-known ancestor in the wheel fitted to the famous little Humberettes of the early 1900's.

Safety rules

Developments today are not so much with regard to the wheel itself but on the steering column and shaft. This is especially true in the U.S., where severe government safety regulations have led to the use of a shaft consisting of two tubes of different diameter connected by a plastic link which will break in the event of a head-on collision. The two tubes telescope, one inside the other. The steering wheel as a device may now be running into obsolescence. Particularly in America, much research is being done on alternative methods of steering to eliminate the potential danger of the wheel in a crash, to permit steering by one hand only at low speeds and to improve steering control.

Of the many systems tried so far, the most satisfactory appears to be the so-called "wrist-twist". This consists of two small wheels five to six inches in diameter mounted at the ends of a T-shaped steering column. A fixed ring gives rest for the thumbs while the fingers grip the two wheels in indentations.

The two wheels are inter-connected so that steering may be done by only one hand; a servo device is used to reduce effort required.

From tiller to a twist of the wrist... in the meantime the present-day driver continues happily with the wheel.

1903 De Dion Populaire (Turin Motor Museum).

1907 Standard. The company was formed in 1903 and the first car was a 6 H.P.

to the right. Bodywork was of the type already known as "tonneau". The 12 H.P. model sold well in 1903 in France, England and America as well as in Italy.

Two more models followed the "12 H.P." within a few months, similar except for their engines. There was a 4181 c.c. which, from its "square" 110 × 110 mm. engine, produced 16 H.P. at 1,000 r.p.m. to give 44 m.p.h., and a 24 H.P. which at first had a hotted-up version of the same engine.

Production figures

Production statistics for 1903 are illuminating. Total world production of motor vehicles was 61,927, of which 30,204 were made in France, 11,235 in the U.S., 9,437 in Great Britain, 6,904 in Germany, 2,839 in Belgium and 1,308 in Italy. These figures show that the big French manufacturers were rapidly expanding, with 25, 30 or even 40 chassis being assembled at a time. Technical progress was world-wide. The "hot tube" was on the way out for ignition, and the magneto on the way in. Single cylinders were going out; two were normal and four were soon to be common. Engine speeds were up to 1,200 and even 1,500 r.p.m., which meant more comfort for motorists as the jolting was replaced by an acceptable rumble.

As far as bodywork was concerned, the closed car was

still to come. This many seem remarkable, but interest in motoring was largely due to the great races and all the cars taking part had been open. Thus the aspiration of those who could afford a car was to own a similar one. But not many years were to pass before common-sense prevailed, with the birth of many cars that could be closed or converted — the coupé, the limousine, the landaulet, the cabriolet, the salon vitre or glass-saloon. In 1903, however, the universal desire was for a "torpedo" — dashing, open and low-built now that engineers had discovered the safety of a low centre of gravity.

Months of waiting

There were signs of things to come — in the Belgian Pipe with overhead valves, in the three-cylinder Mandsley with a magnetic clutch, certain Fiats with compressed air starting, the small French company Dombret with its monobloc engines having the gearbox in the sump, and the Wilson and Pilcher "10 H.P." in England with an early type of automatic transmission.

But it was a long way from the modern situation where the customer goes to the Motor Show or to a dealer and chooses his car, either driving it away or waiting for delivery. In either case, he has little else to do but pay. In the early years of the century the first item bought was the chassis; and then began months of discussion, contemplation and patience. The coachbuilder probably was still working on an custom-built basis, each successive body being different and difficult to classify.

Most bodies were built by men who had come from the horse-drawn carriage trade and wanted to innovate as possible. They transferred in entirety the techniques and methods that were inappropriate for the new field. Thus their products were often masterpieces of finish and ornament, but were impractical and inefficient.

A beauty which has not aged. An elegant 1906 Rolls-Royce Silver Ghost attracts its young admirers.

1902-1903 Fiat 12 H.P. with four cylinder 3,370 c.c. engine developing 14 H.P. Three speeds plus reverse and leather cone clutch. Top speed — 45 m.p.h.

From the "torpedo" to the "char-à-banc" A 1911 14 H.P. Renault showing the stepped seating.

An 1898 Opel 4 H.P. "System Lutzmann" with single cylinder water cooled engine, chain drive, 2 speeds plus reverse, top speed 10 to 13 m.p.h. Cost, at today's prices: about £ 4,000.

front view of a 1908 6/8 H.P. LEGNANO MODEL "A"

engine - front mounted twin
bore and stroke - 85 × 100 mm.
capacity - 1,135 c.c.
output - 8 H.P. at 1,100 r.p.m.
ignition - high tension magneto
clutch - inverse leather cone
gearchange - 3 speeds plus reverse
transmission - cardan shaft

Two cars purpose-built for their markets. A 1909 Rolls-Royce Silver Ghost in dream-like surroundings and, below, a Fiat 500 "Topolino" of 1936.

CHAPTER NINE
RACE WITHOUT A FINISH

The last and most dramatic of the great European capital-to-capital races was the Paris-Madrid of 1903. Only the first stage, Paris to Bordeaux, was run and this was remembered by a chain of tragedies. The reasons were varied. There was the enormous increase in the power which manufacturers had given their cars, arising from their experience in the earlier big races. Drivers were relatively inexperienced in controlling such monsters, which had inefficient brakes and precarious road-holding, and the authorities were inexperienced in organising and controlling such a race.

Finally, there was the lack of discipline on the part of the spectators, who were enthusiastic but extremely ignorant of the potential danger of these hurtling machines. Even the members of the army and police who lined the route were unable to discipline the public, precisely because no-one was aware of the risks.

The Paris-Vienna of the previous year had provided a foretaste of the increase in power, and the major competitors who presented themselves for the Paris-Madrid race had vehicles capable of speeds which had been unthinkable only a few months earlier.

So far as the public was concerned, between Paris and Bordeaux there were several hundreds of thousands of spectators. Ten dead and an uncounted number of injured, was the terrible result of the one day's racing. The drastic suspension of the race was inevitable.

It was not until 1927, with another formula, that major road racing was to be held again. This was the Mille Miglia, and that was also to be finally banned for the same reason — the number of accidents to the public. The Paris-Madrid race was organised jointly by the Spanish and French automobile clubs. It was agreed that the race should be run in three stages — Versailles to Bordeaux, passing through Chartres, Tours, Poitiers and Angoulême; Bordeaux to Vitoria by way of Bayonne; and Vitoria to Madrid through Burgos and Valladolid.

Baron P. de Crawhez' Panhard-Levassor arrives in fifth place at Bordeaux in the Paris-Madrid race.

More than 300 cars entered and, even after the inevitable withdrawals, there was still 275 starters. Alongside many amateur drivers were several professional racing teams, such as that sent by De Dietrich with 12 of their new low cars. Mors had 14 cars entered, one of them driven by Fournier. Panhard had 15 and Renault four cars, two being driven by Louis and Marcel. There were also teams from De Dion, Mercedes, Wolseley and Ader, and there was one Fiat entered.

Cyclists' escort

A number of the regulations represented new ideas in motor racing. For example, as a safety measure it was ruled that time spent in crossing cities should not be counted in the race. On approaching a city, each competitor was stopped, his time of arrival registered, and he

J. B. Warden in a Mercedes 60 H.P. arrives at Bordeaux in sixth place.

was escorted by cyclists at a slow pace through the city, where his time of departure was then recorded. The cars had a sort of post-box into which "counters" were placed at each control point to register its departure. A sign of things to come was the presence in this race of lady competitors. Madame du Gast drove a new Dietrich, Madame Lockert an Ader and Mademoiselle Jollivet a motor-cycle.

The vast gatherings of spectators turned the race into a national event. The Italian newspaper "Corriere della Sera" of 24 May reported, "Last night 100,000 Parisians were making their way to Versailles to see the start of the Paris-Madrid race. From the Bastille to the Madeleine all the cafes, restaurants and night clubs, brilliantly lit, had every table occupied by diners who had their cars, motor cycles and bicycles outside, waiting to take them to Versailles.

"The great boulevards of Paris presented an extraordinary sight. Every minute two, four or even six cars passed amidst clouds of dust and enthusiasm! There was a sort of pre-race competition among the competitors going to Versailles, where the race was to start at 3.30 a.m. It was almost impossible to move in the streets. Still people continue to come from every part. Order was maintained only by battalions of troops and gendarmes".

Waiting to start

At the "Pièce d'Eau de Suisse", the start of the race, the last preparations were being completed. In the ranks of the drivers waiting alongside their cars were many who had won fame in earlier races. There was Charles Jarrott, a large Englishman, whose 45 H.P. Dietrich had a great novelty, an electric headlamp; he had been selected by lot as first away. Louis and Marcel Renault,

De Knyff, Lorraine-Barrow, Théry and Fournier were also there.

At last the signal was given and Jarrott set off; at two-minute intervals the rest followed. Louis Renault was sixth to leave and at once set out to overtake those ahead of him.

Cathedral close

Dust was the universal enemy; it blinded the drivers, blocked engines, covered goggles and hid curves. The only way to avoid it was to overtake everyone else, and Renault passed driver after driver until, in sight of Chartres Cathedral, he finally overtook Jarrott's Dietrich. Up to this point he had averaged 70 m.p.h.

With no slowing down, Renault increased his lead over Jarrott at an astounding rate. At Poitiers he was

The Hon. C. S. Rolls just before he founded Rolls-Royce seen at the wheel of a 70 H.P. Mors of the type that took part in the Paris-Madrid.

Tragedy for the Renault—Fernand tells Louis that their brother Marcel, who crashed at Couché-Verac, is dying. The mechanic, who has heard nothing because of the noise of the engine, smiles unknowingly. Spectators point—and the race goes on.

20 minutes ahead, at Angoulême 23, and he ended the stage in Bordeaux 35 minutes in the lead, arriving there at an average of just over 60 m.p.h.

This drive enabled him to take second place in the general classification to Gabriel, in a 70 H.P. Mors, who had driven an even more remarkable race. He had left carrying the number 168 and arrived fourth at Bordeaux, at an average speed of over 65 m.p.h. Jarrott was third in the general classification and Warden fourth in a Mercedes.

Battleground

The race had been a battleground for the cars, not more than 100 finishing the stage. This was probably due to the fantastic pace set by Louis Renault as the cars were, in fact, much stronger than those that had taken part in the Paris-Vienna in the previous year.

Public opinion was to be more shocked by the reports in the Press throughout Europe of a more serious massacre — this time of people.

A foretaste of what was to happen was given at Ablis, where a spectator who had leaned too far forward was hit by one of the cars but not fatally injured.

A little while later, 20 miles south of Poitiers, Marcel Renault first passed Farman and then set out to pass Théry. The two cars ran side by side at high speed until they came to a right-angled bend at the entrance to the village of Couché-Vérac. Théry, who was in the lead, saw it in time, slowed down and rounded the bend. Renault, blinded by Théry's dust, saw the danger too late and shot off the road into a deep ditch, turning over several times.

Théry, who probably had no idea what had happened, continued on his way and it was not until Farman came by a few minutes later that the accident was discovered. Marcel Renault was already unconscious and died the next day in the little hospital at Couhé-Vérac.

His brother, Louis, was told of the accident when he arrived at Bordeaux. When it was confirmed that his brother had died, he retired the whole Renault team as a sign of mourning.

Marcel's death was to have important consequences in the works at Billancourt. Louis was full of remorse and he even thought of closing the Renault factory, but a third brother Fernand shut his own button factory to enter the company, and resolved the family crisis.

Level crossing

A short while after Marcel Renault's accident, in which his mechanic Vauthier was also seriously injured, Théry

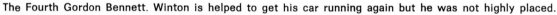
The Fourth Gordon Bennett. Winton is helped to get his car running again but he was not highly placed.

132

Veterans in the sunshine. Backs to the lakes from left to right, a 1929 Fiat 514, a 1923 Citroën 5 H.P. and a 1913 Zebre "A3".

A 1912 Zebre.

was hurt. While he was trying to overtake Porter in a Wolseley, he ran into a ditch; the petrol tank exploded, seriously burning both driver and mechanic. Then Porter himself was involved in a crash. Blinded by the dust of a vehicle in front, he did not see that a level-crossing barrier was descending at Bonneval. His machine hit the barrier and caught fire, and his mechanic was killed. Another driver, Tourand, swerving to miss a little girl, finished in the crowd. A woman and two soldiers were killed; Tourand himself was gravely injured, and so shocked that his brain was damaged for the rest of his life.

A similar tragedy marked the arrival of the drivers at Angoulême. "Corriere della Sera" reported, "A young girl tried to cross the road just as a car came by. Private Dupuy of the 1st Company of the 107th Infantry Regiment rushed out to save her and was struck by car N. 23. The driver tried to avoid them but struck a tree, killing a spectator and a mechanic and seriously injuring another spectator. The mechanic of the car was also

The accent was on comfort. The stirring times of the pioneers were ending in 1907 when this Renault "type X" series B "Double touring saloon" was built. It had a 3,051 c.c. 4 cylinder engine and a speed of 40 m.p.h.

MR. CHARTER'S "WATER ENGINE"

To build a self-propelled vehicle powered by an engine using substances supplied by nature in abundance, air and water, has often been the dream of automotive designers. Unfortunately, water and air will not combine together to release useable energy.

All the same, a car fitted with a "water" engine was once built and ran on the roads of America about 1903.

Wishful Thinking

It was the Charter, a phaeton produced after years of experiment by James A. Charter.

It should be made clear that the expression "water engine" was given to the car by the public, probably out of wishful thinking. In fact, Mr Charter's feet were more firmly on the ground and he himself called it the "water-gasoline" engine.

It was, in any case, a strange vehicle. At that time, in spite of the considerable advances made since the days of the "horseless carriage", carburation was a long way from being perfect.

Bizarre and peculiar devices were designed to achieve the miracle of a perfect mixture of air and petrol vapour whatever the circumstances of the engine — at low and high speeds, climbing, descending, hot or cold, under load or not, wet or dry.

Even today, after tremendous advances have been made, the problems have not been completely solved.

James Charter decided he could improve carburation by obtaining the oxygen necessary for combustion from water, where oxygen certainly exists in abundance, rather than from air. He used a mixture of two parts of petrol to one part water.

The weakness of his engine lay in maintaining it at the correct temperature, which had to be high enough to cause the instant vaporisation of the mixture droplets drawn into the cylinder by the pistons, while not being so hot as to cause overheating and pre-ignition.

Under the seats

The system that Charter used to indicate overheating in the engine was also somewhat unusual. He placed the engine directly under the seats of the driver and passenger. In this way the sensitivity of the occupants themselves showed when it was necessary to stop the car and cool off the engine as soon as it became overheated.

Charter's car, it might be added, had only a short life.

1902 racing De Dion-Bouton with a two cylinder engine. This car took part in the Paris-Madrid.

killed. At the time of the accident the car was travelling at 80 m.p.h.".

Lorraine-Barrow's mechanic in a Dietrich was pinned against a tree when the driver tried to avoid a dog. Lorraine-Barrow himself was seriously injured and died two weeks later. Like Porter, another driver, Gras, hit a closed level-crossing barrier and his car caught fire; fortunately both driver and mechanic were saved. A journalist, Rodolphe Darzens, skidded off the road at

60 m.p.h. but though his car rolled over, he escaped without a scratch.

Stead, in a fierce duel, hit another car with his Dietrich and, losing control, ran off the road. His car ended upside down with Stead trapped underneath. Madame du Gast arrived and gave first-aid, later continuing and coming in 77th; she had also stopped when Marcel Renault crashed. Just before the end of the stage Richard hit a horse and cart and seriously injured three people.

Faced with the horror of this wholesale killing, the authorities made drastic decisions. The Prime Minister himself signed a decree which not only stopped the race but banned the competitors from returning to Paris under their own power. The cars were even forced to leave the city of Bordeaux at once, drawn by horses. At the railway station of Saint-Jean they were loaded on to railway trucks and sent back to Paris.

Still steaming

Though this was a bitter and inglorious end to the intended Paris-Madrid race, it had indicated considerable development. The big cars could now average 60 m.p.h. and more. Even light cars — with 12 to 30 H.P. engines — could complete long journeys at high speeds. This fact was yet another blow at steam cars, whose depleted ranks still raced despite the increasing inadequacy of their vehicles. In this case the vanquished were Le Blon and Chanlaud. But steam cars were not quite finished, and three years later one such vehicle was to put up an astounding speed.

Finally, tyres — nearly all were Michelin — were impro-

Publicity for the Lanza in 1897.

The first Humber, built in 1900 at Coventry and designed by Alec Craig. This car had a single-spoked steering wheel.

A 1904 Marchand "12/16 H.P.". This was one of the more successful cars produced by O.M. in Piacenza. It had a 5,429 c.c. 4 cylinder engine producing 12 H.P. at 1,000 r.p.m. Four speeds plus reverse and chain transmission. Below a 1908 Itala on a present-day track.

ved and were now able to stand up to the mechanical and heat stresses of a major road race.

Shortly after the disastrous Paris-Madrid race, the fourth Gordon Bennett Cup race was run. This valuable trophy had been won the year before by S. F. Edge in his Napier, as one of the stages of the Paris-Vienna race.

Over to Ireland

In accordance with the regulations, the race now had to be held in England. There was, however, the insurmountable obstacle of the rigid laws imposing a maximum speed of 20 m.p.h., which was to remain in force until the end of the first World War. The organisers of the race found an acceptable solution. They decided to hold the race in Ireland, where it was relatively easy to suspend the traffic regulations by means of a local decree.

Just before the race the situation changed dramatically when fire in the Mercedes factory at Cannstatt destroyed five of the six specially prepared 80 H.P. cars. Jellinek — who had become manager for Mercedes — decided to enter the race just the same, using some 60 H.P. touring cars which were awaiting delivery to customers.

Hasty modifications were made and the cars were sent straight to Ireland.

At the same time, a large French contingent set sail for Dublin and Ballyshannon — the start of the race — in a specially chartered ship, the Ferdinand de Lesseps. The race was disastrous for the Americans. Neither Winton nor Owen in Wintons, nor Mooers in his own Peerless was placed. Of the three Napiers nominated to represent England only one, driven by Edge, finished the race and that was disqualified, because Edge was assisted by a spectator at some stage.

The Red Devil

Thus the race became a duel between the French and German teams, and was won by one of the 60 H.P. Mercedes entered by Jellinek. This car was driven by the Belgian, Jenatzy, who had recently set up a world record in his electric car, the "Jamais Contente". Jenatzy was to remain prominent in racing and to acquire the

Wrapped up for the Paris-Madrid race — a car in the touring category sets off with good wishes.

A 1906 Peugeot "torpedo" 81B with 2,208 c.c. four cylinder engine, four speeds plus reverse and chain drive (Peugeot Museum).

A 1906 1,100 c.c. single cylinder OTAV photographed in Italy in 1957. Top speed was 12 m.p.h.

title of "Red Devil". From one point of view, the victory of the German touring car was probably even more impressive than if a racing car had won.

Behind Jenatzy, who averaged almost 50 m.p.h., came three French cars, De Knyff's and Farman's 80 H.P. Panhards and Gabriel's 60 H.P. Mors.

Rolls and Royce

The year 1903 saw the birth of the first Rolls-Royce engine. Then, as 66 years later, the name stood for engineering perfection. The two founders were able to impose and maintain standards of absolute integrity and skill. It should be said at once that the official date of the birth of the Rolls-Royce is not 1903, but 1904. But it was in 1903 that Henry Royce, in his factory in Cook Street, Manchester built his first engine characterised by the same high standards which were to mark the products of the company not yet born.

Royce in 1903 was 40 years old. He was at that time a brilliant electrical engineer on whom fortune had smiled modestly. He was concerned with electric cranes but he had time to spare; he used this time to design and build an i.c. engine without the faults which his able and fastidious mind had found in a 10 H.P. two-cylinder Decauville which he had bought. He had quickly decided that modifications to the engine of this car were not worth while, and that the only way to have a really good engine was to build it himself.

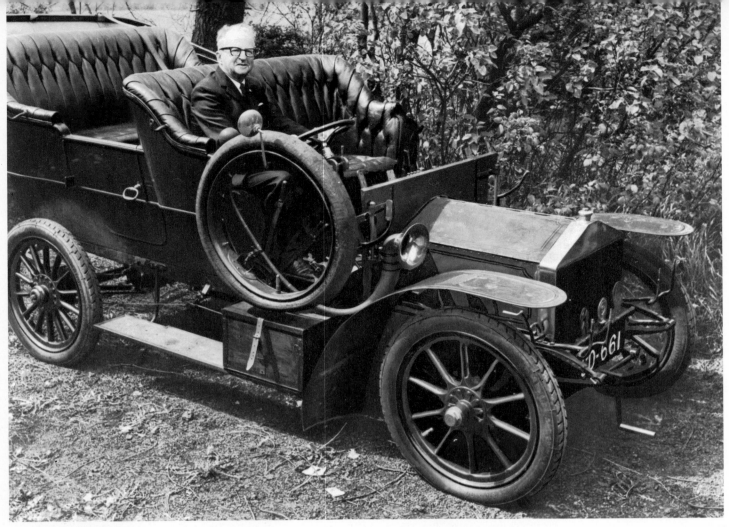

A sentimental journey for 80-year-old Ernie Wooler, who returned to England many years after emigrating to the U.S. He returned to the factory where he had been an apprentice, and was able to drive a 1904 Rolls-Royce which he had helped to build.

In fact, Royce built three cars — one for himself, one for his partner, A. E. Claremont, and one for Henry Edmunds, a friend who had recently been made a director of Royce Ltd. Edmunds was enthusiastic about his car. The Honourable C. S. Rolls and his partner Claude Johnson were equally impressed and Rolls, who had been selling imported cars for cars for some years, saw at once that Royce's car was the one to meet all the requirements of his customers.

Royce's first engine was a 10 H.P. 1,800 c.c. twin. It was quiet, reliable and clean — properties which were not common to cars of that period. When Rolls-Royce was formed in 1904 a variety of cars was produced, consisting of a 10 H.P. twin, a 15 H.P. three-cylinder, a 20 H.P. four-cylinder and a 30 H.P. six-cylinder. In 1905 Rolls entered two of the 20 H.P. cars in the Tourist Trophy, coming in second; in 1906 he won at an average of 40.2 m.p.h.

Only one model

It was in 1906 that the next Rolls-Royce was produced. This was a remarkable V8 engined car, governed down to 20 m.p.h. and thus called the "Legalimit". It was as clean, quiet and as vibration-free as an electric car. For 1907 Rolls-Royce Ltd. decided to concentrate on only

one model, which was to be the finest car in the world. Royce, who designed, built and personally tested all the previous cars, set to work.

The result was exhibited at the Olympia Motor Show at the end of 1906 — and so was exhibited one of the finest cars ever built. The 40/50 Rolls-Royce had a six-cylinder in-line engine with bore and stroke of 114 × 120 mm., and gave a capacity of 7,434 c.c. There was dual ignition (coil and magneto) and valves were at the side. The whole car was built with fantastic precision.

One of the early cars was referred to as a "silver ghost" because of its silent running — and the name at once stuck, the car being known ever since as the "40/50 Silver Ghost". In addition to being silent, the car was long-lived and free from breakdowns. It was kept in production for 19 years — a record surpassed only by the front-wheel drive Citroën.

Though the car was never intended for racing, it was decided to demonstrate its qualities in endurance tests and trials, and one "Silver Ghost" was entered for the Scottish Reliability Trials in 1907. It won a gold medal for its class, and then went on to complete 15,000 miles without the engine stopping. This it did, apart for a stop in error for one minute. The car was then stripped down and all replacements necessary were made to bring it back to its former condition. The cost came to less than £2 5s.

front view of a 1908 FIAT "18/24 H.P."

engine - front mounted 4 cylinder in 2 blocks
bore and stroke - 105 × 130 mm.
capacity - 4,500 c.c.
output - 18 H.P. at 1,400 r.p.m.
ignition - low tension magneto
clutch - multiplate
gearchange - 4 speeds plus reverse
transmission - chain
weight - 3,870 lbs.

American styling simplified over the years — the 1967 Oldsmobile "Cutlass" (above) and the 1958 Cadillac "Coupe de Ville" below.

CHAPTER TEN
"TIN LIZZIE" IS BORN

The creation of the Ford Motor Company was to play a vital role in the development of the motor car. It was the first to set up genuine large scale production; it also created a commercial and special concept hitherto unheard of. This concept presented the car as a vehicle designed for mass consumption and therefore designed with robustness and durability; at the same time, everything superfluous or irrational was eliminated. So was anything which would prevent the price being kept as low as possible. Ideas like this were revolutionary for their time.

Henry Ford — who was always the heart and soul and undisputed head of the huge factory, notwithstanding the presence of major shareholders — also introduced a number of organisational and social reforms inspired by certain principles. In particular, he held that the greatest number of people should benefit from the use of a sound product at a low price, and that as many as possible should share in the material benefits created by its production.

In 1903 the tremendous social and technical differences between the Old and the New World, were illustrated

1905 Ford model "C" 2-4 seater. All the rear body is detachable along the sloping joint.

Steam-powered vehicles were still being produced before World War I. Here is a 1913 Stanley Steamer.

by the beginnings of Rolls-Royce and the establishment the Ford Motor Company. One was to become the byword for refinement and the other for robust, almost spartan, simplicity. The fortunes of both companies were based on technical honesty and on the absolute refusal of both founders to accept anything but the best solutions for their (differing) purposes, without which neither company would have had lasting success. In later years Henry Ford was to drive a Rolls-Royce.

Publicity Value

When Ford was involved with his first racing cars he demonstrated the relationship between the end desired and the means to be used. This was to remain typical of all the acts of the great manufacturer.

Building racing cars was not an end in itself for Ford but after his disappointments and losses on his earlier cars, he knew the value of the publicity and popularity that came from winning races.

He had his first personal success against Winton and later successes with his second car, the "Arrow", and with the third, the "999", in the hands of the popular Barney Oldfield.

Ford in three years won a fame and popularity which in themselves meant little to him but which he judged sufficient to enable him for the third time to become a manufacturer of popular cars.

On 16 June, 1903, the Ford Motor Company was set up with a capital of 150,000 dollars. Henry Ford himself became vice-President, Head of Engineering and General Manager. Among the shareholders were John and Horace Dodge, ex-mechanics who had for some time had their own bicycle business using ball-bearings designed and patented by themselves. At the moment when Ford suggested they should take shares in his company they had a factory producing transmission components for Olds. Against all the advice of their friends, who considered the new enterprise much too risky, the Dodge brothers accepted Ford's offer of 10 per cent of his company in return for equipping the new factory with

1905 Ford model "B".

1907 Ford model "R".

The start of the 1909 transcontinental race. Below, the 1909 Ford model "T" had a separate rear seat called "the mother-in-law's seat".

machine tools and for the temporary manufacture of Ford engines in their own factory.

This decision enabled them to receive 25,000,000 dollars in 1919 in exchange for their initial investment of 20,000.

Strong competition

Among the founder-shareholders in the Ford Motor Company was Andrew Strelow, who contributed his metalworking factory in which Ford intended to set up his first assembly line; Alexander Y. Malcolmson, who supplied 7,000 dollars; Charles J. Woodall and James Couzens, both employees of Malcolmson; John S. Gray, a banker; two lawyers, John W. Anderson and Horace H. Rackhan; an estate agent called Vernon Fry; and finally Charles H. Bennett, an inventor and manufacturer of air rifles.

The beginnings of the Ford Motor Company were not easy. There was strong competition from already established companies such as Cadillac, Oldsmobile, Reo (Olds' company after he left the one bearing his own name) and Packard.

Ford used an unusual system for naming his models — only letters of the alphabet. This was typical of his direct and simple approach in an era when other manufacturers were using horse-power or powerful-sounding names to impress the public.

Ford's cars, however, only vaguely reflected his personality. This is understandable enough as they were built in different factories headed by ex-craftsmen who each tried to impose his habits and point of view. Both the first and second models, the "A" of 1905 and the "B"

of 1904, were of fairly conventional type, though the third in 1905, naturally called the "C", exhibited some originality. For example, two rear seats were provided in a "tonneau" body and could be easily erected or taken down.

The "C" was followed by the flat twin "F" and then in 1906-1907 by the "K", which was an attempt to enter the luxury market. It had a six-cylinder engine (the earlier types had had two or four cylinders) and was put on sale at 2,400 dollars, though the cost of production was considerably more.

Ford at this moment was obviously uncertain which road to follow. The "K" had a 7,040 c.c. engine and its

OPEL Darracq 1902

Europe continued to progress. Out of experiments and errors came practical vehicles like this 1902 Opel Darracq, the 1909 "Doktorwagen" and the 1902 "Tonneau".

The "N" had certain aspects which were later to gain the "T" its name of "spider" — relatively large wheels of wide track with a small body mounted high above the ground.

In 1907 and the beginning of 1908 two further predecessors of the "T" were introduced. These were the "R" and the "S", de luxe versions of the "N", with which Ford neared his target of a car for the masses. They both followed the general lines of the "N", with the same policy of low price and growing commercial success. Both rear and front suspensions were improved.

Criticism silenced

At last in 1908 came one of the most famous cars in history of motoring, the Ford model "T". The "Lizzie"

OPEL Doktorwagen 1909

two speeds and reverse foreshadowed the model "T" yet to come. Its appearance was similar to that of the best European luxury cars of the time.

With the model "N", introduced in 1906, Ford set out for the first time to win the mass market. This four-cylinder model was put on sale first at 500 and then at 600 dollars — a competitive price compared with the single-cylinder cars of other manufacturers. Though popular, it did not make much money as Ford had not yet introduced the manufacturing techniques used later for the "T".

was to be known to millions of Americans — "Tin Lizzie" at first to its detractors before its fantastic success soon made such jibes ridiculous. It was officially born on 1 October, 1908, with a commercial launch which anticipated the publicity techniques of the future and was due to Flanders, one of Ford's most active colleagues.

This was a date on which not only a technically advanced model was produced but also creation of a manufacturing and commercial organisation based on the principles of large scale production.

Thus before the birth of that first car, which was to be the forerunner of over 15,000,000 others, there had been the task of finding and testing new materials, of completely reorganising the machine shops, of setting up assembly lines and of ensuring the full co-operation of sub-contractors.

OPEL Tonneau 1902

1915 Ford model "T". It cost 440 dollars.

For this last operation, Ford was not particular about the means he used, preferring to buy them up to protect himself against commercial antagonism.

This gigantic work of preparation, undoubtedly without precedent, absorbed the last financial resources of Ford and his partners. Couzens, for instance, borrowed his sister Rosetta's last 100 dollars for the launch. Inevitably the crisis raised doubts among some shareholders, especially in the Malcolmson group, and it is easy to imagine the state of nerves in which the "Lizzie" was made ready.

At last the car was launched, all black as its creator had wished in order to maintain the principles of economy and simplicity. It was for this car that Ford laid down his famous dictum — his customers "could have any colour they liked so long as it was black".

The first thing that struck Americans, who had waited

Road conditions were against this forlorn car; the driver has gone to find a horse for a tow.

147

with mounting curiosity for the launch, was the apparent fragility of the new car. At first sight the "T" was disconcerting, giving the impression of little resistance to wear and normal use. It was built largely of vanadium steel, a great technological innovation as it was much stronger than normal steel.

This enabled so much material to be saved that it more than offset its higher cost and gave a bonus in reduced weight. The use of vanadium was one of the most brilliant ideas of Harold C. Wills, a young engineer whom Henry Ford had brought to New York and entrusted with the overall design of the new car. To him was due the fact the chassis of the "T" was reduced to proportions which could stand up to the buffeting from the American roads of the time. This chassis was supported, front and rear, by transverse leaf springs.

The extreme lightness of the steel, which Wills also used for less essential parts of the car, had a considerable effect on the appearance of other items such as the

Above a 1914 Ford "T". Below, veteran cars parked in present-day Virginia City, Nevada.

Styling evolution in clothes and cars. A Ford "Thunderbird" and below, a "T". Ford's one-model policy was a great success but it continued too long, and by 1927 it brought the company near to disaster.

light mudguards and running boards. But the innovations on the "T" did not stop here.

The engine, a four-cylinder, 2,898 c.c. (95 × 101 mm. bore and stroke) had its block cast in one piece and the valves were all on one side. The cylinder head was detachable, which allowed much simpler casting and gave easy access to valves and cylinders.

At first it developed 20 H.P.; this was later raised to 22 H.P., which was a reasonable figure for such a light car and which gave it an acceleration that contributed to its commercial success. Its top speed, however, was only 40 m.p.h. which is astonishing if it is recalled that the "T" stayed in production until 1927.

Ignition and transmission

The most remarkable details of the "T" lay in its ignition and transmission systems. Ignition was by fly-wheel magneto running in an oil bath. This system was invented and patented by John Heinze and Ford remained faithful to it for many years, in spite of certain drawbacks.

The transmission was the result of much hard work by Ford technicians, and was revolutionary. It consisted of an epicyclic gearbox with only two speeds, all that was necessary in view of the low top speed of the car and the low revving engine with its maximum of 1,500 r.p.m. (deliberately designed this way by Ford to ensure a long life).

The gear change was by pedal and, to make this possible, the accelerator was a lever placed near the driver's left hand and near the other manual control, the ignition

From left to right — 1910 DEP, 1909 Léon Peugeot, 1914 Renault. 1914 Benz.

advance/retard lever. The clutch, however, could be operated in two ways, either by the handbrake lever or by the gearchange pedal itself.

To put the "T" in motion a number of unusual procedures had to be followed, the result of Ford's simplification of the various mechanical elements in the cause of ease of production. These procedures were to become familiar to millions of Americans — the model "T" owners — while the rest of the world controlled its motor cars in a way very similar to the methods used today.

In order to start the "T", light pressure had to be put on the gear-change pedal, having provided a "neutral". It was then necessary to release the hand-brake lever which worked on the rear wheels. So long as this was

A 1911 Clément Bayard AC2A passing various versions of the Fiat "508 Balilla". Below a 1907 Bianchi Pantheon.

applied it disengaged the clutch, but allowed it to engage as soon as it was released.

With the brake thus released and the clutch disengaged, further pressure on the gear-change pedal engaged both first gear and the clutch. With the car in motion the foot could be gradually raised until top gear was engaged. It was at this point that the inexperienced driver could achieve an astounding series of bounds.

Into swift reverse

To stop the "T" was simple. The brake pedal, which worked on the transmission, was pressed and at the same time the hand-brake was applied to brake the rear wheels and simultaneously disengage the clutch. Two other methods of stopping the "T" were also possible.

The first of these was to stamp on the brake pedal and the gear-change pedal at the same time, thus engaging first gear and so slowing the car down rapidly. The second was to be used only in the most emergency because of the possibility of dire consequences to the machinery. This consisted simply of engaging reverse gear directly by pressing on a third pedal, and at the same time stamping on the brake pedal.

The astonishing fact is that such a manoeuvre, which would result in the immediate disintegration of the gearbox and much else in the modern car, rarely resulted in a breakdown in the "T".

Spanner and hammer

It is difficult to imagine road conditions in America in those days. Whilst it is true that in the period 1908 to 1927, the production years of the "T", there was tremendous expansion of the first-class road and motorway network, this was anything but true of the secondary and local road systems.

The U. S. had a relatively short existence so that there was nothing like the vast European transport system that served drivers there until roads fit for the motor car were built.

This explains why such a car as the "T", though quickly overtaken by its competitors in terms of comfort and modernity, and even starting behind many in terms of speed, rapidly became a major social phenomenon and stayed so for many years.

The "T" had excellent road holding, was capable of

Above a 1909 Buick and below a 1911 Vauxhall.

Ford had escaped from the format of the "T" by 1930. A model "A" roadster.

The Morris factory at Oxford in 1912, with a line-up of models.

The motor car has revolutionised land transport but it itself is now delivered over long distances by train. From early days road transporters have been used for shorter journeys (below).

being driven through mud, over rough ground and through fords and pools. Its legendary robustness and ease of maintenance — for most repairs only a spanner and a hammer were necessary — made it ideal for the conditions in which it operated.

The fact was also important, and unusual at the time, that it came fully equipped not only with body and seats but also with a hood with which to face the weather and a long journey across the prairie. Of course, later the model "T" was also sold as a chassis only, on which a wide variety of bodies were fitted.

Finally, there was its price to convince millions and millions of Americans that at last a car was in the reach of their purses. At its launch the "T" cost 500 dollars; the price was gradually brought down until it was less than 400.

These are the reasons that 15 million were sold in nine years of production and that Ford sales rose from 8,000 in 1908 to 250,000 in 1914.

The commercial success of the "T", and to a lesser extent of the cars which preceded it, would have been impossible in any economy other than that of the U. S. between 1910 and 1929.

In the first year of its production, Ford profits rose from one million to 27 million dollars. Even in 1908 Ford was able to introduce a 40-hour week in his factories and to pay his manual workers five dollars a day against the 2½ dollars in other factories.

Rosetta's 100 dollars

Alexander Malcomson's 7,000-dollar investment had become 175,000 in three years (the figure is known because Malcolmson was paid off after disagreements with Ford); and Rosetta Couzens' 100 dollars, invested just before the birth of the "T", had become 260,000 by 1919.

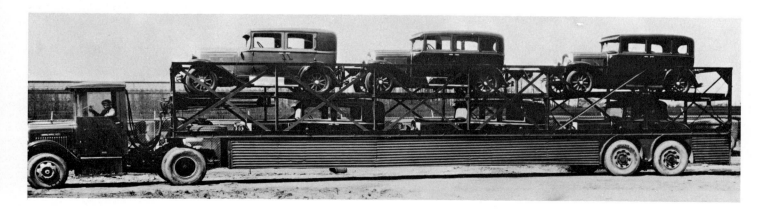

GAS TO THE RESCUE

The strange variations of cars fuelled by gas is now no more than a memory for most motorists. Such cars, which had their heyday in the wartime 40's, represented an emergency device which was thankfully given up as soon as circumstances permitted. But when petrol was rationed or non-existent for civilian use in many countries of Europe, the gas-driven cars fulfilled a useful role. The earliest experiments with gas had been conducted in France and Germany by Panhard & Levassor, Renault, D.K.W. and Gepaa. In Italy apparatus was built by Pignone-Hag and Scaglia.

Trials using coal gas as a fuel for motor vehicles were also run between 1920 and 1930. But they were abandoned because of the major drawbacks involved, including the high cost, the inconvenience and the short time that the gas lasted.

Variety of fuels

While these drawbacks were deciding factors in peacetime, they became less important in face of wartime petrol shortages. This was why gas was utilised all over the continent from 1940. The most widespread use was in Italy, which of all the countries at war had the greatest difficulty in maintaining petrol supplies.

In the case of producer gas or water gas, the installation could use a variety of fuels such as peat, anthracite, coal and wood, though the quantity of gas produced obviously varied. Whatever fuel was used, the basic feature was a unit producing gas by distillation.

This was a furnace lined with refractory materials, the bottom consisting of a grill, below which was a cinder tray. A water tank was heated by the fire, and from this tank the water vapour came into contact with the red-hot coals or coke.

Carbon dioxide and hydrogen were formed, and this mixture was conducted to the carburettor and engine via a series of subsidiary devices — the cleaner, cooler, drier and separator.

The use of this gas on a large scale was encouraged by several governments. But it had one defect more important than all the others as far as the motorist was concerned: it was extremely difficult to start a car when

it was using gas. It was necessary first to heat the car for a half hour before starting up; it was then difficult to get the mixture to fire the engine until the cylinder block itself was hot.

In theory the engine might have been warmed up on petrol, but this would have led to a serious risk of explosion in the gas system.

Another though less important difficulty — provided the car could operate on gas — was the need to carry around a large quantity of fuel. Towards the end of the war, both wood and coal themselves became scarce in many countries. In many war-ravaged territories heating homes was more essential than moving cars. Nevertheless, the use of gas made possible many thousands of miles of war-time motoring which otherwise would have been impossible.

Some of these journeys were not without incident. In Italy, for instance, it was not unusual to see a bus at rest while its passengers went foraging along the roadside. They were looking for fuel to complete their trip.

front view of a 1908 BRASIER

engine - front mounted vertical twin
output - 10 H.P.
gearchange - 3 speeds plus reverse
speed - 28 m.p.h.

Above — a 1967 Chevrolet Corvette. Below — a 1918 Chevrolet saloon, produced the year in which the company became part of General Motors.

CHAPTER ELEVEN
THE EMBRYO GIANT

The second big American motor group, General Motors — today one of the most powerful commercial complexes in the world — was officially created in September, 1908. It was the peak of the work of an oustanding individual, William Capo Durant. The establishment of the company began in 1904, contemporaneously with Ford, but the ambitions and methods of the two men were very different.

Ford was basically an engineer with clear commercial ideas, but all springing from an enthusiasm for the motor car. Durant was, above all, a business organiser and company promoter. He was a man who, like others of

Above — an Oldsmobile of 1908, the year in which Durant formed General Motors and bought Champion and Oldsmobile. Below — a 1919 Oldsmobile. While different from the 1908 model above, car styling has obviously not undergone a revolution.

his time, realised the financial potential of the motor car, and decided to involve himself as deeply as possible in the boom which he so clearly foresaw.

The grandson of a governor of Michigan, in the early 1900's "Billy" Durant was already a millionaire, having founded and successfully developed a carriage factory with his partner and friend, Josiah Dallas Dort, an ex-merchant of fancy goods. Mainly because of Durant's enthusiasm, they decided to turn their plant in Flint — which was a coachbuilding centre — into a car factory. The problem, from a purely commercial point of view, was to find a well-established make of car that was in

financial difficulties and might be revived by the investment of capital. The chance was offered by Buick.

David Dunbar Buick was an ex-tinsmith, also from Michigan, who had made a small fortune from his patents for vitreous enamelling of cast iron, and then decided to build motor cars as did so many craftsmen of his time. Thanks to his engineering expertise, his first light tourer was quickly accepted. The engine was well balanced, the styling was elegant and the car had some practical ideas such as positively actuated overhead valves.

The financial state of the company, the Buick Manufactur-

ing Company, was not so encouraging. By 1903, only one year after its foundation, it had to reform itself as the Buick Motor Car Company with a large injection of capital from the brothers Vincent and Benjamin Briscoe, who had been among those who had earlier financed Olds.

Buick's association with the Briscoes did not last long, however. Business was bad and the brothers withdrew from the company. Buick, in spite of his ideas and his excellent cars, found himself on the point of bankruptcy. Thus Durant, on 1 November, 1904, was able to gain control of his first established motor company. In his capacity of financier, Durant at once increased the capital of 75,000 dollars first to 300,000 then to 500,000. He moved the factory to the wagon works at Flint, with which he had come to an agreement.

Forming a trust

The impetus that Durant gave to this new activity was fantastic. From 28 Buicks built in 1904, production soared to 626 in 1905 and 2,300 in 1906. By 1908 Buick production was so satisfactory that Durant felt strong enough to make another step on the way to the motoring throne which he so clearly coveted.

Instead of looking round for another company in difficulty, Durant's ideas were much more ambitious — no less than a motor trust that would bring together all or nearly all of America's major manufacturers to form a group capable of producing the fantastic figure of 50,000 cars a year.

Without wasting time Durant founded his new company, with the impressive-sounding name of "The International Motor Company", and then sent emissaries to his competitors to propose the union. Ford, clearly the most important objective in this large scale operation, gave a decided no, as did Maxwell-Briscoe and Reo.

Durant, never one to waste his time up blind alleys, at once abandoned the idea and on 16 September, 1908, formed another company, the General Motors Company, with a capital of 12,500,000 dollars. Its job was to shore up any tottering companies — including accessory

A 1903 Cadillac model "A" with 1,609 c.c. engine, two speeds, chain transmission. For many years the name has been associated with luxury cars. In the early days of the company, however, Cadillac was renowned for robustness and low price.

For the first time an English monarch travels in a car. The date is 12 April 1902. Edward VII is at the side of John Scott-Montagu in a new 24 H.P. Daimler. After a ride through the New Forest, the King bought one for his family. Below: from Sunbeamland to Sunbeam. The first 1903, Sunbeam.

manufacturing businesses — in order to form a base for new industrial activity.

The first companies thus absorbed were Dow, a wheel company, Ewing Automobile, the Carter Car Company and Elmore. These were small companies which had previously been grouped in the International Motor Company. Then followed Weston Mott, of Utica (which specialised in axle production) and then the first big purchase, Champion, the sparking plug factory set up by Albert Champion, the French racing driver.

Persisting in his plan to buy up all the accessory manufacturers necessary for his group, Durant absorbed Briscoe, which made mudguards, and then his first big motor car company. This was Oldsmobile, big in reputation though commercially small; like Briscoe, Oldsmobile changed its mind after an earlier refusal.

All these purchases, including also the coachbuilders, W. F. Stewart, took place over four months and Durant distributed 245,000 dollars in dividends — not so much because of trading success as out of necessity to maintain the enthusiasm of his partners. Durant was now in full cry and on 28 July, 1909, the great Cadillac, already famous for quality, was bought at a price of 4,400,000 dollars.

Ill-timed offer

At this point he conceived the most ambitious scheme of his financial career — yet another approach to Ford. "Fabulous Billy", as Durant was already known in Wall Street, offered to buy the Ford Motor Company for the

1901 Columbia, built in the U.S.A. by the Electric Vehicle Company. This car belonged to Queen Alexandra.

astronomical sum of eight million dollars. Naturally, Durant was acting for a group of financiers, and these, as will be seen, were quick to withdraw their support at the first sign of crisis.

The huge offer once again fell on deaf ears, but only for a piece of ill-timing. Ford, in spite of the notable success of the "T", had been having a difficult time, above all because of his dispute over the Selden patent. In fact, Durant's offer arrived just as Ford became certain of winning his legal battle and was free from the nightmare of having to pay huge arrears of royalties to the then holders of the patent.

Ford's refusal was the beginning of Durant's decline. In keeping with what was typical behaviour at the time by American big business, the unlimited faith which it had placed in Durant rapidly turned to uneasiness at the size and ambitious nature of his ideas and then into open alarm. Wall Street turned its back on him and replaced him with Charles W. Nash.

Nash was an old colleague of Durant's, having worked in the cart and carriage factory in Flint, and had set up the first assembly line of the type that was to become typical of every motor manufacturer. Appointed President of Buick after Durant had bought it, he quickly

A 1910 Lion Peugeot on the seafront.

took the old company to a prosperity it had never known before. It is not surprising that General Motors shareholders saw in him a more realistic man with whom to replace the capricious "Billy". (The name "Nash" was to become even more familiar to the mass of American motorists after 1917, when he set up his own company).

It should be noted that this was not the end of Durant who, five years later in 1915, returned triumphantly to the head of General Motors thanks to his success with Chevrolet. He left the company finally as the result of a crisis which saw General Motor shares fall from 400 dollars to 12 dollars. He still persisted in the car industry, however, and his name was associated with a number of makes such as Durant, Dort, Star and Mason, until the world crisis of 1929 sent him finally into obscurity. He died in 1947.

Huge misunderstanding

The "Selden question", mentioned earlier, was a strange affair which had considerable influence on the early American motor industry. The affair has been called a

1912 La Ponette.

1909 Humber 8 H.P. It had a 1,525 c.c. twin cylinder engine with h.t. magneto ignition and three speeds plus reverse.

The first Singer, built in 1904.

1911 Hillman coupé.

huge misunderstanding, but others have referred to it as a racket imposed by violence. Its beginnings were at the show held in Philadelphia in 1876 when a young lawyer, George Baldwin Selden, admired George Brayton's i.c.-engine exhibited there; three years later he patented a development of that engine, which he had subsequently applied to a vehicle.

The patent was the centre of an amazing complex of interests which continued to have an effect for many years.

As soon as car manufacturing became established on an industrial basis in the last decade of the century, Selden decided to exploit his old patent, of which he had made virtually no use previously as he had no interest in manufacture on his own behalf. He succeeded in obtaining a second patent, number 549,160, being granted on 5 November, 1895. This patent was possible only because Selden was a competent lawyer and because the patents officials were, at best, incompetent.

1911 Opel "Stadt coupé".

A noted car: the 1913 "Bebé" Peugeot, which did over 60 miles to the gallon.

Waited for opportunity

The patent covered everything that might be called an automobile. The original text stated "... the combination, in a road locomotive equipped with an appropriate transmission, driving wheels and steering, of a hydrocarbon engine of one or more cylinders, a fuel tank, a transmission shaft designed to run at a speed higher than that of the driving wheels, a clutch and coachwork adapted for the transport of persons or goods...".

With considerable foresight Selden was able to have the new patent back-dated to the old one, and he then sat back to wait for an occasion to profit by it.

The opportunity came when Col. Albert A. Pope, of Hartford, in the name of his company, the Electric Vehicle Company, requested a licence to manufacture small cars for use as taxis. The request arose on the advice of Pope's lawyer, who had discovered the existence of Selden's patent.

1903 Panhard-Levassor 7 H.P., a much copied car. The twin cylinder engine had 1,654 c.c., 3 speeds and chain drive. Lord Montagu at the wheel.

Selden, of course, granted the licence and, with the confidence of a first success behind him, did not hesitate to start a legal action to establish his "monopoly rights". The victim selected was the Winton Motor Carriage Company of Cleveland. Winton was a genuine manufacturer, who hardly deserved to be sued in this way, and even less deserved the sentence of the court that he should pay arrears of royalties and damages to Selden. This verdict had the effect of causing 10 manufacturers, including Pope, Winton, Olds and Packard to form ALAM — the Association of Licensed Automobile Manufacturers — to defend themselves against further demands from Selden. Selden agreed, in return for a royalty of 1.25 per cent, to prosecute any competitor who was not a member of ALAM.

This situation, particularly absurd because Selden had no part in the motor industry, was to continue — at least legally — until 12 November, 1912. Cars manufactured by members of ALAM displayed a plaque which said that they were manufactured "under the Selden licence". The final crisis came with Selden's attempts to withhold recognition from manufacturers who were not members of the association.

Soon he found he had to fight on two fronts. On the one hand, there were the European manufacturers who were not worried as long as their products were sold outside America, but who protested strongly at attempts to enforce payment on cars exported to America. On the other, a growing number of American manufacturers were seeking to avoid the threat of legal action.

Ford alliance

These latter, at a critical time, were joined by Henry Ford, against whom a legal battle was then commenced. Ford's reaction was to form an alliance with some of the major Europeans, including Panhard-Levassor and Jeantaud. They found ample justification for breaking Selden's patent, not the least being the back-dating of the 1895 patent to 1879, and by showing that there were dozens of precedents.

Finally, in 1911, the Federal Appeal Court — reversing a verdict of the District Court — recognized Selden's patent as "valid but not violated". ALAM was at once dissolved and, in spite of the efforts of the owners of the patent, the Supreme Court confirmed the Federal sentence on 12 November, 1912, and finally put an end to a ridiculous legal and technical situation.

The Vanderbilt Cup

The years of expansion of American motoring produced, as might be expected, an important race of international significance in the U. S. This was the Vanderbilt Cup race, which was to have a parallel role to that of the Gordon Bennett Cup in Europe. First held in 1904, the race had many regulations in common with its European counter-part, including one requiring competing cars to be entirely built in their country of origin. The only major difference was in the second clause, which said that the race should always be held on American territory.

The designer and promoter of this race was William K.

Vanderbilt, Jr. who was a rich amateur racing driver. The Long Island circuit was chosen for the race and its nearness to New York attracted tens of thousands of spectators right from the start. Though this ensured financial success it also brought organisational problems, most important of which was safety. One incident illustrates the problem. A famous race official, Fred Wagner, once had to use a compressed air pipe on the spectators to force enough room for the cars to pass. Successive Vanderbilt Cup races were to grow in importance. Unfortunately they did not lack tragedy. After being run seven times in the East (first at Long Island and then in Savannah) it was transferred to Milwaukee for 1912. The last two editions, those of 1913 and 1915, were held in California.

'Wrecking race'

The first edition in 1904 was marked by so many breakdowns that it was called the "wrecking race". There were two strong sources of competition from Europe. The French had three Panhards driven by Heath, Teste and Tart, Gabriel in a De Dietrich, and Clément in a Clément-Bayard. The Germans sent five Mercedes, four

A postcard of the 1904 Gordon Bennett Cup.

THE MIGHTY "FIGURE 8" ENGINE

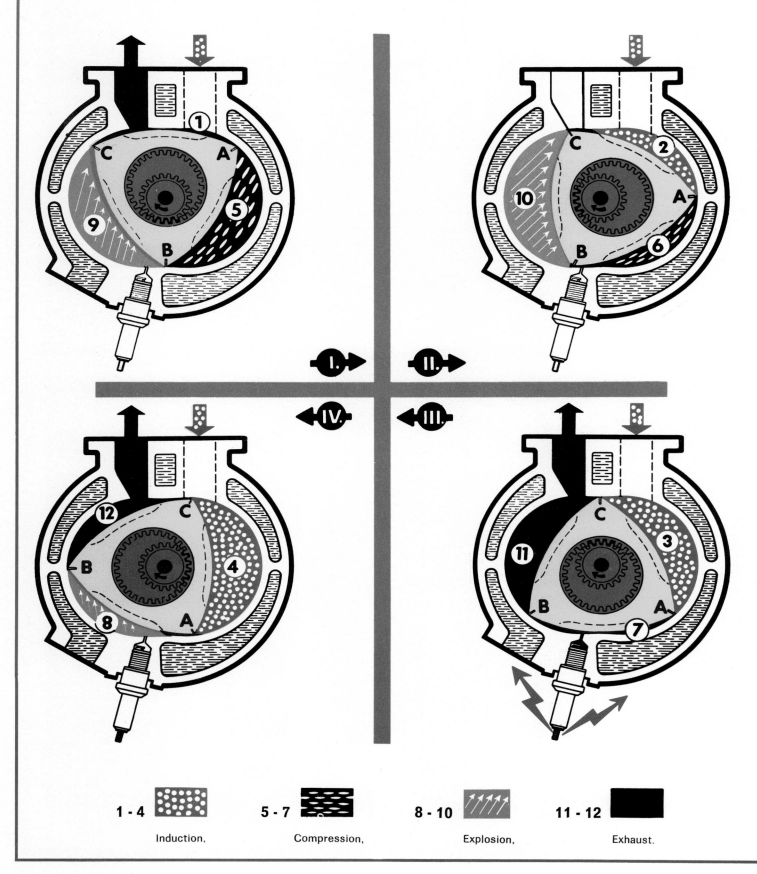

1 - 4	5 - 7	8 - 10	11 - 12
Induction.	Compression.	Explosion.	Exhaust.

From the early days of the invention of the petrol engine thousands have been built which were based on principles or cycles different from those of the classic two or four stroke cycle. Of these, one type has laboriously approached a satisfactory state of development after years of study and experiment — the rotary piston engine or, nowadays commonly, the "Wankel" engine. The first car to fit such an engine in series production was the NSU two seater sports car, and it created much interest in motoring circles for its smoothness, very small size, and for the amazing power developed by its half-litre capacity (though this is not comparable with the half-litre of a reciprocating piston engine, as we shall see).

What is the "Wankel" engine? Its principles are not easy to describe and before doing so it will be useful to look at the engine's history. Its origins lie in 1951 when Felix Wankel, who was in charge of a technical research department in Lindau, made his first contacts with NSU engineers to study the problems of sealing irregular spaces. These studies resulted in the discovery that a more or less triangular rotor (but with convex sides) rotating in a chamber which had, roughly, a figure-eight shape (the descriptions are, of course, mathematically very inexact) could give rise to a true four stroke cycle.

The first application of the principle was in the form of a compressor for the 50 c.c. NSU two-stroke engine with which world records were taken at Utah in 1956. The rotary compressor enabled this small engine to develop 260 b.h.p. per litre. This gave the small car a speed of nearly 100 m.p.h.

In 1958 Wankel agreed with the American company Curtiss-Wright for joint experiments towards the building of a large engine based on his principles. Later, tests were begun with cars powered by various forms of Wankel engines of varying characteristics. Between then and 1963 the engine gradually took definitive form and was then fitted in the small NSU two seater, which was introduced at the Frankfort Motor Show in the autmn of 1963. Since then a licence has been granted, among others, to Mazda in Japan, who have a twin rotor version in commercial sale.

Perhaps the best example, is the magnificent twin-rotor NSU RO 80, which went into series production in October, 1967; the righthand drive version was introduced on the British market at the end of 1968.

This, then, is how the engine works. In essentials it consists of a chamber whose internal shape approaches a figure of eight, as shown in the diagram. Inside this revolves the somewhat triangular rotor — the piston — which revolves eccentrically in relation to the crankshaft, or mainshaft of the engine. The shapes of these two elements are such that while the corners of the pistons are always equidistant from the walls of the chamber — and very close to them, thus forming a seal — they successively enlarge and reduce the space between the convex sides of the "triangle" — the rotor — and the chamber walls.

The NSU sports with Wankel engine.

Three phases

Thus, if a mixture is injected into one of the chambers as it is increasing in size, it will be compressed on the subsequent decrease in volume as the rotor, or "piston" rotates. As may be seen from the diagram it is therefore clear that in this way the classical four stroke cycle of induction, compression, firing and exhaust is produced, and furthermore that the three faces of the rotor are at three different phases of the cycle at the same time. In the diagram the face CA of the rotor can be seen in positions 1 to 4 gradually passing through successive stages of the first phase, that of induction, of drawing in the explosive air-petrol mixture into the chamber. Now go back to diagram I and look at side AB. This is now beginning the next phase to that which AC has reached in diagram IV, that of compression. This phase may be followed through positions 5 to 7.

As soon as this point is reached the single sparking plug fires, and the expanding gases may be seen in position 8 providing the power to drive the rotor.

In position 9 and 10, side BC can be seen passing through the phase of explosion and expansion. Then in positions 11 and 12 it sweeps the burnt mixture out of the exhaust port for the exhaust stroke of the cycle. As we have said, three phases of the cycle are being passed through respectively by the three sides of the rotor, displaced 120° one from the other, and this explains why a "500 c.c." Wankel engine can easily develop 50 b.h.p. The 500 c.c. referred to is that volume between the chamber and one side of the rotor and, as we have seen, this is multiplied by three by the three sides of the rotor.

For and against

The advantages of the Wankel engine over the normal reciprocating piston type are many. In first place is the absence of vibration due to the fact that there is only a rotary movement, and this in turn means less wear and longer life. The consumption of the Wankel engine is rather less than that of the conventional. It can be made significantly smaller and the number of components is fewer, and the engine is therefore inherently less complicated.

It is obvious that there must be drawbacks to explain why this type of engine has not been seized upon at once by the world's manufacturers. Certainly the Wankel engine also presents technical and technological problems. Briefly, these concern a rather inelastic power curve and problems of maintaining a seal between the corners of the rotor and the faces of the chamber, the latter causing difficulty in the maintenance of production tolerances as well as of design.

What is certain is that today there are cars on commercial sale which perform satisfactorily. Whether the complex of design, performance, production and commercial advantages and disadvantages will come down in favour of the "rotary piston" engine is something that we shall see within the next few years.

168

Goux in a Léon Peugeot at the Grand Prix des Voiturettes at Dieppe in 1908.

1906 corre seen in Monaco.

1904 Gordon Bennett Cup. Girling at the wheel of a Wolseley "75 H.P."

"60 H.P." and one "90 H.P.", all driven by Americans. There were also two Fiats which, however, quickly fell out of the race with clutch failure. America was represented by Royal, Pope-Toledo and Simplex, which were hotted-up tourers, and by the Pope-Toledo Special and Packard "Grey Wolf" racing cars.

Within a few minutes of the start one of the Mercedes overturned, killing the mechanic. Later the other four Mercedes broke down and, with other retirements, the race reduced itself to a duel between Heath and Clément, resolving itself in favour of the former by a small margin. His average was 52 m.p.h. and he won by two minutes. This foreign victory was not isolated and it was not until 1908 that an American car won the Vanderbilt Cup.

Official approval

In 1904 the fifth Gordon Bennett was held in Europe, this time in Germany after the Mercedes victory in Ireland the previous year. The course was near Frankfurt-on-Main in the Taunus mountains where an 87-mile track had to be lapped four times. For the first time the race had official approval marked by the presence of the German Emperor, Wilhelm II. It is said that his interest in motor cars dated from the time when one of his own court, Rausch, overtook the Kaiser's galloping horse in a car.

There was a large number of entrants for the race, a possibility due to modifications that had been made to the rigid regulations. Thus there were three French cars, three Belgian, three British, three German, three Austrian, three Italian and one Swiss.

The French entrants were Théry in an 80 H.P. Richard-Brasier, Salleron in a 100 H.P. Mors and Rougier in a 100 H.P. Turcat-Méry. The German entries Jenatzy, Werner and Warden all had 90 H.P. Mercedes. Among the British were Girling — future brake manufacturer — Edge and Jarrot. Italy had Lancia, Cagno and Storero in 65 H.P. Fiats.

This was a breathtaking race. The spectators was excited by the desperate duel between the French car driven by Théry and the German car driven by the Belgian Jenatzy. At the end of the first lap Théry had only one minute's lead. At the end of the second it was one minute 15 seconds and finally Théry, thanks to the better road-holding of his Richard-Brasier, won by 11 minutes. Wilhelm II himself congratulated the winner and his mechanic, Miller, and sent a telegram of congratulations to the French President, Loubet.

The good performance of the Fiats — Lancia and Cagno finished eighth and tenth respectively — was a portent of their excellent showing the following year in the sixth and last Gordon Bennett. In this race Lancia just missed victory due to a radiator fault, while Nazzaro and Cagno were second and third behind the winner, who was again Théry, still driving a Richard-Brasier. It is interesting to explain the death of such an important race as the Gordon Bennett. The rules had been severely

1905 Gordon Bennett. Tracy in the Locomobile 90 H.P.

1905 Gordon Bennett. Jenatzy in the 120 H.P. Mercedes at the Rochefort bend.

1905 Gordon Bennett. The Clifford-Earp team in a Napier 90 H.P.

One of Peugeot's first "Babies", built in 1903. The car was a great success in England as well as in France.

criticised from the start, most of all by the Automobile Club de France which, in particular, wanted a greater number of competitors. This was quite reasonable considering the large number of manufacturers in France,

A 1903 De Dietrich 24 H.P. with a 5,428 c.c. four cylinder engine. A car such as this took part in the first Vanderbilt Cup race.

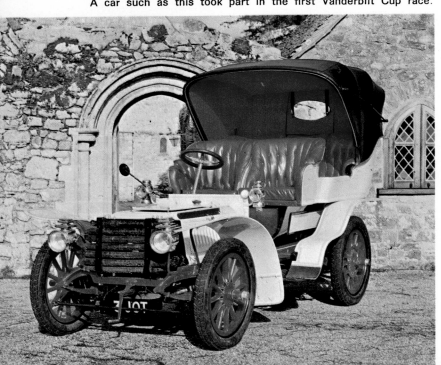

and selection there was always a long and bitter process. The British, Germans, Italians, Austrians and Swiss opposed any change, however, and when nominating their team for the 1905 race the French declared that it would be the last they would enter. This automatically decided the fate of the race.

This last race, held in France because of Théry's win the previous year, was on a difficult course chosen by Michelin to the west of Clermont-Ferrand. The circuit had to be completed five times for a total of about 350 miles.

The idolised Théry won after a bitter battle with Lancia (although they only just lost, Fiat called their car the "Gordon Bennett"). Average speed was 77.7 k.p.h. (about 48 m.p.h.).

The American team had a disastrous race. Of the 90 H.P. Locomobile and two Pope-Toledos entered, only one of the latter finished the race. The driver, Lyttle, was so slow, however, that he finished 2½ hours after Théry, who was just finishing as Lyttle completed his second lap.

front view of a 1909 ROLLAND-PILAIN

engine - front mounted vertical 4 cylinder
bore and stroke - 80 × 110 mm.
capacity - 2,100 c.c.
output - 8 H.P.

Above, Fiat Dino Spider. Below, the company's 1952 V8 which reached 129 m.p.h. Over recent years cars' performance has increased only slightly.

CHAPTER TWELVE

EUROPE IN TOP GEAR

Already, towards the end of the first decade of the twentieth century, two quite different but not altogether independent trails were being blazed in the world of motor cars.

There was the normal production industry to supply the needs of the ever-growing numbers of motorists who had no particular leanings towards competitive events. There was the sporting side, which even at that time had started to brand its cars, conceived and built exclusively for racing, with its own unmistakable identities.

So, in the same years that saw the most exciting battles in motor racing fought out in Europe and America — and motor racing will always be romantic and exciting even though the thrills come no longer from catastrophic breakdowns but more from fantastic speeds and brilliant driving — equally important events and developments were taking place in the motor factories, out of sight of the public.

It was here that technical progress took its greatest strides, here that cars even nearer to perfection were born and continually brought up to date in the light of

research directed towards the future. Evolution was even more rapid then than now. The cars of today are, perhaps, too near to technical perfection to admit of rapid change, other than in detail and styling modification. This early progress cannot be traced in all of its detail, since this would involve extensive technical descriptions. The interest and, it might be said, the charm of those

Wolseley 6 H.P. 1,302 c.c. single cylinder engine with three speeds and belt drive, built from 1904 to 1906.

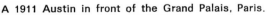

A 1911 Austin in front of the Grand Palais, Paris.

cars of long ago are best experienced by standing in the presence of a "veteran", and for preference one which is in working order. The now numerous veteran car enthusiasts have for many years understood this.

In the first decade were born models and marques which stand as pointers in technical evolution, and many famous factories came into being.

Two makes dominate

Because of the legislation of the Locomotives Act of 1865, Britain was deprived of the honour of inventing the first effective petrol-engined car, although she had pioneered steam cars.

It can, however, be said that the first British petrol-driven four-wheeled car — the 1895 Lanchester — was unquestionably a thoroughly modern motor, with its worm drive, epicyclic gearing, pneumatic tyres and racy appearance.

Two splendid survivals — a 1925 "40/50 Silver Ghost" Rolls-Royce in front of the clipper "Cutty Sark". This Rolls was built at Springfield. Massachusetts, where the company had set up a factory.

Meanwhile the British Motor Syndicate started to make Daimlers, and the two names Lanchester and Daimler dominated the early history of automobilism in Britain. Today they both belong to another "syndicate" — British Motor Holdings. Among the names of individual men who really founded the industry were those of the Lanchester brothers, F. R. Simms, Henry Hewetson, J. H. Knight, Sir D. Salomons, H. J. Lawson and E. J. Pennington, whilst the editors of the motor Press and executives of motoring associations had no small influence.

By the end of the century it was clear that the petrol motor was to reign supreme, although steam and electric vehicles still had a stake in the business for many years. Moreover, the general specification of the car seemed fairly well established, at any rate in respect of the broad principles of having an internal combustion engine, electric ignition, wheel steering, pneumatic tyres, chain or shaft drive and sliding-cog gearbox.

The British motor industry was becoming more influen-

tial because of the formation of adequate and unified representation, too. In 1897 Simms founded the R.A.C., almost at his own expense, and in 1902 he established the Society of Motor Manufacturers and Traders, as watchdog of the expanding industry.

With the start of the 20th century, motors and affairs began to move forward more rapidly, and competition became more vigorous. Since no history of automobilism can be complete without reference to Rolls-Royce, let us refer to the immortal designer Henry Royce immediately. The brilliant, painstaking Northamptonshire miller's son put the firm on the map with the 40/50 Silver Ghost, and over 6,000 of these hand-built quality cars were made between 1906 and 1925, when the Phantoms and smaller cars were introduced.

Large quality cars such as the Rolls-Royce are still in considerable demand, but today mini-cars are more acceptable to most people than large limousines. The BMC — now a baby Leyland! — is a phenomenon of the age. An early version was called the Austin Seven, and

preserved the line of descent from Herbert Austin's little wonder, although Alex Issigonis was and is the new genius.

The Austin Motor Company was founded in 1905. Herbert Austin, who later became Lord Austin, was born in 1866 at Little Missenden, Buckinghamshire, but at the age of 18 emigrated to Australia to work as a foundryman. After richly varied technical experiences, during which he pursued his studies in engineering, Austin returned to England and built a number of experimental prototype cars almost single handed. He started with a lightweight three-wheeler in 1895, following it with a further car the following year, this being exhibited at the Crystal Palace.

Royal patronage

In the meantime he had been made general manager of the Wolseley Sheep-Shearing Machine Co. In 1899 he brought out the first four-wheeled Wolseley car and this twin-cylinder machine was a prizewinner in the Thousand Miles Trial of the Automobile Club — an event which went far towards establishing motoring in Britain — especially as King Edward VII (then Prince of Wales) followed it enthusiastically and soon took to motoring himself.

Austin founded the Austin Motor Company in 1906 and built the nucleus of the Longbridge factory that is still there today and which is indeed the nerve centre of the Austin-Morris Group. In the same year the first Austin — a 4 cylinder 25-30 H.P. — was put into production and was followed by other models so that by 1908 there were 17 types from 17 to 50 H.P.

A 1914 Standard. Below a 1907 Daimler "Open Tourer" with a 10,604 c.c. 45 H.P. side valve engine, four speeds and chain drive.

There was even an "Austin Seven" in 1909 but this single-cylinder utility car only theoretically anticipated the historic best-seller of 1922 — the famous Chummy, a four-cylinder 10 H.P. car which stayed in production until 1938-9, with progressive development.

Daimler is another marque that now serves under the B.M.H. banner, with Leyland overlord. Originally the Daimler car was German, but H. J. Lawson founded the British company in 1896 and bought a factory site in Coventry. Jaguar-Daimler themselves have said; "This represented the laying of the British motor industry's largest foundation stone".

From 1897 onwards, new Daimler models — Coventry-built — appeared in rapid succession, and between that year and 1903 twelve different power units were used,

varying in size from one to 4½ litres, and of two or four cylinders. It has been noted that the Prince of Wales interested himself in the Thousand Miles Trial and it was the award-winning Daimler cars that interested him most — so much so that he bought a British Daimler with Hooper body, a four-seater mail phaeton. This was the beginning of the many years of Daimler Royal motoring.

Daimlers took 11 awards in the Thousand Miles Trial; their 13 cars all finished the course. This success in competitions became a habit and went on right up to the first world war.

A particularly interesting Daimler model — again bought by Edward, now the monarch — was the 1904 28/36 which was offered with the option of coil ignition or

In 1902 the magazine "Nature and Art" showed an illustration of a "dog and cat ambulance" for English animal lovers.

Its designer, Louis Coatelen, at the wheel of the 1907 Hillman.

the Eisemann magneto, which was then very modernistic, but the engine still had an exposed camshaft! The King's particular car had revolving chairs in the back.

An interesting sidelight on Daimler history is that even the very early cars had the fluted radiator which is now still simulated on "Jaguar-Daimlers".

Daimler adopted the sleeve-valve engine in 1909, with great success, and retained it until the middle '30s. The 50 H.P. Double Six of 1926 was probably the most impressive Daimler ever made.

Some of the earliest motorcar manufacturers bear the great names of companies now in the Chrysler-controlled Rootes Group. The famous Humber Company made superb bicycles for some years, then started on the production of equally excellent light cars, with the lovely little 5 H.P. Humberette in 1902-3. Dozens of these early "minis" still take part in veteran car events, and are among the most reliable and economical of the real "oldies". The company soon started making bigger cars, such as the 1909 20 H.P. model, but they brought back the name Humberette for an unusual smallwheeled cycle car in 1912.

Rootes's "Imp family" now embraces Sunbeam, Singer and Hillman models, and as rival companies these were all going strongly in the early 1900s. Typical of early Sunbeams was a 12 H.P. four-cylinder tourer of smart appearance and "upright carriage". This was a conventional car; hardly the same can be said of the 1901 Sunbeam-Mabley light car, the machine with one wheel at front, one at the back, and two wheels abreast in the middle! The famous designer, Louis Coatalen, operated for both Sunbeam and Hillman. Singers made their first car in 1905 and it had a White and Poppe engine; their most successful early car, however, was the 10 H.P. of 1912, and this was where Rootes came into the picture for the first time, the Maidstone agent William Rootes taking the entire first year's production.

Henry de Rothschild's 21 H.P. Daimler at the start of the Chantaloup hill climb in 1900.

1914 25 H.P. Lanchester. It was the first British car to have electric lighting as standard. The foot brake was through discs on the transmission. The handbrake worked on the rear wheels. 4 cylinder 3,299 c.c. engine with preselector epicyclic box.

The motoring fraternity nowadays tends to lose sight of the importance of the earliest Vauxhall cars, although the vintage enthusiasts venerate the big 30/98 cars of later years. The Vauxhall Iron Works of London made engines and pumps only, at first, and they were very good ones. Then they came out with a remarkably advanced small car in 1902, followed by a three-cylinder version a year or two later. The little 6 H.P. had an automatic inlet valve and even had a hot-spot system for the carburetter. Speed control was by varying the tension of the inlet valve spring. Coil ignition was employed and pump cooling was a feature.

Ahead of its time

The car had a two-speed and reverse transmission and — wonder of wonders! — a steering-column gear-shift. Admittedly it had a tiller instead of a steering wheel, but the column-change was about 50 years ahead of its time. Another interesting fact was the use of hub-type freewheel mechanism instead of a differential.

Already, in 1905, one saw the beginnings of those well-known flutes on the bonnet of the Vauxhall, which were retained in some form or another until a few years ago.

In 1904, moreover, the company moved to Luton, where it nowadays has a whole town of its own. And one of the first-ever thoroughbred sports cars worthy of the name was surely the Prince Henry 3-litre car, from which was derived the 30/98 — that beloved, imposing piece of historic machinery so well represented in vintage events.

The Napier story is an important one, although the name has passed out of the automotive field many years ago. The Napier concern made a highly successful car in 1900. In fact, an example was entered in the Thousand Miles Trial and did well. This event itself was an extremely important one; in fact, it really put the whole industry on a firm footing at a time when it was very shaky, due to prejudice and hidebound tradition, associated with an undue reverence for the horse.

The Thousand Miles Trial was organised by the Royal Automobile Club — a body which also was responsible for getting the new "horror" of motoring accepted in circles that mattered — with the twin objects of letting people up and down the country see the incredible monsters, and proving that these devices could travel great distances without breaking down too often. The route was from London to Edinburgh via Bristol, Birmingham, Manchester, and Carlisle on the outward

179

leg and Newcastle, Leeds, Sheffield and Nottingham on the way back.

One of the most enthusiastic supporters of the great trial was the Prince of Wales, later King Edward VII. Indeed, this member of the Royal Family was keen on every aspect of motors, and without his patronage the industry might have been much slower to develop.

It was the Australian pioneer motorist S. F. Edge who got Napiers into the "big time" and out of their little works in Lambeth Walk. Persuaded by this far-sighted extrovert, the company went racing in Europe with great success, their crowning achievement being to win the Gordon Bennett Cup Race in 1902. Then in 1907 S. F. Edge took a Napier to the already famous Brooklands track — now "underneath" an aircraft factory — and established a 24-hour record of 1581 miles at an average of 65 m.p.h., which no one managed to crack for nearly 20 years.

Type of caravan

From 1904, when the company introduced their 18 H.P. model, the name Napier became associated with precision-built luxurious six-cylinder cars, right up to the years just after the first World War, when they went over to aero-engine production. But even just before the second World War, lordly Napiers were to be seen in use as hire cars, hearses etc. The company, incidentally, made an export model — a kind of motor caravan,

almost, with a hood that could be converted into a tent, and seats that could be made into bunks.

Among the names of all the historic marques that now come under the banner of Leylands is that of Morris, and many people think that it is the oldest. This is not so — not by a long way, for William Morris was selling and making cycles when the earliest cars began to take the roads, and he did not start manufacturing until much later. The famous Bullnose Morris, in fact, did not delight the motoring world until 1913, but Morris had a profound influence on the motoring scene thereafter. Lord Nuffield still attended new model presentations until the middle 1950s.

Leylands were pioneers in the steam wagon business rather than in cars, but it should not be forgotten that one of the directors of the firm that became Leylands actually built a steam tricar in 1895. And, of course, there were Leyland cars and Trojan cars later on, in the early '20s.

Rover and Riley (also now Leyland names) were pioneer cars. There were Rover tricars and a single-cylinder four-wheeler in 1904. The latter boasted a tubular backbone type chassis, rack-and-pinion steering and three-speed gearbox. In 1907 a Rover car won the classic Tourist Trophy race, and the marque has always had a reputation for quality and performance. One of the nicest cars of the early 20s was the Rover 8 air-cooled twin — a real sporty little disc-wheeled roadster that caught the eyes of the flappers.

There was a Riley car as early as 1898, and although

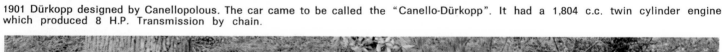

1901 Dürkopp designed by Canellopolous. The car came to be called the "Canello-Dürkopp". It had a 1,804 c.c. twin cylinder engine which produced 8 H.P. Transmission by chain.

1905 Prosper-Lambert, one of the many small companies that disappeared in the 1909 crisis. This car had a 2,545 c.c. engine, 3 speeds and shaft transmission.

it was a prototype, the Riley company had fair justification, later, for coining the catchphrase "As old as the industry, as modern as the hour". Various three and four-wheeled models followed, and led to the exciting Redwing and the illustrious Nines of later years.

It is not always appreciated that Standards bear one of the oldest names, or that they had a vital influence on the progress of the industry. They introduced a 6 H.P. single-cylinder model as early as 1903, and it had a three-speed transmission, sloping steering column, flexible couplings for the shafting, drum-type rear brakes and leaf-type suspension, front and rear. "Quantity" production began in 1905 with the 16-20 H.P. tourer, then there was the 15 H.P. car in 1911 and a 20/25 H.P. model in 1916. Today's Standard-Triumph concern is part of the Leyland Group.

The Lagonda car — or tricar, as it was then — first saw the light of day at Staines in 1904, where an American opera singer took the mellifluent name of the marque from the Indian-sounding Lagonda Creek, Ohio. One could still obtain Lagonda spares at Staines in 1950, and the cars were being made at the old Hanworth aerodrome

when Prince Philip bought one in 1954. They were to be seen there with their sister Aston Martins until only a few years ago, when Aston Martin Lagonda took over the historic Tickford coachbuilding works at Newport Pagnell.

The first taxis

The contribution of France to motoring started with the remarkable steam carriage made by Cugnot and often claimed as the first "car" but one of the most important events of the pioneer motoring years was De Dion Bouton's launching of the "Populaire" in 1903. It had the rear axle and transmission arrangement, which has become a classic and is still in use on some of the finest cars today.

The Renault history is an important one, of course, and Louis Renault's car designed in 1898 bristled with advanced characteristics, including shaft drive, direct-drive top gear and a tubular chassis. Louis and Marcel, his brother, slaved away in a tiny shed in their father's

DYNAMO AND ALTERNATOR

A small technical revolution — the advent of the alternator — has been taking place in the contemporary car. The majority of motorists are beginning to realise that the dynamo, that good old faithful servant whose duty for many years has been to supply electricity to the battery, it being ousted by the alternator.

It is generally agreed that this development carries with it certain technical advantages, but it is not always obvious what they are.

Perhaps the first questions are why this replacement of the dynamo by the alternator should be proceeding so slowly and why, considering the advantages claimed for the alternator, not all motor car manufacturers have yet been persuaded to fit it. The alternator and control gear assembly at present costs more, but it is likely this will cause little difficulty, as the difference in cost is fairly small.

Paradox

Before illustrating the technical advantages, it would be useful to run over the operating principles of the dynamo and compare them with those of the alternator.

The role of both is that of battery-charger. The battery is a large reservoir of electrical energy. Both dynamo and alternator replace in it the "deficit" of electricity used in supplying the car's various electrical apparatus. The battery accepts and delivers only direct current. Here we strike an apparent paradox, since it would be thought that the most suitable device would be the dynamo, by its very nature generating direct current, rather than the alternator, which, as its name implies, produces alternating current that must be rectified before being put into the battery.

In fact, this complication does not exist. Indeed, there is a considerable simplification in using the alternator, because of the type of input system which it requires and because of the transistors, which perform two essential tasks in the control gear.

The dynamo works on Faraday's and Pacinotti's principles. Electro-magnetic induction generates a direct current in the copper wire coil wound on a soft-iron armature, which rotates in the electro-magnetic field provided by an electro-magnet (the inductor). Since the coil is continually in rotation, the electric current generated in it is collected by brushes in contact with the commutator, which is integral with the armature.

The voltage of the current supplied by the dynamo is, roughly speaking, directly proportional to its speed

which, in turn, is strictly related to the engine speed. Hence, at low speeds, the induced voltage is very low. To prevent a current reversal, in which the higher voltage of the battery would drive current through the dynamo — which would then act as an electric motor — it is necessary to insert an automatic cut-out in the circuit. At high speeds, however, the voltage of the current supplied by the dynamo is excessively high, so it is also necessary to insert a voltage regulator in the circuit to avoid burning out the battery.

These complications do not arise with the alternator. Theoretically speaking, the mode of operation of the alternator is different from that of the dynamo. The induced current is not generated in a rotating coil but in the winding of a stationary element (the stator), inside which a concentric inductor rotates, so that the commutator and brushes are no longer necessary.

Apart from the fact that in dynamos these are the parts which are most subject to wear and which therefore demand the most frequent maintenance operations, the substantially greater robustness of the alternator also assists the saving in maintenance.

There is, of course, the question of rectifying the alternating current. This is done by using silicon diodes (transistors), which have the property of allowing current to pass in one direction only and so act as current rectifier valves. But the transistors in the alternator also perform the function of the automatic cut-out.

Because of their semi-conductor properties they effectively prevent any counter-current flowing from battery to dynamo.

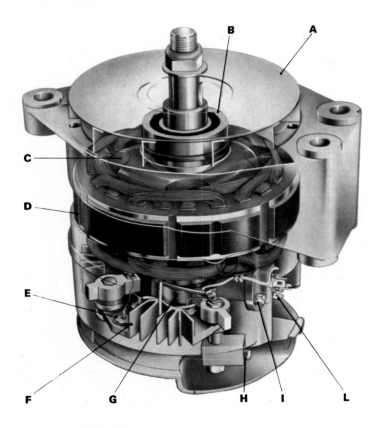

Section of C.A.V. Alternator
A - fan B - bearing C - rotor D - stator E - silicon diode F - wing G - contact ring H - positive terminal I - brush mounting L - negative terminal.

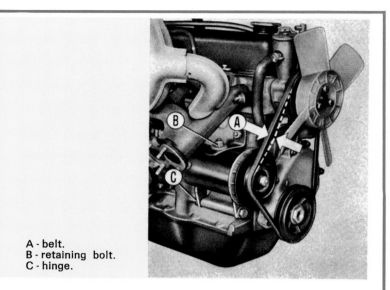

A - belt.
B - retaining bolt.
C - hinge.

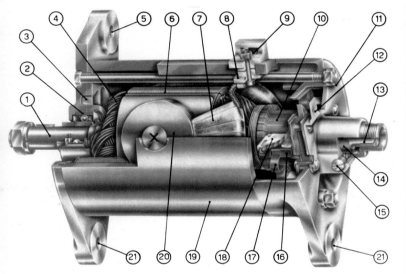

Section of Magneti Marelli Dynamo
1 - pulley shaft 2 - ball bearing 3 - end plate 4 - induction windings
5 - mounting holes 6 - field stack 7 - field windings 8 - earth terminal
9 - terminal 10 - commutator 11 - end plate 12 - positive terminal
13 - tachometer drive 14 - bush 15 - oil nipple 16 - brush 17 - brush
spring 18 - brush holder 19 - body 20 - earth 21 - mounting hole.

The voltage regulator is also simplified because the alternator and dynamo have different input curves; changes in voltage between low and high speeds are smaller in the alternator. Furthermore, the voltage is already satisfactorily high when the engine, and therefore the alternator, is running slowly.

Increased demand

This is one of the useful advantages of the alternator, since it means that the battery does not discharge so quickly under particularly heavy conditions of working. These include urban use in winter when, apart from the inadequate charging, there is increased demand by the electrical installations of the car (the lighting system, windscreen wipers, fog lamps, radio, heater, etc.). There is no doubt that the use of alternators is becoming more widespread, not only because of the progressive reduction in manufacturing costs, but also because of the electrical "extras" now available in many cars.

garden. It is still there — in the forecourt of the great Renault factory in Paris — with the bench, lathe, drilling machine etc. In March 1899 Renault Frères was founded.

A highlight in the fortunes of the company was the production of the first taxis in 1905, and some of the popular Renault cabs were used in London, too. The Paris cabs were "enlisted" in the first World War and did great work at the front.

In those early years Renault also produced a two-cylinder 10 H.P. car and a four-cylinder 14 H.P. model developed from the prototype that won the Paris-Vienna event. Luxurious coachwork was mounted on this chassis and it came to be adopted for many official functions. Other firms that came into the picture early, were Sizaire & Naudin, and Delage. The former specialised from the start in making sports cars; one of the first — the 8 H.P. — had independent front suspension. Louis Delage's firm produced both tourers and racers. Both these firms did quite well in competitive events. Panhard-Levassor were among the pioneer concerns, of course, and made cars as early as 1891. Levassor was responsible for the first sliding-cog type of gearbox. The marque was noteworthy for its racing record, right up to the early 1900s.

Pages from the Lancia catalogue.

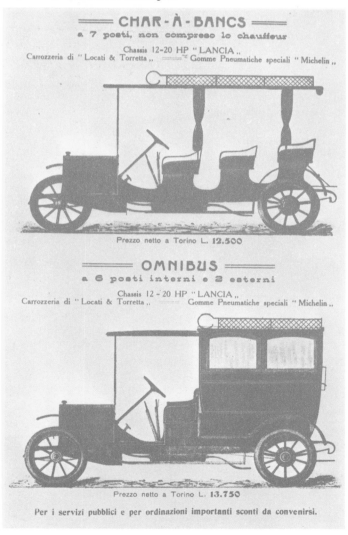

1904 Renault. Note the functional but elegant clothing. Below the 1906 Renault "Grand Prix".

1906 Renault.

Other important French pioneer marques were Peugeot, Decauville, Gobron-Brillie, Gladiator, Delahaye, De Dietrich and Bugatti.

Among the earliest Italian cars were the Giusti and the Miari which were designed by Bernardi and built in 1896, whilst in the same year, several motorcars were constructed by Michele Lanza. In 1898 Ceirano (later associated with the Itala) manufactured the Welleyes. A year later, the Fiat concern — now the largest European motor manufacturer of all — was founded, on the first day of July.

In November of 1899, 10 3 H.P. cars were completed

A superb racing car — the 1911 Fiat S74, which weighed 3,300 lbs. and had a four-cylinder 190 H.P. engine of over 14 litres.

The famous 1909 Itala "Palombella" complete with steps.

Nazzaro in the Fiat F2 on the Landinier straight, in the 1907 French Grand Prix.

and work was about to start on 6 H.P. models. This was the beginning of a great endeavour, and it was unfortunate that the designer of the Welleyes car — the earliest Fiat — died in poverty after renouncing his profession.

Giovanni Agnelli was the industrial genius behind Fiat and its employees included Lancia and Nazzaro, themselves soon to become famous.

From that early start in Corso Dante, the Fabbrica Italiana Automobili Torino grew steadily during the first decade of the century, and a good deal more quickly after the first world war. Much of its early success was due to racing, even as early as 1902, and a Fiat race car did 128 m.p.h. in 1906. The firm went on racing for another 20 years, then withdrew, like most mass producers, but continued to build sports cars.

The company had other important interests, including aviation and the production of industrial engines, marine engines etc.

In the three major motor races of 1907, Agnelli entered three different models with quite different features. The car for the Targa Florio was the 28-40 H.P. model, of 7358 c.c. with a maximum speed of 60 m.p.h. The Taunus model, with which Nazzaro won the Kaiserpreis was an eight-litre machine with a maximum of 80 m.p.h.

A 1909 Alfa in a racing version. Below Merosi, the designer, at the wheel of the 1914 Alfa "Grand Prix".

For the Grand Prix of the French Automobile Club the entry was a spectacular vehicle of 16 litre capacity and a 110 m.p.h. maximum.

The illustrious Lancia concern was founded in November 1906 by Vincenzo Lancia and Claudio Fogolin. There was a disastrous fire almost immediately, but this did not deter the pioneers, who soon started the Greek alphabetical series with the Alpha 24 H.P. model, following it in 1908 with the Dialpha, the first 6 cylinder, and the Beta, Gamma etc.

The firm then moved to a larger factory and from the new premises emerged the first Lancia to achieve real commercial success. This was the Theta, which had a capacity of almost 5000 c.c. and developed 70 H.P. at 2200 r.p.m. Lancia was always on good terms with

Fiat's Agnelli and in the early years of his own industrial efforts, still raced for Fiat.

Darracq Italiana was founded in Naples in 1906, for the purpose of building the same models as the parent company in Paris. In fact it was really an assembly plant. The company ran into difficulties and was rescued by a Milan bank which insisted that a new car be designed, suitable for touring and racing. The new company was called Anonima Lombarda Fabbrica Automobili, hence Alfa, and the designation Alfa Romeo came in 1920.

The fame of Itala — another notable name in Italian early history — was consolidated after the epic Pekin-Paris race, which was won by one of the marque, driven by Prince Scipio Borghese. The firm had been set up in 1904 by Matteo Ceirano. A very special Itala was

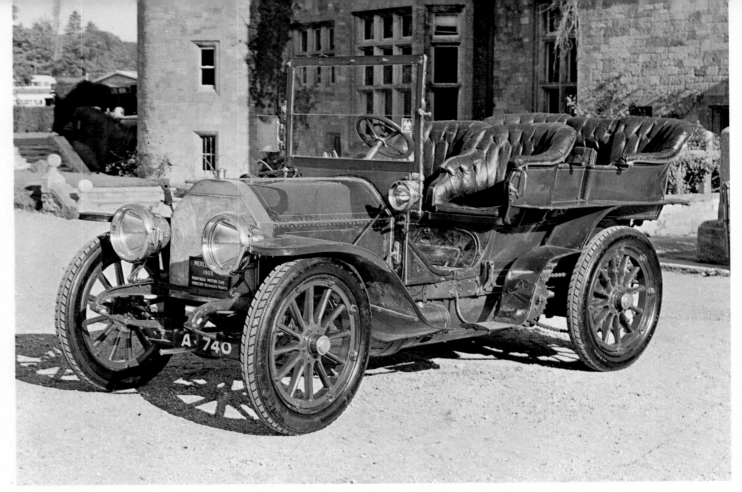

A much admired G.T. car—a 1903 Mercedes 60 H.P. with a 9,230 c.c. four-cylinder engine. The electric lights on this car were fitted in 1910.

that owned by the Queen of Italy and nicknamed by her Palombella. It can be seen in Turin's motor museum. Apropos of Italian Royalty and the motorcar, King Victor Emanuel III rivalled the Kaiser and King Edward VII as a motoring enthusiast. Emanuel and his Queen Elena were involved in a somewhat sobering incident when they tried out an electric car and it got out of control and went backwards, hitting a tree and flinging them out. The Queen sprained her ankle but they both remained enthusiasts.

In 1906 the firms of Brixia-Zust, Aquila Italiana and Legnano came into existence. The first of these distinguished itself mainly by reason of its vertical three-cylinder engines, built in various sizes. The 1500 c.c. example powered a fine touring car and gave it a maximum speed of 40 m.p.h. In 1918 Brixia-Zust and Officine Meccaniche of Milan merged and this resulted in a new company later called O.M. - Fabbrica Bresciana di Automobili. This, still later, became a part of the Fiat group. Aquila Italiana of Turin made sports cars under the engineer Cappa. Some of the cars boasted such advanced features as monobloc engines, aluminium pistons, ball-bearing crankshafts and engine sub-frames.

The Legnano company had a somewhat short life but produced some excellent cars, including the 6-8 H.P. twin, with a circular radiator well-known to veteran enthusiasts.

The most interesting German machine of the first decade of the century was the 60 H.P. Mercedes, the excellent qualities of which were demonstrated in the fourth Gordon Bennett Cup Race. At this time, the firm had lost their new 80 H.P. models prepared specially for the competition to be held that year in Ireland, because fire

had swept through the factory. But they wanted to see a team at the starting line so they hurriedly converted three of the 60 H.P. tourers and these did well in the event. The model had a four-cylinder 9200 c.c. engine.

Elegance in the Valentino Park at Turin.

front view of a 1910 RENAULT "A. G. FIACRE PARIS"

engine - front mounted separate vertical twin
bore and stroke - 80 × 120 mm.
capacity - 1,206 c.c.
output - 7 H.P. at 1,800 r.p.m.
ignition - high tension magneto
clutch - inverse leather cone
gearchange - 3 speeds plus reverse
transmission - cardan shaft
weight - 1,900 lbs.

Smoother lines all round. A Hillman "Californian" with feminine appeal. A similar setting below for a Citroen and lady driver of the 20's.

CHAPTER THIRTEEN

BY CAR ROUND THE WORLD

The long-distance motor races and trials are already legends, heroic achievements of a time never to return, though hardly fifty years have passed since they were run. Already it is almost impossible to imagine the enthusiasm, admiration and worship for the drivers who took part in those long, long drives over impossible roads in far-away and exotic places.

Certainly these exploits, in addition to testing the car to its absolute limit and of demonstrating that this means of transport had reached the state where it could carry people to almost any point on earth, also fascinated a large public — a public much greater than the number of potential purchasers. The feminine element, too, was affected by the thrill of motoring, seeing the drivers through the eyes of newspaper accounts as knights of the new mechanical civilisation.

Brief mentions have been made of some of the early exploits of this type — Winton's adventurous journeys from Cleveland to New York in 1897 and 1899; Chapin's eventful drive between Detroit and New York in 1902; the first coast-to-coast drives by various Americans in 1903; the "Passe Partout" trip of Lehwess and Cudell; and the fantastic journey made by Charles Glidden of 50,000 miles round the world in his indefatigable Napier.

Glidden's journey between 1902 and 1907 touched continental Europe, Scandinavia to the Arctic Circle, North America, Australia, Malaysia, New Zealand, China and Japan.

One may well wonder if the roads of many of these places were in a sufficiently good state to allow a car

A Rover 6 H.P. of 1906. It was in a car of this type that R. S. Jefferson made his long journey.

of those times to survive such a severe mechanical test for five years. The answer is obviously that they were not; the prudent Glidden had the foresight to equip his Napier with a set of interchangeable wheels by means of which it was possible, when the roads were too bad or when they did not exist at all, to continue by another means — on the railway track. He fitted his car on the rails and boldly forged ahead like a small locomotive. In Glidden's honour (he was a native of Lowell, Massachusetts) a number of transcontinental trials were held in America which provided a splendid opportunity for the leading transatlantic motoring figures to meet periodically. The last of these commemorative trials was held as late as 1947.

R. S. Jefferson was another who figured in an exploit similar to Glidden's, also impressive and exciting even though it was shorter in time and distance. Like many other motorists he was attracted by the prospect of adventure which the Balkans and above all the Ottoman Empire still held at the beginning of the century for European eyes. In 1905 there were only two cars in Serbia and none in Bulgaria, while in Turkey they were

For years roads in America were terrible. It was not until 1912 that the first bitumen road was built. In the picture — the official parade at the opening of the road to the New York State Fair.

The development of motor roads has changed the aspect and sometimes the geography of the countryside. This photograph and the photograph of the preceding page are of the same place.

outright prohibited for reasons which were partly religious and partly political. Not only mechanical and logistic difficulties but also major diplomatic problems had so far prevented any Balkan trial, but the tenacious Jefferson set out to overcome them.

Fuel stop

Firstly, he got Rover to build him a strengthened version of their 8 H.P., a car whose mechanical elements had a suitable strength and simplicity, including a single cylinder engine. He then got into contact with the countries through which he was to pass and soon obtained enough permissions to get through Serbia and Bulgaria — though in neither country was it possible to find petrol. The Turks were much more obstinate, however, and to get anywhere Jefferson had to ask the British Ambassador to intervene.

The Rover set off from Coventry and after crossing that part of Western Europe which had decent roads quickly reached the Hungarian frontier. Here Jefferson encountered the first of two pleasant surprises — the plain which had no roads whatsoever, where he had envisaged tremendous difficulties, proved to have a firm, hard surface over which he could boldly make his way. His troubles began when he had to cross rivers or swamps and more than once the courageous driver was put to a severe test of his ingenuity.

He continued his adventurous way across the frontier, which he passed at full speed, giving a military salute to the startled guards (this inevitably ended up as a

Rover has maintained its traditions for solidly built cars since the days of Jefferson's journey. A Land Rover is particularly suitable for difficult terrain.

CAR
AS LIGHT
AS A
FEATHER

One of the cars which had a major influence on styling was the Panhard-Levassor "Skiff", built in 1911 by Henri Labourdette, a well-known French coachbuilder. Up to then, in spite of one or two tries only partially successful, no-one had definitely broken away from the early styling of the century. It was René de Knyff, who has figured a number of times in our story as a daring and successful racing driver and who subsequently became manager of Panhard-Levassor, who put Labourdette on the right lines.

De Knyff wanted a 20 H.P. sleeve-valve engined car for his own use, but not the usual heavy body with consequently lower performance. He asked Labourdette for a car to be "light as a feather" and preferably of new streamlined appearance. He suggested that aeroplane techniques might be used in the construction, that field having already passed beyond the canvas and plywood stage.

Thus Labourdette, impressed, too, by the commercial importance of his client, set to work to produce something

new — not only from the technical point of view but also from that of appearance.

Labourdette produced something which was a cross between a canoe and an aeroplane, with no doors and covered in a light triple sheathing. In styling, the "Skiff" was equally revolutionary, with a long smooth bonnet flowing into the low inclined windscreen and with a low hood.

This was the forerunner of the long series of sports cars which still persists today. The spoked wheels contributed to an unusual and attractive appearance and are echoed on the G.T. cars of today.

The "Skiff" had a tremendous effect on the motoring world, so much so that Labourdette had orders to build many variants, all of which took the name of "cab-skiff". It is hardly necessary to say that with this method of construction they were very expensive, but for those who could afford them it was money well spent — not least for the suggestion that with a machine like this the owner was superior to ordinary motorists of the time.

From top to bottom — 1904 Humberette, 1904 Vauxhall and a 1903 Panhard-Levassor. The three cars were photographed at the 1964 Prescott hill climb.

`diplomatic incident). When he reached the Turkish frontier, however, things took a turn for the worse as the frontier guards had not been informed of his special permission to enter Turkey. In the end this matter, too, was resolved and then Jefferson had his second pleasant surprise — the Turkish roads were unexpectedly smooth and well-maintained, though this turned out to be true only of the frontier zone.

The journey towards Constantinople quickly took on the more normal character of cross-country "navigation" but it aroused delirious enthusiasm among the local population, who were able to see the first car ever to enter the Ottoman Empire. It was only when in sight of the Turkish capital that the Rover had its first serious breakdown — a broken valve — but the motoring conquest of the Balkans was already achieved.

The fantastic Pekin-Paris

The greatest and most exciting of all the long-distance trials was immortalised in the reports of Luigi Barzini, who took part as special correspondent of the "Daily Telegraph" and the Italian "Corriere della Sera", and in reports by Edgardo Longoni of "Secolo", Jean Taillis of "Le Matin" and of one of the competitors, Georges Cormier. To try to drive from the Chinese capital to Paris in 1907 was considered sheer madness, considering that to the lack of roads and bridges were added other obstacles unknown in early trials — swamps, mountains, narrow gullies and unknown territories where the only means of passage were doubtful tracks. Nevertheless, there was an immediate and enthusiastic response from a small group of keen motorists when Le Matin proposed the idea to all the countries of the world. Soon after the announcement the editor received entries from 25 volunteers, but later when the entries had to be confirmed in a more tangible way — by the payment of 2,000 francs — they decreased to five.

There were four Frenchmen — Cormier and Collignon, both with two cylinder 8-10 H.P. De Dion - Boutons, Godard with a four cylinder 15 H.P. Dutch Spyker and Ponts with a Contal tricycle — and one Italian, Prince Scipione Borghese with a 35-45 H.P. Itala. The drivers quickly paired with journalists, for the big newspapers were aware of the interest such a race would arouse in the public. Barzini travelled with Borghese, Longoni with Cormier and Jean Taillis with Godard.

At once their respective newspapers began the pre-race publicity and diplomatic channels hummed with activity as the French, Dutch and Italian authorities made contact with those of Pekin. The latter exhibited great diffidence towards the undertaking which to them was quite inexplicable. As Luigi Barzini was to be told later when in China "The reactionary Mandarins, who hold the power at Court, are afraid that the race is really an

effort to see how long it would take to invade China by car".

Nor was this the only suspicious interpretation of the race. Some Chinese officials saw the competitors as saboteurs who were to discredit the Kalgan railway, and still others saw them as military spies under the command of Prince Borghese.

Getting permits to cross the various frontiers proved a difficult task and was a test for the nerves of the organizers. One minor incident occurred when the request for the translation of a permit into Mongol was turned down by the Chinese for fear of the effect on their uneducated soldiery of the word "fire-cart" — the only way of translating the words "motor car". In the meantime logistic problems seemed almost insurmountable. All the competitors had renounced any sort of comfort during the race, but petrol had to be made available en route. Finally, dumps were formed by mule and camel transport. Meanwhile the vehicles were shipped from Marseilles and Naples for the long sea voyage to Shanghai and then by Trans-Siberian railway to Pekin. The race started on 10 June, 1907, at 7 a.m., saluted by the band of the French garrison at Pekin. Paris was

1898 De Dion-Bouton and a 1902 experimental Royal Enfield quadricycle, fitted with a single cylinder 244 c.c. De Dion-Bouton engine.

The famous Itala of the Pekin-Paris race. It had a 7,433 c.c. 4 cylinder engine which produced 45 H.P. at 1,250 r.p.m.

10,000 miles away. Right from the start Prince Borghese took the lead which he was never to lose. Thus began the impressive performance of his Itala, and its enthusiastic driver who was never able to drive a cautious race such as the innumerable and unknown difficulties ahead might have suggested.

The first region to cross was the terrible, mountainous area of Kangal, 800 miles of impossible "road". When mountains were met, it was necessary, wrote Barzini, "to haul the cars up — the way a cannon is manhandled into place". Boulders had to be moved; undergrowth and roots blocked the way and had to be wearily cut through with axes. The steep slopes were too much for the brakes and it was necessary to call on local peasants to fasten ropes to the rear of the cars and slow their downhill progress.

If one of the objects of this race was to spread knowledge of the motor car in those out-of-the-way places, it was not achieved. There were plenty of acts of generous

The Itala driving on the track of the Trans-Siberian railway.

197

VLADIMIR
MOSCOW
COMPIEGNE
SNOSSIOS
CHARLEVILLE
PARIS
HANNOVER
AIX-LA-CHAPELLE
BERLIN
POZNAN
WARSAW BREST

hospitality and spontaneous help from the populations met en route, but absolutely no curiosity towards the unknown device from the Chinese peasants.

Across the Steppes

Finally they were through the mountains, with the immense Mongol plain to cross. Pons' tricycle dropped out of the race and one of the five competitors was gone. Behind the Itala, which continued to forge ahead, the two De Dions drove along together, experiencing no serious mechanical troubles (nor were they to do so, finishing the race in fine style) while the Spyker was already in trouble.

On 25th June, two weeks after the start, the long awaited frontier between Russia and China was reached at Kyakhta—and three days later Cormier and Collignon saw their first "civilized" bed since they had set off. In the meantime Borghese was galloping over the horizon. Now the cars began to use the only road available to

them, in the valley of the Trans-Siberian Railway, alternating with short stretches of Siberian road where the simple sign-posting made it possible for the drivers not to lose the way in the Steppes. It was, in fact, in the Steppes that an accident which was to become famous in motoring annals befell the Itala.

A wheel broke down, the ends of the spokes coming out of their seats in the rim. It seemed impossible to go on, but Borghese had a bright idea. Remembering the famous cry "Water on the ropes!" he thought he could effect a repair by causing the wood to swell in water.

The only suitable place for this operation was in the public baths of the small town where they happened to be. That night he booked a cabin and the Italian wheel went into the Russian bath. The repair did not last and the wheel finally broke after a few miles. Only the work of a Siberian blacksmith enabled the Itala to carry on to victory.

As they reached Kazan the drivers began to find roads

The Itala in difficulty.

One of the early stages.

KAZAN
ELABUGA
BIISK
ZLATOUS
KURGAN
URAL Mts.
VOLGA
SIBERIA
SIBERIA
TOMSK
KRASNOYARSK
KANSK
IRKUTSK
Lake BAIKAL
KYAKHTA
GOBI
PEKIN

that gradually became more and more "civilized". Cormier told how he nearly fainted when he found a road-roller at the entrance to one city!

Nijni-Novgorod, Moscow, Warsaw... Borghese dashed towards the finish while the others were still on the Russian plain, and on the 10th August the Itala was in Paris — to be received with delirious enthusiasm. Borghese had covered 10,000 miles in 60 days exactly and the other three competitors arrived together 21 days later!

Found in warehouse

Let us see how this wonderful Itala was built. It had a front mounted, vertical four cylinder engine which developed 45 H.P. at 1,250 r.p.m. from its 7,433 c.c. It had a four speed gearbox plus reverse, transmission by prop-shaft and the whole car weighed about 27 cwts. The car did just over 8 m.p.g., and a single rear seat was squeezed between the two supplementary petrol tanks which contained a total of 70 gallons.

Behind the tanks was a large box full of tools and spare parts, but most of these were thrown overboard during the race to lighten the car. Hidden away were two other tanks of 12 gallons each, one for oil and one for water. Pirelli had manufactured special tyres for the Itala, capable of lasting "as much as 2,500 miles".

Today the 35-45 H.P. Itala of Prince Borghese is preserved in the Turin Motor Museum. Even after the great race it had a romantic history. Abandoned in a disused warehouse by Itala, it was found almost by accident in 1923. Carlo Biscaretti, later to found the museum, who was then publicity manager of Itala, arranged for its restoration. Unfortunately today it lacks the four famous mudguards which played an important part in

199

A 1903 De Dion-Bouton and a 1909 Humber.

the Pekin - Paris race. Made out of strong steel, they could be detached and placed under the wheels to cross streams and marshes.

Somewhat unjustly, history which has celebrated the driver (nobleman, militant politician, journalist and above all a keen motorist) and tenacious reporter, has neglected the third member of the team, Ettore Guizzardi, the mechanic. "When he had nothing else to do he would stretch out under the car and examine it all, nut by nut, bolt by bolt, piece by piece", wrote Barzini, "and he would spend a long time in this strange communion with his machine".

As was inevitable, the Pekin - Paris generated a spirit of emulation. Thus another newspaper, this time across the Atlantic, the "New York Times", planned an even more ambitious race all round the world. The idea was for the competitors to leave from New York and, after having gone north-west across the American continent, to cross the Behring Straits from Alaska to Asia. From there, covering much of the route of the Pekin-Paris, they would arrive in the French capital. The distance to be covered was 18,341 miles and there was a terrible enemy to conquer — the North American winter.

The start was fixed for 12 February, 1908 at 10 a.m. and there were present — after the inevitable withdrawals — six cars. There were three French (Bourcier, Hansen and Autran's De Dion, Godard, Hue and Livier's Monobloc, and Pons, Deschamps and Berthe's Sizaire-

The start of the New York-Paris race on the morning of the 12th February, 1908. Below the 1907 20-30 H.P. Spyker.

Naudin), one Italian (Scalfoglio, Sartori and Haaga's Züst), one German (Koppel, Knappe and Maas' Protos), and one American (Schuster, Roberts and Williams' Thomas "Flyer").

Once again a good part of those entered consisted of journalists for whom these great adventures were beginning to offer opportunities for a type of story sure to attract the public as proved by Barzini.

At least 50,000 people were present at the start from Times Square and another 150,000 lined the streets of Broadway between 42nd and 20th Streets. Similar enthusiasm had been shown for European competitors when leaving their respective capitals and the Kaiser himself had sent his best wishes to the German team. Most of the press, both American and European, criticized the choice of the time of year for the race. Everyone forecast its premature end on the outskirts of New York or at least in Illinois. They underestimated, however, the spirit of the competitors who, amidst every kind of difficulty (snow chains were used for the first time in this race) advanced slowly across the continent, over vast expanses of snow where tracks were barely visible, and on the railway track beds where necessary,

as they were authorized to do. Competitors even helped one another out of difficulty in a spirit of understanding though occasionally less orthodox methods were used, Koppel being literally forced to help Schuster on one occasion.

Guidance in the snow

The inhabitants of the areas which were crossed, watched the progress of the competitors with ever-increasing amazement as the race went on relentlessly. They also gave tremendous help of all kinds. In Schenectady they showed the way after a particularly heavy snowfall by laying coloured streamers across the snow.

In spite of all this only four machines reached the Pacific coast at San Francisco. The Sizaire-Naudin had never even left New York State and the Monobloc fell out finally at Cedar Rapids, Iowa. The first to enter San Francisco was the Thomas, 42 days after the start, six days ahead of the Züst and 14 days ahead of the De Dion. The Protos was out of the race for the time being, stuck in the mud in Wyoming.

Schuster's team at once set sail for Valdez in Alaska,

from where they were to drive to None. The team had been changed to: Schuster, driver; Miller, mechanic; Hansen, navigator; and Macadam, a journalist from the "New York Times". While the team was on its way, however, the organisers changed their minds, afraid of the terrible state of the roads between Valdez and None.

Ship recalled

Thus the ship was recalled to Seattle, where the American team was joined by the other three to sail for Japan. The Germans had been hauled out of the "quicksand" and had been sent on by train to San Francisco. While the teams were sailing to Japan there was tremendous supply activity in Siberia as sledge teams hauled drums of petrol to supply points. The experience of the Pekin - Paris race proved very useful, indicating what to do and what not to do and when the race began again after another sea crossing between Japan and the Asian continent, it turned into a speed competition between the Thomas and the Protos. First prizes of 1,000 dollars each gave an excellent incentive on the successive stages into which the race was divided. Almost at once the American car was held back by a series of misfortunes. First the transmission broke, causing the loss of precious lubricant which they tried to replace with tallow. Then the gearbox broke down. Schuster had to leave his car and go on horseback to the nearest town to try to get an emergency gear made. Almost at the same time the Protos became stuck in a sea of mud; the same thing happened to the Züst and the De Dion, both of which had to give up the race.

Getting free once again, the Germans set off before Schuster was able to get his machine going and, arriving at China first, won the 1,000 dollars offered by the Trans-Siberian Railway. Then, alternately passing and re-passing, the Americans and the Germans reached the area of Lake Baikal, where the Germans arrived first and the Americans had the misfortune of seeing their adversaries disappear into a ferry while they had to wait another 24 hours. Although it recovered the time lost in a dash to the Russian frontier, Schuster had once more to give way to the Germans, who thus won the 1,000 dollars offered by the Russian Automobile Club.

The Protos was already on good European roads and the Thomas had no more chance to catch up. Thus the Germans arrived in Paris on 26 July at 6.15 p.m., just at the time when the Americans were leaving Berlin. All the same, the victory was quite correctly given to the Thomas, which arrived four days later. The Protos received a thirty day penalty for having crossed part of America by train and for having refused to go to Alaska — it was because of the German refusal that the organizers had changed the route.

Amidst Parisians once more in the throes of delirium the four Americans, bedecked with a huge "Stars and Stripes", arrived at the finish to be proclaimed the winners of the toughest of races.

Back to the factory

The winning machine, which had been in the race for 170 days — 88 of which it had been on the road — and had averaged over 150 miles per day (with a maximum of 400 in 24 hours), stayed only five days in France before being shipped back to the factory in Buffalo. There the bonnet was sealed and it did a 600 mile test run, after which the bonnet was opened. In the presence of witnesses, it was shown that the valves, spark plugs and bearings were those fitted before the race.

This remarkable technical achievement did not give the hoped for prosperity to the small American company. It was a victim of large scale competition and four years later it was closed down.

The triumphal arrival of the Protos team on the 26th July, 1908.

front view of a 1912 PANHARD · LEVASSOR "X17SS"

engine · front mounted 4 cylinder in two blocks
bore and stroke · 80 × 130 mm.
capacity · 2614 c.c.
output · 15 H.P. at 1200 r.p.m.
ignition · high tension magneto
clutch · single plate
gearchange · 4 speeds plus reverse
transmission · cardan shaft
weight · 2750 lb.

The car has become an instrument of daily living, but as a social symbol it accurately represents the public taste of its time. Above, the 1967 Oldsmobile convertible complete with model passenger and umbrella. Below, a 1930 Bentley 4 ½-litre with Gurney Nutting body.

CHAPTER FOURTEEN
THE GRAND PRIX MONSTERS

In 1905 the last race for the Gordon Bennett Cup was run on the Auvergne circuit; in 1906 was born the Grand Prix de l'Automobile Club de France. The succession was a natural one.

There was much opposition to the Gordon Bennett Cup rule that required that every part of a competing vehicle be made in the country it represented; many manufacturers who were excluded from taking part suffered material damage by not being able to share in the publicity created by the races — publicity which was an important commercial factor. These considerations had led l'Automobile Club de France to announce that, after 1905, it would take no further part in the Cup races. This withdrawal, which deprived the race of its most important entries, caused its end, and it was natural and logical for France to create another major competition to replace it, the Grand Prix. It is said that this competition signalled the birth of "formula" racing in

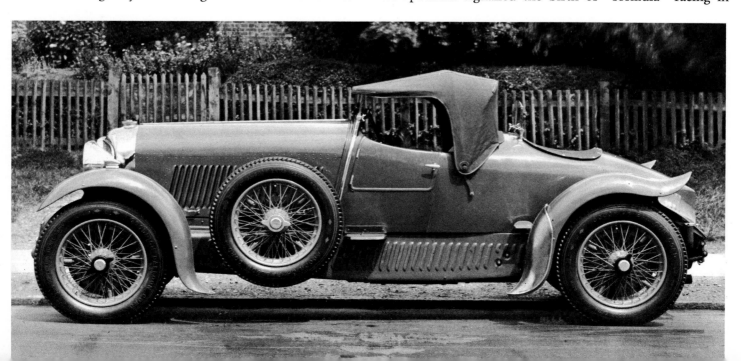

Two racing Wolseleys. The one above was photographed in 1905; the one below, in less formal pose, was photographed the year before.

the modern sense of the word. For the first time in a major international race, technical limits were laid down for participating cars in a very similar way to the method used today.

The most important requirement was that weight should not exceed 1,000 kgs. (about 2,200 lbs.) though an extra 7 kgs. were allowed for cars with electric ignitions. The driver and mechanic had to weigh at least 60 kgs. (132 lbs.) each and, as in the Gordon Bennett races, no manufacturer could enter more than three machines.

There were also more severe regulations, such as the requirement that breakdowns could be repaired only by the driver and his mechanic. The race was to be over a distance of 1,248 kilometres (almost 780 miles) run in two days, with the machines put in bond under the control of three inspectors during the intervening night.

The course was unusual — a large circuit near Le Mans, created by building new wood-paved roads through Vibraye forest and near Saint-Calais. All the rest of the 65-mile circuit was thickly paved with asphalt to avoid the terrible dust which was characteristic of other race tracks.

The asphalting was one of the earliest of its kind and derived from the attempts of the Swiss doctor, Guglielminetti and an engineer, Legavlian, to imprison the dust under a covering of tar. The first roads so treated showed encouraging results, leading to the use of the method for the first time on a large scale at Le Mans. In practice, the remedy for dust proved to be worse than the complaint as high road temperatures played havoc with tyres on a hot June day.

The new race created a new craze among the public.

A 1904 racing De Dietrich. Note the finned tube radiator.

For the first time tens of thousands of enthusiasts came to Le Mans, then almost unknown, though later to play an important part in the story of European motoring. There it was possible, from dawn of 26 June until dusk the following day, to admire the most beautiful cars of the time. Hotels and inns were invaded for miles around and special trains poured visitors into the local stations.

At the start there were 32 cars (23 French, six Italian and three German). It was a surprising array, with nearly all the most important French and Italian makes represented, but not one from England, where it seemed the new race had aroused little interest. Among the makes taking part were Panhard-Levassor, Hotchkiss, Lorraine-De Dietrich, Darracq, Renault, Clément-Bayard, Richard-Brasier, Itala, Fiat and Mercedes.

Because the regulations put no limitation on engine capacity or power, many manufacturers had built monster prototypes with very light chassis and huge engines with capacities ranging from 12 to 18 litres and horsepower from 90 to 130. These unusual vehicles were typical of racing cars for some years, until they were defeated by much lighter vehicles of a new technical age. An example was the 90 H.P. Renault with its 13 litre four cylinder engine which had magneto ignition, sidevalves and a three-speed gearbox. There were brakes on the rear wheels only.

The race was won by a Renault and one of the reasons was that the machine, like the Fiats and Italas in the race, had detachable rims which could be removed by unscrewing eight nuts. This was a Michelin invention which in those days was revolutionary. In fact, a number

Collapse of a car. This 1905 Gordon Bennett Napier had a long and glorious career until 12 August 1933, when it lost a wheel and was damaged beyond repair. The occupants received only minor injuries.

A 1908 G. P. Austin. It had a 9,677 c.c., six cylinder, 100 H.P. engine with h.t. magneto and 4 speeds.

Make a law and someone will find a way round it! When the regulations limited the bore to 80 mm, manufacturers increased the stroke to exaggerated lengths. One result was this 1910 racing Peugeot.

of people had no faith in removable wheels and considered them very dangerous.

Changing a tyre

The most frequent repair, which the regulations required should be done only by the driver and mechanic, was changing the tyres. This was always a performance against time. First the remnants of the old tyre had to be removed from the rim — often a knife was necessary — and the new tyre had to be fitted with safety bolts. This often caused difficulties, then followed the inflation of the tyres; and finally an 18-litre engine had to be started by hand! When it is remembered that this process might be necessary ten or twelve times (in that first Grand Prix Rougier took the record with fourteen changes) some idea can be obtained of the efforts required from the competitors.

At the start, at 6 a.m., the race was led by Gabriel in a Lorraine-Dietrich followed by Lancia and Nazzaro in Fiats, Szisz in a Renault and Héméry in a Darracq. The first part of the race was marked by the high speeds of the three Brasiers driven by Barillier, Baras and Pierry (Baras did the first lap at 75 m.p.h.) but they began to have mechanical troubles at the beginning of the second lap and quickly disappeared from the scene.

Nazzaro in the Fiat did the second lap at 80 m.p.h. but then he had to stop and Szisz in a Renault went into first place, which he held for the rest of the day, covering the course in 5 hours, 45 minutes and 30 seconds at an average of just over 65 m.p.h. He was followed by a Clément-Bayard, Nazzaro in a Fiat and Shepard in a Hotchkiss.

On the second day the duel between Szisz and Nazzaro began at once, and the whole of that day's race consisted of a vain attempt by the Italian driver to overtake the leader. At the finish less than a minute separated the two machines and the Renault was given a winning total time of 12 hours, fourteen minutes and 7 seconds at an average of just over 63 m.p.h.

The blinding tar

Photographs of the race show another torture undergone by the drivers, blinding by hot liquid tar thrown up by the wheels on those two extremely hot days. Szisz had actually to be led by the hand at the finish to the prize-giving with his eyes covered.

It is a curious fact that the second French Grand Prix

You can never be too careful. This 1910 Wolseley seen in a veteran race is equipped with a modern fire extinguisher.

In 1912 Leslie Howard built two prototype "people's cars" One of these still exists, shown here. it has a 4 cylinder 1,253 c.c., 10 H.P. engine, with two epicyclic gears and h.t. magneto.

Foreign influence. This 1904 Brusch, made in England, was built to American ideas as its single cylinder engine and desmodromic valve gear show

had the positions of the leader and runner-up reversed, Nazzaro winning in a 16-litre Fiat with Szisz, still faithful to Renault, coming in second. Fiat attached a growing importance to racing in those years, having prepared three prototypes for the major races of 1907. The lawyer Carlo Cavalli, who despite his profession was the designer of all racing cars for Fiat at that time, had designed for this Grand Prix the 130 H.P.

A Fiat 130 H.P. prototype prepared for the 1907 French Grand Prix.

monster which could reach 100 m.p.h. at 1,600 r.p.m. The choice of this car was due to the new regulations for the 1907 race. In addition to the weight limit, fuel consumption could not to exceed 30 litres every 100 kilometres (about 9 m.p.g.) and the drivers had to do 10 laps of a 47-mile circuit without an interruption, the two-day formula having been abandoned. Cars were to start at one-minute intervals.

High bonnets

The first to start was Vincenzo Lancia, who at once went into the lead and stayed there for most of the race. On the last lap clutch trouble caused him to lose some minutes and cost him the race. The race was won by Nazzaro who, following his usual practice, had started cautiously, partly to save petrol in view of the regulation, then becoming faster and faster to a final lap at almost 75 m.p.h. After Nazzaro had won, at an average of about 71 m.p.h., his petrol consumption was found to be 3 gallons less than the limit required, which is another indication of the driver's prudence. The Grand Prix was the third of Fiat's great victories in 1907, having been preceded by the second Targa Florio and the Emperor's Cup.

Henry Cissac's Panhard-Levassor before the start of the race in which he was killed. Below the French Grand Prix driver Szisz is escorted from his car with his face burned by the hot tar on the course.

Renault's gas turbine car, the "Etoile filante".

TURBINES FOR THE FUTURE

Over the past 20 years, several important automotive concerns have built and tested gas-turbine cars or commercial vehicles, whilst in long-distance racing, as well as the land speed record, the turbine is already established as an effective prime mover.

The Rover Company made world news with JET 1, the first practicable turbo-car, in 1950. There was a notable Fiat turbine sports car in 1954 and Renault set new standards of performance with their Étoile Filante race car a few years later. Rover produced later versions of their car, which were driven by Prince Philip and Princess Margaret.

Test driving

Other manufacturers, including Leyland in the commercial field and Austin with both cars and lorries, have developed the gas turbine. The result is that it is now a production possibility, if not today at least in the reasonably near future.

Wide research has been carried out by Ford and Chrysler, as well as General Motors. Ford and GM have been more interested in application to heavy vehicles but Chrysler have produced saloon cars with this type of engine. By 1964, in fact, Chrysler had made a pre-production run of 200 such cars, derived from an unusually handsome Ghia-styled prototype which has been demonstrated all over the world.

These cars were lent to 200 ordinary motorists who undertook to use them in certain conditions and to keep records on their working, defects, breakdowns etc.

More than 1000 drivers were in fact involved, because after 12,000 miles each car was passed to a new user. The basic principles of the gas turbine are very simple, though there are a number of possible ways of building such units in practice. The principal element is a kind of fly-wheel on the circumference of which is fixed a large number of vanes. A mixture of hot air and burning gas is directed on to this, causing the wheel to turn. In practice, the gas turbine is a much less simple affair and there are various types, provided with one or more compression stages or turbine wheels or combinations of these multiple units. In the most commonly adopted layout of such an engine for use on land the air is first compressed and then mixed with vaporised liquid fuel, which is ignited in a burner.

As the mixture issues at high velocity from the burner it strikes the blades of the twin turbines, of which the first stage serves to drive the auxiliaries and the second initiates movement of the transmission. There are also devices to make use of the high temperature of the exhaust gases, whereby a heat exchanger passes heat to the air as it is taken into the compressor. The exhaust gases themselves pass out through the exhaust cones.

Easier construction

The principal problems of a motor car or lorry turbine lie in the method of controlling the power developed, to produce acceleration or deceleration. In the Chrysler car a double system is used. The angle of incidence of the turbine blades to the income gases is variable, while

The experimental Rover "Jet 1" of 1950, the first gas turbine car.

Interior of the Chrysler gas turbine car.

it is also possible to vary the direction of entry of the gases. This system even enables the direction of rotation of the turbine wheel to be reversed, producing a deceleration or braking effect.

The advantages of the gas turbine for land use compared to a reciprocating i.c. engine lie in its lower weight and smaller engine, in the "cleanness" of its exhaust gases, its silence, and its greater simplicity for production as there are no valves or clutch and the electrical circuit is much simpler.

There are fewer moving parts (about one fifth of those of a i.c. engine) and there is no vibration, making the design inherently more durable. Moreover, the gas turbine has greater torque and crude fuels can be used. The principal obstacles concern the major technical problems involved. Temperatures of 2,200°C are reached in the burner and the turbine wheels revolve at around 50,000 r.p.m. Production costs are high, and other disadvantages include a flat power curve and lag in response in application of power.

The Fiat gas turbine car of 1954.

The winner of the second Targa Florio on the Madonie circuit on 21 April was the "20-B", the 28-40 H.P. which had a top speed of 60 m.p.h. This car was designed particularly for the "Targa" in view of the limits placed on cylinder bore by the race regulations. This led to long-stroke engines and very high bonnets to contain them, thus giving this type of car its distinctive appearance.

Vincenzo Florio had received forty entries for the race and among machines represented were Fiat, De Dietrich, Isotta-Fraschini, Clément-Bayard, Itala, Darracq, Gobron-Brillié Benz and Berliet. The list of drivers included Wagner, Hémery, Duray, Gabriel, Hanthiot, Opel, Sorel and Rigal — all famous at the time. Some of the cars had the new shaft drive, but it was generally considered less reliable than chain.

The race, which also adopted interval starts, was exciting from beginning to end. At the finish Duray led, followed by Lancia and Nazzaro, and the public acclaimed Duray as winner. Then it was announced that Felice Nazzaro had registered the shortest time to cover the 280-mile circuit, followed by Lancia 15 minutes behind, Fabbry 10 minutes later and Duray at 26 minutes. Nazzaro's average was just over 35 m.p.h. and Lancia did the fastest lap.

This second edition of the Targa Florio was driven in a "scientific" way by the leading drivers present. For example, Nazzaro showed 23 seconds difference in lap times and Lancia even fewer, 20 seconds. This may

A 1907 Hispano-Suiza, one of the first cars built by the company.

1907 "La Buire", particularly interesting for its six cylinder engine with twin carburettors. The model shown is a "double phaeton"

The winning Mercedes in the third French G. P. in 1908. Lautenschlager is changing a wheel.

A laden Daimler seen in the 1907 Herkomer Trophy.

1905. Siddeley 100 H.P.

serve to correct the impression of the latter as having been too impulsive and undisciplined as a driver.

Fiat and Nazzaro's third success in 1907 was in the "Kaiserpreis", the Emperor's Cup. The "Taunus", a 72 H.P. 8 litre (the maximum capacity allowed by the regulations) was used, which also conformed to the weight limit of 1,175 kgs. (about 2,585 lbs.).

The race was run less than two months after the Targa Florio on a circuit in the Taunus mountains in Germany, on roads very similar to those which had seen Théry win the fourth Gordon Bennett Cup in his Brasier. The organization of the race was carried out with a precision that was unusual for the time. For example, for 200 yards before every curve the tree trunks were painted white to a height of 6 feet and a series of white discs on the side of the road indicated dangerous inclines. The Emperor's Cup was held on 14 June in the presence of Kaiser Wilhelm II. There were 33 German, 20 French, 19 Italian, 10 Belgian, four English, three Swiss and two Austrian cars, representing practically every make of the times.

The large number of entrants at once gave rise to safety problems. It seemed unwise to allow so many competitors to race on such a twisting circuit, made even more

dangerous by two narrow sections. So it was decided to run two heats, the first 20 in each of which were to enter the final, consisting of four laps of the 75-mile circuit. The heats consisted of two laps only.

Nazzaro won heat and final — and the useful sum of 50,000 lire in special prizes.

Racetrack in the pines

The circuit of Le Mans, one of the first in Europe specially designed for car racing, was built in 1907. A little more than a year earlier, on our own side of the Channel, another track had been inaugurated, at Brooklands in Surrey. This had very different characteristics from Le Mans because it was intended for record attempts and out-and-out speed racing. It was to be one of the most important tracks in Europe up to the outbreak of the second World War.

The track was built in a forest of pine trees through which ran by the small river Wey and at first belonged to Napier, who intended to use it not only for testing the firm's six-cylinder prototypes but also for publicity by challenging competitor manufacturers. One of the

A line-up of Austins — from left to right 1911 17 H.P., 1908 100 H.P. "Grand Prix", 1936 "Twin Cam" 750 c.c., 1926 "Gordon England" and a 1931 "Swallow" 7.

Before the start of the 1960 Prescott Hill Climb — a 4 ½-litre Vinot-Deguingand and the 14.432 c.c. Itala, both built in 1908.

most famous of the challenges was that given by S. F. Edge, Napier's official driver, to Fiat.

Felice Nazzaro was chosen to defend Fiat's colour in the race, which took place on 8 June 1908.

He won in his "SB-4" (Mephistopheles) after a broken crankshaft had put the Napier out of the race. The "SB-4" had a 4 cylinder oversquare 18,146 c.c. engine

The "Blitzen Benz".

with bore and stroke of 190 mm. and 160 mm. — a rare formula for an engine of this size. It developed 175 H.P. at 1,200 r.p.m. and the car weighed 23½ cwts.

At Brooklands in June the previous year had already been sensational when Edge, in a six-cylinder Napier, set up a record by running for 24 hours at an average speed of 65 m.p.h. — over 1,500 miles covered in spite of 1 hour and 40 minutes spent in the pits changing tyres. The Press of the time showed imaginative illustrations of the great car hurtling through the night in its race against time, with the edge of the track picked out by torches.

After this successful attempt, for forty years Brooklands was host to outstanding motoring events. Here may be mentioned the flying kilometre of the Frenchman Goux in a Peugeot at a speed of 170.868 k.p.h. (nearly 106 m.p.h.) and the "one-hour" record set by Percy Lambert in a Talbot 4½-litre at almost 105 m.p.h. During the second World War, Brooklands was taken over for military use and was considerably damaged. Afterwards, for a number of reasons, it was unfortunately lost to motor racing, and today is the site of an aircraft factory although parts of the circuit can still be seen.

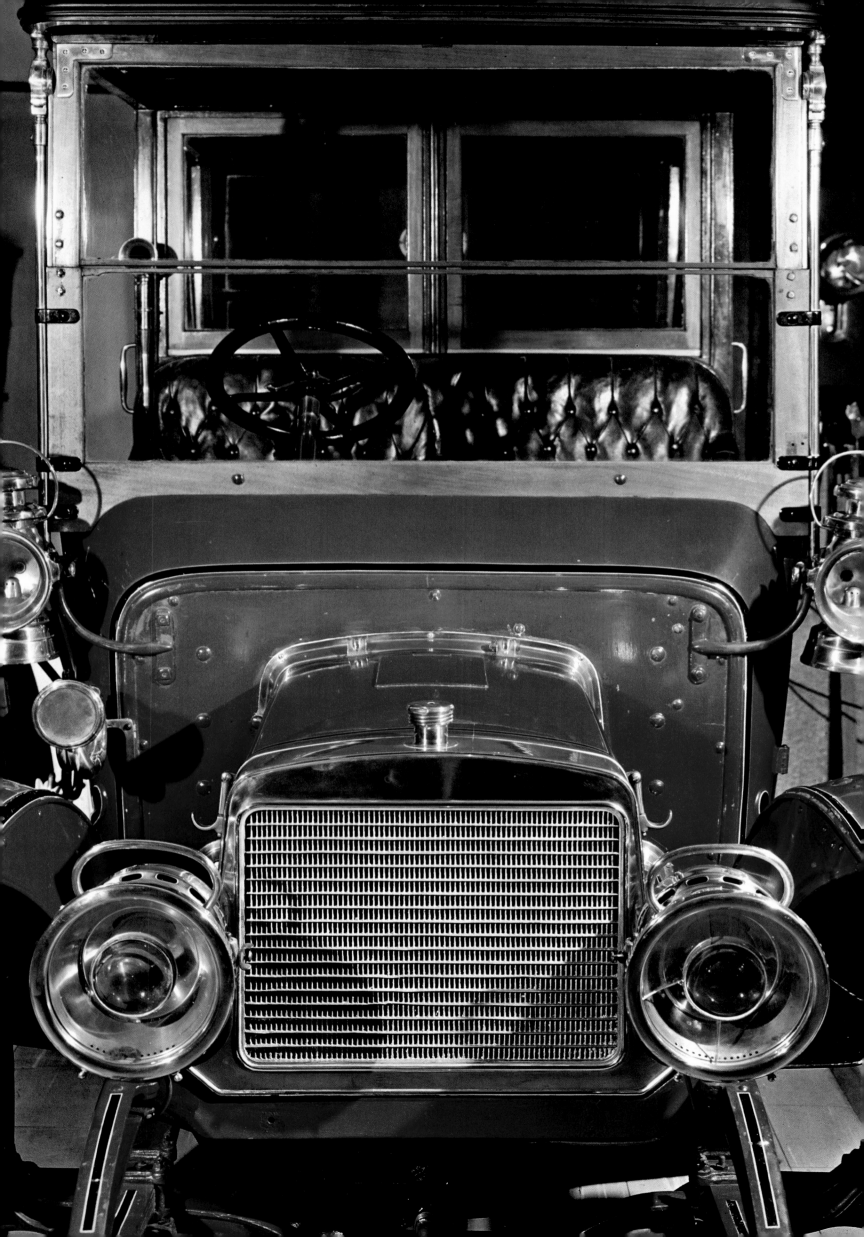

front view of 1912 ADLER "K 7/15 H.P."

engine - front mounted 4 in line
bore and stroke - 75 × 103 mm.
capacity - 1816 c.c.
output - 17 H.P. at 1400 r.p.m.
ignition - low tension magneto and battery
clutch - multiplate
gearchange - 3 speeds plus reverse
transmission - cardan shaft
weight - 2200 lb.

Six cylinder engines began to built around 1908. The fact that the four cylinder is more common in Europe is due to present and past fiscal measures. Above — the V6 cylinder Lancia "Flaminia". Below — the 8 cylinder Lancia "Dilambda Speciale".

CHAPTER FIFTEEN
COMFORT AND CONVENIENCE

The year 1907 was important for major sporting events. In another sphere of motoring, however, it was important as it marked the perfection of the "valveless" engine by the Wisconsin agriculturist Charles Knight. Its primary object was the elimination of valve gear, which was then very noisy partly owing to the considerable "play" between cams, tappets and valves, which the techniques of the times demanded to cope with expansion caused by heating.

After early studies that began in 1901, he built his first experimental engine with a friend, L. B. Kilbourne. It had a somewhat rudimentary system of letting in the mixture and letting out the exhaust gases by alternately raising and lowering the cylinder itself, and in so doing uncovering inlet and outlet ports. The device was over-complicated and Knight devised an improved system. His first production engine saw the light of day in 1907.

In this engine a sleeve was introduced between piston and cylinder. The sleeve was windowed and it reciprocated in such a way as to cover and uncover inlet and outlet ports. The first of these sleeve-valve engines was fitted in a Panhard imported into the United States,

and performed well both from the points of view of silence and of general performance.

In 1908 Knight and the English Daimler Company made an agreement whereby the more luxurious Daimlers would be fitted with sleeve-valve engines. The finest

King George V enters his impressive Daimler in 1910.

example of this collaboration, which was to last for many years, was the Daimler Double-Six V12 of 1926. This car had a seven-litre sleeve valve engine, and the Royal cars were converted to take the new engine, although the King bought five new Double Sixes in 1931.

Destroyed in practice

Not only Daimler, but many other European and American makes adopted the silent and flexible Knight engine, including Willys and Stearn in America, Panhard, Mors, Voisiny, Peugeot, Clément and Delaguère-Clayette in France and Minerva in Belgium.

The fashion of the non-poppet-valves engine, whose convenience was quickly appreciated (not so highly its performance, however) led to similar attempts by other designs, for example the Scots "Imperia" and the better known Itala, an Italian design.

Between 1911 and 1915 over 400 "valveless" engines were produced with outputs ranging from 25 to 50 H.P. Even a prototype racing car with this type of engine was built, but this car was destroyed in an accident in the 1913 Grand Prix practices at Dieppe.

If a motorist of the day had to have a car with poppet-

Even the dog takes part in the great day when the first car is delivered! A 1902 Brushmobile.

A 1913 Delahaye. 10-12 H.P. 1,953 c.c. four-cylinders, high-tension magneto. The body is made of wood.

A double sleeve valve Itala driven by Nazzaro in the 1913 French Grand Prix.

Two great pre-war cars. Above — the splendid 1907 6 cylinder, 7,046 c.c. 40/50 H.P. Rolls Royce "Silver Ghost". Below — the 1912 3,615 c.c., 15.9 H.P. Hispano-Suiza.

valves, the 6-cylinder engine was always smoother than a twin or four. The enormous popularity of this type of engine around 1908-1910, and the large number built, can only partly be explained by its undoubted technical advantages, such as increased silence and the sense of power which it has always given to drivers. It is probable that there was another psychological motive at work, this being related to the long aggressive bonnet which an in-line six imposed on the car. This led to modification of other elements in the coachwork and gave the cars of the period their distinctive styling. On the other hand the six-cylinder engine was far from perfect, suffering as it did from whip and torsional deformation in the crankshaft, which was too long and complicated for the production technology of the day. Among other multi-cylinder layouts were the V8 De Dion of 1910, which was produced only a few years after the abandonment of the single-cylinder formula to which De Dion had been faithful for so long; Winton's double-four engine; an overhead valve V12 by Marvel-Schebler in the United States; the narrow V8 of Delahaye and the V4's built between 1910 and 1916 by Aries in France and Buick in America. These engines never went into quantity production, however, as they were ahead of the mass manufacturing techniques available at the time.

Keeping windscreen clean

About 1910 the motor car began to acquire a number of accessories which were of secondary importance but which were essential to its efficiency and comfort. First there was the windscreen wiper which, when it arrived, made obsolete all the complicated arrangements for maintaining some visibility in case of rain.

In America the bumper began to appear, born of the necessity of protecting the car as more and more vehicles used the roads. In Europe it was not adopted until later, because the need was hardly so acute. "Safety" glass was also introduced at this time; it was a type which consisted of glass and Celluloid.

Unfortunately it was considered a mere luxury for a long time, and as such was reserved for the more expensive cars. It was not until the late 30's that its fitting became generally obligatory, and then only for the front screen.

At the end of the first decade of the century great strides were made in carburation, a constant problem for engine designers and not only in that era. In this period around 1909 it was appreciated that the carburettor had to be cured of its many weaknesses; it caused many stoppages and required too much maintenance. The necessity for frequent blowing through

In 1909 Sizaire et Naudin were still building single cylinder engines. This was a 1½ litre.

225

Lanchester with a 2,470 c.c., four-cylinder engine, three epicyclic gears, footbrake operating on the rear wheels and hand-brake by disc also on the rear wheels.

Vauxhalls in the 1914 Isle of Man T.T.

the jets and continual cleaning of the bowl was sometimes due of course, to the problems of preventing the contamination of the fuel by dirt and dust.

Important progress was made, however, by two French industrialists, Maurice Goudard and Marcel Mennesson. In 1910 they decided to devote themselves to the design and production of more advanced types of carburettor to replace the primitive devices manufacturers still usually fitted in the most inaccessible place possible. The name of their product, Solex, was decided upon after a competition, and appears to have no particular meaning.

The success of the new company was assured from the start and about the same time a second major manufacturer of carburettors was born, the British concern, Zenith. These two have remained among the largest producers ever since.

The difficult problem of four-wheel braking was also nearing solution at this time by modification of existing systems. In theory, the need for braking all four (or three) wheels had been known from the beginning of the century, but it had been held to be impossible to brake the front wheels efficiently in practice because of their steering requirements. The difficulty was not in transmitting braking force to the wheels, but rather in ensuring that this force did not change the position of the wheels, cancelling out the efficiency of the brakes and creating new dangers.

Braking difficulties

The problem consisted of the need — as can easily be seen today in the light of experience — to design steering geometry which was mechanically effective and able to keep the effects of steering and braking separate. This goal was finally achieved in practical and effective form by a Scotsman, Henry Perrot, though many before him, including Maybach, had tried and failed. Perrot helped to design the first car with four-wheel brakes which were considered safe; they were produced by the company for which he worked, Argyll.

The adoption of four-wheel brakes was extraordinarily slow, nevertheless, in part due to the prejudices of manufacturers, and in part due to fear of their customers' attitudes. These early motorists feared front-wheel skids. Progress in pneumatic tyre design was also slow. Their performance had been adequate for years apart from two major defects — their short life and the frequency with which they punctured. Before the first World War they had an average life of less than 2,000 miles. Improvements made by the use of new materials and

A 1909 Bianchi 20 - 30 H.P.

better construction of the cover of the tyre were only to come later.

On the other hand, progress in meeting the consequences of punctures was made at this time by the general adoption of inter-changeable rims, fixed to the wheel by a number of bolts (it has been recorded how the 1906 Grand Prix was decided by the use of such a device for the first time by the winning Renault).

A most important step forward, when the whole wheel became removable, was due mainly to the British manufacturers Sankey and Rudge-Whitworth. It was due to Michelin, in the years immediately following, that the first wheels were produced in pressed steel.

1911 Bedelia 8 H.P. with front mounted V twin engine. Bore and Stroke 82 × 100 mm. Capacity 1,056 c.c. Ignition by h.t. magneto. 2 speeds, no reverse. Belt drive. Weight — 4621 lb.

Leather face mask, goggles and gauntlets —almost a return to the middle ages. Danny Druce at the wheel of "Mooneyes".

HOT-ROD RODEOS

There is perhaps more than an ocean between Europe and America from the point of view of motoring competition. The differences are well known not only so far as the kinds of cars, tracks and racing regulations are concerned, but also in the attitude of the public. This does not mean, of course, that there can be no point of contact between these two worlds or that drivers cannot take part in races on the other side. Indeed, there has been a considerable increase in such activity in recent years with European drivers and cars at classic U. S. events and American drivers in Europe.

Little resemblance

There is, however, one type of motoring competition which has only recently begun to be popular in Europe — "hotrodding".
Hotrodding — it is the official, if somewhat illogical, term — describes acceleration races through one quarter of a mile from a standing start. For this purpose specially developed vehicles are used which bear little resemblance to any other form of land vehicle.
Hotrodding should not be considered the prerogative

of a small group of rich devotees in the U. S. On the contrary, it is practised by tens of thousands of people, mostly young.
They work rigidly within the regulations of their appropriate federation, the National Hot Rod Association. These regulations have 72 different sub-classes of vehicle according to capacity and weight, and are grouped together in eight major categories, as follows:
Stock cars, which are derived from standard cars and to which only certain limited modifications may be made to increase safety. By accurate tuning they can have considerable acceleration. Stock cars are the only ones in the Association which run distance races on the trace.
Road cars, which are production vehicles considerably modified for sprints but still legally capable of road use. There are three categories of these.
"Moderate" competition cars, which are again derived from production cars but to which modifications are not limited by the need to keep them legally suitable for road use.
Competition cars, similar to the above but even more highly modified.
Experimental cars, or prototypes.
European-type sports cars.

American Mickey Thompson, dragster champion, in action behind his car's smoke screen. Its engine develops 1,000 H.P.

The principal modifications made to a standard production car consist of chopping and channelling, or of lowering the roof and the interior of the car until it almost touches the ground.

In addition to these eight categories which still preserve some resemblance to motor cars, there are two other categories: the "dragsters" and the "fuel dragsters".

These are vehicles built exclusively for quarter of a mile acceleration competition. They are of distinctive appearance, with two light small wheels in front, two very large wide ones at the rear and often a parachute for braking. Everything that is inessential for acceleration is eliminated or reduced to the minimum. The chassis consists or two simple tubes; front suspension is rudimentary and rear suspension does not exist. There are brakes only at the rear. The driver is cantilevered out behind the rear axle.

Although great liberty is given to dragster builders — who are often the drivers themselves — the vehicles still have to conform with certain requirements as to weight, wheel base and track.

A typical "Hot Rod".

Special tracks

The "fuel dragsters" are a special category, the most esoteric of all. Any sort of fuel is permissible in these machines. These vehicles use fuels such as nitro-methane, and are always liable to explode. The engines are usually uncooled and sometimes without lubricant, to reduce loss of power to the minimum. Engines are switched off as soon as possible.

Hot rod competitions take place on special tracks all over the United States. The most important are at Daytona and Bonneville Salt Flats, where even the back-room boys of big companies go, often finding something interesting among the bright ideas of the builders.

The vehicles run in pairs, with the front-wheels lifting sometimes as much as two feet amidst clouds of smoke from the rear, caused by slip between tyres and the surface.

The skill of the driver in getting full power from the engine and using it immediately at full power is best exhibited by the way he controls the wheel spin to achieve maximum adherence.

Young people who take up hotrodding and drag racing in America work miracles of improvisation, often picking up parts cheaply from motor junk yards.

The races themselves present a scene typical of modern American entertainment. With their profusion of bright colours, publicity, designs and symbols of every type they are the rodeos of the present-day mechanical age.

From zero to 190 m.p.h. in eight seconds! Tony Nancy's dragster takes off. Below the same vehicle brakes by parachute.

The Mercedes team cars in the 1914 French Grand Prix. Lautenschlager drove the car on the right and Salzer the car on the left. Below a 1912 French 6 cylinder — the 35 H.P. Renault.

In the period 1910 to 1914, vital years in the evolution of the motor car, the first attempts were made to solve suspension problems. Here, too, there had been earlier efforts but it was only in 1912 and 1913 that hydraulic shock absorbers went into general production.

Yet another change directed towards better road-holding and stability on poor road surfaces was made by lowering of the centre of gravity. Before this was to become general, some years had to pass. But there were some interesting solutions before the first World War by "underslinging" the chassis, or making it pass under the axle. The more prominent companies in this field were Stabilia in France and Underslung in America.

Back to open-top

The question of bodywork of the car at the end of the decade, however, moved in what seems an absurd direction — back to the open car. After dominating early motoring at the time when it was the hobby of the wealthy enthusiast, the open-top had been replaced by the closed "carriage" as the car came into common use. Though such closed bodywork was not to disappear completely, there was a marked return to popularity of the open car, mainly due to the well-publicised sporting successes of the goggled and heavily accoutred racing drivers between 1905 and 1910.

Aerodynamic styling, child of the new and rapidly developing field of aeroplane design, began to influence the motor car. It influenced the design of the "torpedoes", open cars which were relatively long and low and whose name gives an idea of explosive power. This picture of the 1910-1914 motor car would not be complete without acknowledging the work of the coachbuilder. The car manufacturer himself frequently supplied only the chassis, and the client selected the type of body he wanted and arranged with the coachbuilder to make it.

In practice, the waiting time for chassis meant that details were settled with the coachbuilder before his small army of highly skilled specialists could start work. This included, of course, the details of design and shape of the body and also the choice of metals, leather, fittings and colours.

Skilled craftsmen

Timber, too, played an important part in the interior of the car, in the widest variety of types from walnut to maple, from mahogany to elm, from beech to oak. The care with which this wood was selected and its seasoning carried out is shown by the perfect condition of the wood-work of many of these veteran cars existing today.

After a long period with the expert joiners and leather workers, the body passed to the skilled metal workers, who carefully built up the panelling, including external bolts and rivets, which were often plated or polished.

All the vast number of fittings were mounted by hand, including the lamp brackets, windscreen, toolbox, running boards and spare wheel supports. Nothing was hurried and craftsmanship was all-important. Finally the whole went for painting; perhaps as many as 16 coats were applied by hand in colours chosen after long discussion with the client.

One last visit to the lighting specialist, whose products of gleaming brass and crystal gave the finishing touch, and the car was on its way to the customer. The bill would be extremely high, as was inevitable for work which had occupied a number of specialists for weeks. But the "belle époque" of the motor car was drawing to a close. On the other side of the Atlantic, mass production was an accomplished fact. Ford had made gigantic strides in this respect and had provided the opportunity for thousands of Americans to own their first car.

In Europe, quantity production was at the half-way stage. Already some manufacturers were producing some part of their production by large-scale methods, fitting standard bodies and supplying a complete machine. About this time a new sort of car was born which was to have a short life. This was the cyclecar. The manu-

A Nazzaro "Type 3" of 1914.

The 1908 Austin 100 H.P. derived from the famous "Grand Prix". It had a six cylinder 9670 c.c. engine with h.t. magneto ignition.

facture of light vehicles was not new to Europe, races for such touring cars often being run before those for their more powerful and heavier sisters. The reasons for the development of the cyclecar were, however, very different from those that led to the voiturette.

In addition to a substantial increase in the price of petrol, new taxes and fiscal charges in many countries were an incentive for manufacturers to produce vehicles less expensive to run. There were still thousands of potential motorists in Europe who could not afford even

A German production car. The 4-8 H.P. Opel "Doktorwagen" of 1908.

A 1902 Cadillac model "P" with single-cylinder engine. Its catalogue advertised, "Price of the runabout 850 dollars. Extra for brass lamps, horn and the picnic basket".

the cheapest product of the day, and a substantial drop in price would open up a new market for the manufacturer who could cut prices and yet still produce an acceptable motor car. This was a factor which Ford already appreciated and which Herbert Austin and others were to exploit.

Cyclecar prospers

The manufacture of cyclecars mushroomed throughout Europe in the years immediately before the first World War mainly because the motor car had reached the state of development similar to that of the electric car in the 1880's. As in the period three decades earlier, the basic problems had been solved and components such as engines, transmission and running gear were now universally available to the chassis builder.

Most cyclecars were built by people with little experience of car design or manufacture. Generally, they were simple, crude, uncomfortable and probably dangerous.

The engine was usually that of a motorbicycle of about one-litre capacity, and air-cooled. Transmission was by chain or even belt. Bodywork was reduced to the minimum of steel sheet, rather like a bath, into which were fitted two crude seats; often one was placed behind the other with the driver in the rear. Braking was often inadequate even for such light vehicles. Reverse gear and clutch were non-existent, and steering layout had much in common with a child's pedal car.

These vehicles were not to be produced for long, though there was to be a brief second wave of popularity after the first World War, this time in America as well as in Europe.

Unlike the light, simple, "real" motor cars which existed alongside them, cyclecars had negligible performance. In their favour was one psychological factor. They introduced the possibility of a self-propelled vehicle to many people who otherwise would have been excluded from motoring. Thus they helped to create the conditions which enabled Austin, Morris and others to offer a satisfactory solution to the problem.

1905 Benz "Tourenwagen" 40 H.P.

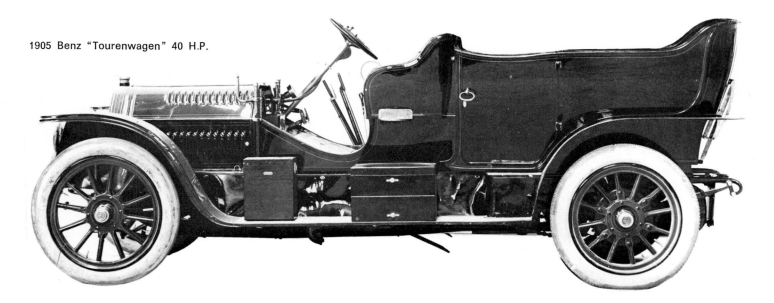

RUDOLF DIESEL - TRAGIC GENIUS

Tragedy on the classic scale marked the life of Rudolf Diesel, whose invention has had such an effect on transport. His childhood and youth were difficult. At the time of Rudolf's birth in 1858 his father, who was of German origin but living in Paris, was extremely poor. Twelve years later he moved with his family to London when the Franco-Prussian war made life impossible for them in the French capital.

Rudolf himself was solitary and taciturn but quickly showed his interest in mechanical things, spending long hours wrestling with theoretical problems.

After the family returned to France, Rudolf attended the Conservatoire des Arts et Métiers and began to study what was to become one of his specialities, refrigeration. A little later, when he was just 20 years old, he published his first paper on the internal combustion engine.

In subsequent years he was to pursue in parallel his studies in these two fields, the former under the guidance of Professor Linde in Berlin, to which he had moved, and the latter on his own account.

In the field of the i.c. engine he turned his back on the direction others were taking — most studies of the time were concerned with gas engines — and devoted his time to an engine powered by ammonia gas, a project on which he wasted much time and money.

At last, however, he got on the right lines and began a series of experiments to perfect an engine in which the mixture of air and fuel was exploded not by a spark or other outside means, but by the extreme heat produced by very high compression.

The first engine of this type — it was patented in 1892 — used coal dust blown into the combustion chamber. It was extremely temperamental, but the first step had been taken, though his adversaries duly claimed that a compression ignition engine was impossible.

Backers enthusiastic

Later experiments with other hydrocarbons, particularly diesel oil (as it is now known) and petrol, were much more successful. As a result the powerful Krupps-Essen and MAN group got in touch with Diesel and entered into an arrangement with him. The consequence was the birth of the first true "diesel" engine, in the sense we know it today, in 1893.

Many technical problems had been overcome, but many remained. Diesel's backers were prepared to continue however, encouraged mainly by the low fuel consumption of the new engine, which proved to be about half that of the petrol engines of the time.

Fortune began to smile on Rudolf Diesel as his engines became more and more widely used for heavy industrial purposes and for marine and stationary uses. He crossed the Atlantic to market his invention in the United States and quickly became wealthy.

With the money he began to speculate on the stock exchange, particularly in petrol shares, and he even tried to set himself up in competition with Rockefeller himself.

Disappears overboard

Then his marvellous intellect began to fail. This at first showed itself in excessive optimism and delusions of grandeur, which led him to be put under medical care. His business affairs were neglected and started to go badly; his mental state deteriorated.

He disappeared from the ship "Dresden" as he was crossing the Channel from Antwerp to Harwich on the night of 29-30 September, 1913. This inevitably gave rise to rumours of commercial espionage and even of the murder having been committed through competitors. It is more likely, however, that the great inventor, much envied and renowned though he was, could no longer live a life in which bitterness and disappointment finally destroyed him.

front view of a 1913 LE ZEBRE

engine · front mounted vertical single cylinder
gearchange · 3 speeds plus reverse
speed · 22 m.p.h.
body · 2 seater phaeton

The Opel Kadett coupé L., designed to satisfy "sporty" tastes with the comfort of a saloon, which the Opel "Puppchen" 4 - 8 H.P. of 1913, below, was also intended to achieve. The "Puppchen" had a four-cylinder engine and could reach 40 m.p.h.

CHAPTER SIXTEEN
HAND PUMPS AND PUNCTURES

The beginning of the second decade of the century experienced one of those pauses in motoring which was to occur from time to time, and there was a general decline in racing interest.

This decline of interest is most clearly exhibited by the fact that the most important European motor race, the French Grand Prix, was suspended from 1909 to 1911.

The reasons were complex in nature: economic, political and perhaps of habit.

Racing magic fades

The car had lost the "magic" of its pioneering years without having gained the enthusiasm of mass participation. Some historians see the drop in popularity as being due in part to the growing interest in aviation, which was competing for public attention, though this is unlikely to have had a major effect.

The pause was not to last for long and interest was to revive before the outbreak of the war.

The French Grand Prix of 1908 was again held on the Dieppe circuit, but it was run to a new formula. Instead of being based on fuel consumption, it demanded that bore be limited to 155 mm. for four cylinder machines

and to 127 mm. for six cylinders. This dubious restriction — which was to be imitated in other races, as indeed it had already been anticipated — was the cause of the "monsters" with an exaggerated long stroke. This led to very high bonnets.

This elongation of the stroke brought about by the "stroke formula" was not, however, the only technical innovation in the race. With increasing engine speeds, lubrication was becoming a more acute problem and

Theodore Roosevelt, back left in the picture, was the first president of the U.S. to use a car for official purposes. Olds is driving the car at Lansing in 1907.

many cars in the 1908 G. P. were equipped with large hand pumps, which the mechanic (who was still an obligatory member of the team) had to operate continuously throughout the race to maintain the supply of lubricant.

The race itself was interesting from another technical point of view, in that it was marked by an extraordinary number of punctures. Power and speeds had notably increased in the past few years but the pneumatic tyre had made little progress. Thus, as in an earlier period, the number of punctures became a deciding factor.

In the race eight French makes, three German (Mercedes, Benz and Opel), two Italian (Fiat and Itala), two English (Austin and Wiegel) and one Belgian (Gemiani) took part, while Napier were excluded because their cars had Rudge Whitworth centre-lock removable wheels which the organisers considered too dangerous. The American company, Thomas, was also represented. One of the French cars had an engine with one of the first overhead camshafts.

Careful tactics

Fiat's hopes of repeating the success of the previous year were dashed when first Lancia, then Wagner and Nazzaro were forced to make long pit stops due to mechanical trouble. The tyre disasters of the drivers soon began with the two Benz of Héméry and Hanriot, joined by Lautenschlager's Mercedes and Rigal's Clément. The punctures continued, and when Rigal had 19 (a record for the race) he retired!

At this point Lautenschlager, Mercedes' chief tester and an experienced racing driver who knew that there were

A 1907 American car — the Rambler "Model 24".

1909, the first Hudson.

no more spare tyres in the Mercedes' pit, began his very intelligent tactics. He accelerated down the straights but took corners gently, the point where most tyre wear occurred. His adversaries were not equally careful and Lautenschlager won by a large margin at the high average speed of 73 m.p.h. Second and third were the Benz of Hémery and Hanriot.

The victory at Dieppe was a triumph for the "120 H.P." Mercedes, designed by Paul Daimler, Gottlieb's son. The engine was a four-cylinder in-line with bore and stroke of 155 mm. × 170 mm. giving 12,781 c.c.s. For the first time the Grand Prix itself had been preceded, on the previous day, by a race for voiturettes, light touring cars.

Long-stroke engines

This represented official approval of a type of competition that had been popular for some years, as the kind of cars which took part were near enough standard production machines. This type of race had begun in 1905 when the French paper "L'Auto", aware of the tremendous publicity value of the great capital-to-capital races, had decided to organise a race for cars weighing less than 700 kgs. (1,540 lbs).

The race, called the "Coupe des Voiturettes" was run in 1906 and won by a single cylinder Sizaire-Naudin. It was the first occasion on which the "stroke" formula was used (90 mm. for two cylinder cars and 106 mm. for single) and, as with the larger cars, it led to the use of a large number of long-stroke engines. Among the

The fearsome front of a 1907 Darracq, with Morgan body.

many manufacturers to adopt this formula between 1905 and 1910 were Hispano-Suiza, Delage, Lion-Peugeot and Isotta Fraschini.

In 1908, the touring car race at Dieppe was won by Guyot in an interesting Delage with a single-cylinder engine of 100 mm. × 150 mm. bore and stroke with four sparking plugs and a double flywheel. This singular vehicle had been designed by the young Louis Delage, who had once worked with Peugeot, and an ex-school friend, Némorin Causin. This led to an association between Delage and Clément and was excellent publicity for Delage, who was to have great success in the future, beginning with the period 1910 to 1913 when nine series of his famous "AB 8" were produced.

Source of ideas

Another interesting touring car present at Dieppe in 1908 was the Ariès with four valves per cylinder with desmodromic actuation. For many years these races were a fountain of ideas, not all successful inevitably, but the source of many major and minor improvements.

The Cadillac factory in 1912.

In the subsequent story of the touring car, or voiturette, the 1910 two-cylinder Peugeot should be mentioned. In this car the long-stroke design went to unprecedented exaggeration — 80 mm. × 280 mm. As time went on, four-cylinder engines became more and usual and a new name was to be found among the manufacturers, that of Bugatti, who had set up his own factory at Molsheim in 1908.

The Grand Prix was not run in 1909 because of the lack of entries, 40 being the minimum number required by the Automobile Club de France. To this was added the serious problem of the exceptionally high cost of preparing a large-engined racing prototype, which already bore little or no resemblance to the ordinary production car. The touring car race proved to be much more useful to the manufacturer, as did a third kind of race which quickly became popular, especially in Germany — road racing.

Road races were run between 1905 and 1911, and this period may be considered in two parts — 1905 to 1907, which included three editions of the Herkomer Cup, and 1908 to 1911. In these latter years four editions of the race were run named after Prince Henry of Prus-

1913 Zebre phaeton has two seats and a single cylinder engine. Top speed — 22 m.p.h. Below a 1912 Delage.

sia, brother of Wilhelm II and a keen motorist, who took part himself in the last. This race, incidentally had no individual classification. The famous Vauxhall sports car took its name from these races.

The races were held over ordinary roads in Germany and Austro-Hungary (in 1911 they were extended to England and Scotland) over a distance of 1,200 to 1,500 miles and lasting a week. Two distinct categories were envisaged for racing cars and touring cars respectively, but the latter were more important. As the series of Prince Henry Cup races went on more and more regulations were made to ensure that the cars were close to normal touring models. Thus coachwork had to be painted and the body had to weigh at least 15 per cent of the total. Many famous owners took part in these races, and the winner of the 1910 race was Ferdinand Porsche in an Austro-Daimler of his own design.

Different formula

The first "post crisis" edition of the French Grand Prix was held in 1912, although there had been a rather poor affair the previous year at Le Mans, when there had been a separate race for the first time for cyclecars. The 1912 race was run to a formula very different from its predecessors. It was run over two days, with a break, for a total of 1,540 kilometres (960 miles), again on

A 1913 two-seater Clément-Bayard tourer, having three speeds and gear change on the steering column. Solex carburettor.

the Dieppe circuit. Forty-seven cars were entered, of which five had the very large engines of previous years while 42 fitted much smaller ones. All these cars raced in one class, however, as there were no regulations except the width of the bodywork.

It was clear from the start that there was going to be a fight between the 14-litre "old-fashioned" Fiats and the "small" 7.6 litre Peugeots. In fact, the race was to be a battle between brute force and advanced design. The Fiats were driven by Bruce Brown, an American, and De Palma, an Italian-American, and Wagner. The Peugeots had relatively high revving engines (2,200 r.p.m.) and interesting cylinder head design with twin overhead camshafts and four valves per cylinder. At

first the Fiats had the advantage, but then both Bruce Brown and De Palma were disqualified for irregularities and the race was between Wagner and Boillot, the leading Peugeot driver.

The Peugeot won and it marked not only a worthy sporting achievement but also the victory of brains over brawn, of technical skill over capacity. Another significant result was the position of three of the four Sunbeams which came in third, fourth and fifth after Wagner, a compact group of cars of only three litres! These performances marked the end of the exaggerated monsters and brought Grand Prix racing back to rational limits.

For the 1913 Grand Prix a new venue was chosen, the

1908 French G. P. The Clément-Bayard team lined up on the track, all "135 H.P.s" driven by (L to R) Rigal, Gabriel and Hautvast.

20-mile Picardy circuit, a group of roads near Amiens including an eight-mile narrow straight. For the racing car category (there were also races for cyclecars, and motorbikes and sidecars) 29 circuits for a total of 580 miles were envisaged. This time there was a new formula with two main requirements — fuel consumption not to exceed 20 litres per 100 kms. (13 m.p.g.) and weight to be between 800 and 1,100 kgs. (1,760 to 2420 lbs.). At this race, too, Peugeot appeared with cars capable of embarrassing all their opponents. These were versions of the previous year's cars but with cylinder capacity reduced to 5,650 c.c. Delage had an unusual car with horizontal overhead valves which led to exhaust pipes higher than the bonnet, and there were sleeve-valve Italas.

Into the canal

The race quickly turned into a battle between Peugeot, Delage and the Sunbeam team whose cars were, as usual, beautifully prepared. These Sunbeams all had six cylinders. An unusual accident to Guyot's mechanic occurred when he was run over by their own Delage, having jumped out too soon at a refuelling stop. This left the Peugeots dominant. Boillot and Goux finished in that order at 72 m.p.h., having consumed petrol at the rate of about 16 m.p.g. Lee Guinness, one of the Sunbeam drivers, ended up in one of the canals which ran parallel to the road.

Perhaps even more interesting than Boillot's victory was the performance of another Peugeot, a new three-litre designed by the Swiss engineer, Henry, which could

reach about 105 m.p.h., thus being capable of beating machines two and three times its capacity. Henry was to have a major influence on engine design up to the early 20's.

The last pre-war Grand Prix in 1914 was also one of the most spectacular. The public was to see on this occasion the battle between a famous and idolized driver and a team working together to a perfectly prepared plan. It is probably not coincidence that the former was French and the latter German.

The man was Boillot, winner of the two previous Grand Prix, and the team was Mercedes, organized to the point

K. Lee Guiness at the wheel of the Sunbeam which won the 1914 Isle of Man T. T.

Still at Dieppe in 1908. The Renault team of 100 H.P.s with Szisz, Caillois and Dimitri (L to R).

Louis Boillot comes out of a bend in the 1913 French Grand Prix.

that it was later referred to as "track militarism" (it should not be forgotten that the Great War was about to begin and there were political undertones to everything,. including the race itself).

Neither the public not the competitors were apparently conscious before the race began of such implications even though there were signs of nerves among the French teams on the eve of the race, with Delage changing first his carburettors, then the system of valve mechanism on his cars, and Peugeot changed his tyres.

Although up to the last moment there was little to indicate the relative potential of the competitors — 34 out of 37 entries were built to the same formula of four cylinders with overhead camshafts — shortly after the race began on the triangular circuit at Giver, near Lyons, it resolved itself into a battle between two makes. Quickly the Delage and Sunbeam entries proved to be not a threat and the battle was between Mercedes and Peugeot. The first move was made by the Mercedes driver, Sailer, who had agreed with his team to be the "hare".

German supremacy

He set off as fast as he could go, using all the capabilities of his car and forcing Boillot to chase after him. In the meantime, the other three Mercedes drivers, Lautenschlager, Wagner and Salzer, kept a distance behind, making certain they did not lose their key positions but also not forcing their cars. On the sixth lap Sailer, as might have been expected, dropped out with a con-rod through the cylinder — but his effort had not been in vain. Boillot went into the lead to the delirious enthusiasm of the crowd, but his machine had been over-stressed in the early part of the race and as his three pursuers gradually increased their pace he began to lose ground.

On the 18th lap Lautenschlager took the lead and on the last lap Boillot's engine, by now running on three cylinders only, broke a valve and dropped out of the race. Boillot was in tears.

Lautenschlager's clear-cut victory at 65 m.p.h. was the first episode of a German supremacy in motor racing which in another period, in the 1930's was to be for a time absolute. This race also saw the first, unsuccessful, appearance of a car which was to have great success after the war. This was the Fiat "S 57/14 B", a four-cylinder 4,492 car with three valves per cylinder and 135 H.P. output, which was capable of over 90 m.p.h.

Change of circuit

Though the Grand Prix de France was the peak of motor racing in Europe before the first World War, it was obviously not the only race. Among the lesser races in Europe, at first run to widely different formulae but

These three cars were photographed in the 1964 Prescott hill climb. From top to bottom, 1913 Lanchester, 1914 T.T. Sunbeam and a 1913 Argyll.

BOTTLED GAS TO PUSH BUTTON

SCAT claimed that their cars were the only ones in Italy with "automatic starting".

If the complete structure of the motor car has undergone a fantastic and gratifying change over the effective 70 years of its existence, so has each of its component parts.

It would be possible to write a long story about every such component, but it is the intention here to comment on the development of electric starting, since its consequences were so significant. For instance, it is not too much to say that it made motoring practicable for women, who before this might have made occasional appearances at the driving wheel. But they would always have to be accompanied by a willing and probably muscular male ever ready to prostrate himself with exhaustion in his efforts to get the machine started or re-started.

One can hardly blame the ladies, since to use a starting handle was a matter requiring great strength and often courage, since there was the possibility of a broken wrist or slipped disc.

It is impossible to state the exact date of the introduction of electric starting. In fact, the early histories of most motor car accessories and components are somewhat confused and inadequate, whilst many of the early cars which have survived and which are equipped with such a device probably had it added years after the date of chassis manufacture.

One fairly reasonable theory gives credit to an American inventor, Charles Kettering who, in 1911, had an electric starter, which he had designed himself, fitted to his Cadillac.

Compressed gas or air

What is certain, however, is that the electric starter was generally accepted only after many European and transatlantic manufacturers had tried numerous other methods of solving the problem of non-manual starting.

One of the many methods involved a device which temporarily connected the combustion chamber of a cylinder to a compressed gas bottle, the pressure from which forced down the piston and caused the crankshaft to turn. The complications of such a system were many and explain the wide variety of solutions.

If exhaust gases were used to charge the bottle (a solution that was relatively simple from a manufacturing point of view) it created a dangerous and evil-smelling source of poisonous gas. If compressed air were used, both a compressor and a reservoir were necessary.

Safety device

Furthermore, if the engine had a single cylinder, a safety device was necessary to permit the compressed air to enter the cylinder only when the piston was past top dead centre, to avoid the engine contra-rotating. If no such device were fitted, it was necessary to turn the engine over by handle to the right point. If, on the other hand, the engine was of a multi-cylinder type, a distributor was necessary to pass the air only to the cylinder in which the piston was past dead top centre. There were also other technical obstacles, particularly the problems of sealing the compressed air lines when the engine was running normally and of fitting a third valve. The complexity of these problems finally defeated even the most obstinate opponents of electric starting, who were dubious about electrical circuits in general (with some reason, considering the frequency of their breakdowns).

The most difficult problem with electric starting was, in fact, ensuring only an intermittent connection (i.e. at the moment of starting) between the starter motor and the crankshaft.

This was solved first with the Bendix drive and, more recently, by electro-magnetic means. The push button starting of an engine has now reached such a stage of perfection that few motorists today could imagine what was involved for the pioneers of 70 years ago.

In an appropriate rural setting, a 1913 Rolls-Royce 40/50 H.P. "Silver Ghost" tourer. Below a 1911 Austin.

becoming more and more similar in style, was the Targa Florio in Italy, which went into a decline in the years immediately before the war.

From 1912 to 1914 the race changed both circuits and name, being run on the coastal roads of the island for a distance of 650 miles and being called the "Tour of Sicily". The difficulties of the new course in 1912 attracted a respectable number of entries, 26 in all, including two Americans. The race was won by an Englishman, Cyril Snipe, in a SCAT car, at an average of 26 m.p.h. The low speed is an indication of the difficulties of the course, but it is also true that the competitors did not over-exert themselves. It is said that when the Englishman reached Sciacca he was so tired he decided to have a couple of hours sleep. His mechanic persuaded him to continue, and the fact that he won suggests that other drivers had a similar nap.

Vincenzo Lancia, who was driving a 60 H.P. Mercedes, had an unusual accident. Blinded by the sun, he turned left when the road turned right and mounted a railway running parallel to the road. Not surprisingly his machine collapsed.

Different conditions

In Europe, the greatest number of races were in France, which before the first World War was undoubtedly the

The start of a race at Silverstone in 1957.

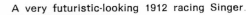

A very futuristic-looking 1912 racing Singer.

leading nation in motor racing. But races were held almost everywhere, even in Central Europe and in Russia, where the Moscow-St. Petersburg race attracted many of the well-known manufacturers. Races were also held in Scandinavia, where the most important was the Gothenburg-Stockholm race.

In Britain during the early days of the century the most important series of races was for the Tourist Trophy. At first the event was run on a fuel consumption basis in the Isle of Man. The winner of this 200-mile race in 1905 was J. S. Napier, on a two-cylinder Arrol-Johnston. The second race in the following year consolidated the reputation of Rolls-Royce, being won by C. S. Rolls. The third race was a victory for Rovers. That was the year when a class of heavy cars was handicapped by making them carry "aerofoils" to *increase* wind resistance.

In 1908 a horsepower formula was introduced and since most engines had a bore of 4 in., it became known as the "Four Inch" race. The winner was W. Watson, with a 5.8-litre Hutton, which was really a Napier. Though from then on until 1914 Brooklands track was the goal of most sporting motorists, the T.T. was run

Two cars on the way to the start of a race at Brooklands.

again in that year in the Isle of Man over a distance of 600 miles. It was spread over two days and the victor was K Lee Guinness (of KLG fame) in a Sunbeam.

The 1914 event was for racing cars, in spite of its title, but this innovation was discontinued. In the race W. O. Bentley drove the smallest car, a French D. F. P., which influenced the design of the original Bentley.

It was not until 1922 that the race was held again, the winner being the Frenchman Chassagne with a Sunbeam, although Sir Algernon Guinness won the 1½-litre event with a Talbot-Darracq, driving without goggles in the blinding rain.

In 1926 the R.A.C. secured the Ards circuit, outside Belfast, and the series took on a new life. The first race was won by Kaye Don with a Lea-Francis, and was the start of a long run of events — from then until the second war — which attracted many of the most illustrious drivers and successful cars of the era. Winners included Caracciola, Nuvolari, Black, Whitcroft, Dodson, Dixon, Comotti and Gerard. These were the great years of the MGs and the sports-racing Rileys.

Ards had to be abandoned after the 1936 race, when

Bruce-Brown and De Palma, the Fiat drivers, ready for the start of the 1912 French G. P.

In 1911 this Renault bus travelled in the jungle.

a car ran into the spectators. But the excellent Donington circuit was available in time for the 1937 and 1938 events, which were now almost on Le Mans lines and were for sports cars little different from those available to the general motorist.

It as 1950 again before the T.T. was in the calendar, with a long series of events to the present day with the exception of 1956 and 1957.

1909 Daimler "Piccadilly" phaeton, with the choice of three engines, 22, 23 or 40 H.P.

The 1914 Fiat S 57/14 B.

front view of a 1913 DIEDERICHS

engine - front mounted vertical 4 cylinder
bore and stroke - 70 × 140 mm.
gearchange - 3 speeds plus reverse.
body - 4 seater tourer

A Citroën of the DC and ID series and, below, the first Citroën, the Model "A".

CHAPTER SEVENTEEN
CLASSIC IN THE RED DUST

Among the major American motor races were some that were "classics" by European standards. One of them was the second Vanderbilt Cup, which was run in 1905 on Long Island. The "European" character of these races was a reflection of their origin, which began as an attempt to take the Gordon Bennett type of racing to America.

The 'great bear'

Once again there was the usual strong contingent from the old world, including Darracq, De Dietrich, Panhard, Mercedes and Fiat. In the American ranks, however, there were some innovations. Alongside "normal" machines — the Locomobile, Matheson and the Pope-Toledo — there were some unusual vehicles such as the air-cooled eight-cylinder in-line Franklin driven by Winchester, a Premier which had a bonnet nearly 10 feet long and the first ever front-wheel drive racing car, a Christie with transverse mounted engine and a complicated system of transmission which caused it to move along in a somewhat zig-zag fashion. The crowd at once christened it "The Great Bear".

Of the U.S. cars, only Tracy's Locomobile ended in an honourable position. The rest of the race was dominated by Europeans. Victor was Héméry in his "light" 80 H.P. Darracq, which won at over 60 m.p.h. Second was Heath in a 120 H.P. Panhard. Behind Tracy's Locomobile came Vincenzo Lancia's Fiat, Szisz in a Renault and then Nazzaro and Sartori in Fiats. In tenth place was Louis Chevrolet, also in a Fiat.

Knipper in a Keeton at Indianapolis in 1914. Below, Victor Demogeot in a Darracq at Daytona beach in 1906.

The Vanderbilt Cup was to be dominated by Europeans for many years to come. In the 1906 edition, in spite of frantic American efforts to make up the technical deficiencies demonstrated in 1905, Wagner won in his 110 H.P. Darracq; at speed across an unguarded level crossing, he had missed a train by a hair's breadth.

In the same period motoring in the U.S. and Cuba introduced a different sort of competition — typically American, even if not only Americans took part. This consisted of straightline speed record attempts on sand in certain suitable localities such as Florida. Representatives of European manufacturers were frequently seen there, especially from France and Italy .

In 1906 Marriott, at Daytona, reached the fantastic speed of 125 m.p.h. before his Stanley Steamer exploded.

Home-made cyclone

In the same year the race between Los Angeles and New York ended in victory for a man whose name was to appear frequently among the lists of successful drivers in America before he was killed in practice in 1908 — Emanuele Cedrino. He raced in a Fiat imported from Italy, but in future years he was to use a machine built by himself from components, which he called Fiat-Cyclone. Ralph de Palma, in effect Cedrino's successor, averaged nearly 75 m.p.h. on the wooden track at Savannah during the first American Grand Prix in 1908.

American industry, so advanced in production cars, was unable to produce racing machines that could compete with those of Europe. This was true even though many race regulations put heavy limitations on European entries, which were not able even to take part officially and could enter only in the name of some American client. All the same, 1908 saw the first American victory in the Vanderbilt Cup — that of Robertson's Locomobile at just under 65 m.p.h. on the modified Long Island circuit, which now included an eight-mile stretch of the newly opened "parkway".

The most interesting American race in 1909 was probably the New York "Motoring 24 Hours", one of the first of a type of race which was quickly to become popular in America. In Europe they were to develop much more slowly. The winner was Raffalovich in a Renault.

S. P. Mills at the wheel of the winning Humber in the 1907 Isle of Man T.T.

According to reports at the time, this European victory was due not only to the merits of his car (to whose preparation the French company had devoted particular care as it was about to attack the American market and wanted some favourable publicity) but also to a "secret weapon". This was mounted at the last moment, and gave Raffalovich an advantage over the other drivers, consisting of straight mudguards mounted just behind the front wheels to protect the driver from flying stones. This hazard nearly always appeared after a number of laps and drivers had to be very cautious when close behind other cars.

In fact, the photographs of the race show this Renault without the mudguards at the beginning of the race, though they were shown at the end.

In 1909 the first race at Crown Point, Indiana, was organized by the Chicago Automobile Club. The race was to be for the western United States what the Vanderbilt Cup, before its migration, was for the east. The race was won by Louis Chevrolet, in a Buick, which towards

Even from the earliest days, racing cars differed greatly from production models, as can be seen in this photograph of Grillon at the wheel of a Hispano-Suiza in 1913.

Though competitive racing stopped in Europe in 1914, races continued in the U.S. This is the arrival at San Francisco of a Hudson after a trans-continental drive in 1916.

A 1914 STAR

the end was running on only three cylinders. Credit for the victory, however, should also go to William Crapo Durant, future founder of General Motors, who at that time was head of Buick and who planned his team's tactics shrewdly.

Free grandstand view

The Crown Point race did not, however, have the success its organisers wanted, above all because of one drawback. As the specially built circuit had a length of 30 miles, anyone who wished could watch the race without paying to go in the grandstands.

But this was a lesson for the rival organisers of the race held at Elgin which, unlike the Crown Point, was to run for many years and become one of the most important in America. It was run on a triangular course inside the town; the organisers persuaded the owners of houses and of land around the circuit to sell tickets for the race — and this time they succeeded in getting half the entrance money themselves.

The Elgin race, first run in 1910, was held until 1933.

The 1912 racing Aquila Italiana.

A 1913 D.F.P. "Type B".

BLENDING IN THE QUALITY

Petrol is a cocktail of many hydrocarbons and additives tailor-made to the needs of the motor engine as a good whisky is blended to suit the individual palate. Petrol is probably the most complex and sophisticated product in normal daily use by the public, and a vast amount of know-how and skill enters into its formulation.

A satisfactory petrol must meet the needs of a large variety of cars, each with its own particular performance chacteristics, driven by a wide variety of drivers in towns, on motorways, in hilly country, in all types of climate. Wherever and whatever he is driving, the motorist expects to have instant starting, rapid warm-up and quick acceleration from cold, freedom from knock, good fuel consumption, smooth engine running, little power loss as the car grows older, and good performance in all weathers. It is no easy matter to build all this into a petrol, and at a reasonable price, but this is precisely what is done in top-quality petrols.

Birthplace of high-grade motor spirit — catalytic cracker at Shell's Stanlow Refinery in Cheshire.

A 24-hour job — pumping units in typical Dutch countryside.

Petrol is essentially a mixture of hydrocarbons, but the mixture can vary widely both in the types of hydrocarbons and in their relative proportions, depending upon the crude oil from which it is derived, and the process used to manufacture it. There are at least ten different processes, ranging from simple refinery distillation to complex cracking and reforming, and there are more kinds of crude oil than of the famous brand of soup.

By judicious selection and blending of petrol components produced by these various processes the characteristics of a petrol can be determined. But the product will still be lacking in certain essential requirements that can be achieved only by the addition of various non-petroleum products. It is this inherent variability of the basic petrol fractions and their sensitivity to additives that makes the formulation of a top-quality petrol so complex.

The refining process

Petrol, as it flows from the crude oil distillation columns in an oil refinery, is a mixture of hydrocarbons with a boiling temperature range between about 30° and 200°C. The vapour of this mixture burns in the presence of air to form carbon dioxide and water, a reaction which releases energy to power the engine.

In the early days of the motor car at the turn of the century, it was this petrol fraction straight from the distillation columns that was sold to the motorist. As the population grew, straight distillation did not produce enough petrol to meet demand without creating a large and wasteful surplus of other oil fractions such as paraffin and fuel oil.

Refiners had to find a way to convert surplus oil fractions into petrol, and so balance supply and demand for all their products. Cracking techniques, first thermal and then catalytic, proved to be the solution. Single hydrocarbon molecules of heavy fractions such as gas oil are broken down — or "cracked" — to form two molecules of lighter fractions such as petrol. Cracking not only produced more petrol, but also of the superior quality (higher anti-knock rating or octane number) needed to fuel the newer engines with higher compression ratios. The engine designer and the fuel designer have worked together to raise performance over the years.

Petrol tailor-made

Most modern refineries are also equipped with reforming plant which improves petrol quality without increasing the volume yield. In such plant individual molecules of the feedstock (petrol from the distillation column) are re-arranged to give a product with a much wider boiling range and a higher anti-knock value.

Petrol from the pump is a blend of components to which are added various chemicals to improve specific aspects of car performance. It is at this stage — in the blending and use of chemical additives — that the petrol is tailor-made to meet the diverse needs of modern cars.

The proportions in which the components are blended to make a petrol are determined by a number of performance criteria. For a car to start from cold, a combustible petrol/air mixture must be present in the cylinder. Thus a very volatile fraction such as butane must be incorporated in the petrol, but not too much or it will create problems of vapour locking and hot re-starting.

Freedom from knock

For quick warm-up and acceleration, the fuel must contain petrol fractions in the lower and middle boiling range; and, for good fuel consumption over a long period, fractions with higher boiling points and greater energy release are needed. Petrol has therefore to be a correctly-proportioned blend of fractions covering a wide range of boiling temperatures.

Another important aspect of performance is freedom from knock. This phenomenon stems from irregular combustion of the petrol/air mixture in the cylinder; it causes loss of power and can damage the engine. Although the steady increase in compression ratios of engines develops more power for less fuel, it also leads to a greater tendency to knock; therefore modern cars require fuels with a very high anti-knock rating. Refinery processes such as cracking and reforming improve anti-knock properties of fuels. Addition of such compounds as tetraethyl lead also produces marked improvement.

Fractionating tower at BP's Gothenburg Refinery, Sweden.

Forerunner of today... this Paris taxi-driver serves himself with petrol during the first World war. Each driver had his own hose and key to the pump; by putting in a disc he released a set quantity of petrol. The pump was invented by a French taximan.

But the anti-knock properties of the finished petrol depend upon careful blending.

Originally the knock rating of a fuel was assessed in terms of a single rating number — in a laboratory test engine, with full throttle knock at low speed. A much higher degree of control has been achieved by the introduction of two more ratings that give a better guide to anti-knock performance at high speed and where

segregation of the fuel/air mixture occurs in the inlet manifold. Fuels are also tested for knock in all standard makes of car engine.

By blending components in the correct proportions, it is possible to produce petrols which have high anti-knock ratings in all motoring conditions and which, at the same time, have the desired volatility range. Petrol performance will, of course, be influenced by climate, and therefore the proportions are amended from summer to winter. So many variables are involved that nowadays it is normal practice to work out the proportions on a computer.

Quality control

To the fuel blend, chemicals are added to control various aspects of long-term engine performance. These additives vary with the brand of petrol, but fairly typical are organo-phosphorus compounds which modify deposits on sparking plugs. Deposits of this kind, which are more likely to form on engines with high compression ratios and in congested driving conditions, lead to spark plug misfire and random ignition.

Elaborate quality control tests are carried out during manufacture, storage and distribution to ensure that the petrol conforms to the prescribed specifications. Ultimately, the reputation of the petrol depends upon specifications being kept up to date with, or ahead of, current motoring requirements.

A customer serves himself at the pump island and another pays at the kiosk in one of National's latest self-service stations, at Birmingham.

About to enter their 1912 Newton. Below, Boillot leans out of his Peugeot during the 1914 French Grand Prix held at Lyons on 4 July. Peugeot used storm tyres after days of heavy rain, but a brilliant sun dried the track and the French cars were at a disadvantage compared with the Mercedes.

A shrouded start at the new track at Indianapolis in 1909 before the famous 500-mile race was introduced two years later. Number 34, a Buick, won the 100-mile race. The day before another Buick had won the 250-mile race.

For a substantial time it had a function for American motor racing equivalent to that of Indianapolis.

The 'Indy' is born

This famous 500-mile race, the principal American motor race, took place for the first time in 1911. The winner was Ray Hudson in a six-cylinder Marmon "Wasp" in front of Ralph Mulford in a Lozier; third was David Bruce-Brown in his Fiat — the car with which he was to win the American Grand Prix in the same year. The winner of the "500" had a rear-view mirror for the first time, and the publicity for the idea led to their swift adoption throughout America.

At Indianapolis a number of races had been held — two of them three-day races — when the track was half built. The construction of this track, marked for many years by its unique pagoda-like tower and built outside a city having many connections with the U.S. motor industry, was due to the efforts of an enthusiastic racing driver, Carl G. Fisher.

As a driver his best performance had been in the Gordon Bennett race in Ireland. His project was clearly inspired by another circuit on which he had run a number of

Indianapolis prestige has always attracted European companies. René Thomas in 1920 at the wheel of a car whose builder, Edouard Ballot, is the severe looking gentleman in the straw hat.

times, Brooklands. To build his track, beginning with the difficult operation of buying the land, Fisher associated himself with three others, James Allison, Frank C. Wheeler and A. C. Newby. The first was an engine manufacturer who was to become well known in America as the builder of an aeroplane for the American forces. The second sold petrol and the third was the president of a small motor company.

Brick track experiment

By the time the track was finished the partners found they had spent a million dollars against initial estimates of about half that sum. Among the major difficulties they had encountered was that of the paving of the track, wood having been rejected as a material. Most American tracks at that date were of wood but as speeds became higher this became less and less suitable; and Fisher, who was always the dominant personality in the group, chose Macadam. The first surface was of this material.

It proved unsuitable, however, because of its rapid wear and Fisher had the idea of using brick and the track was rebuilt in this unusual way. Wear was no less than

The 1914 Opel which took part in the 1914 Grand Prix at Lyons.

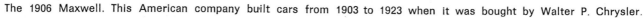

The 1906 Maxwell. This American company built cars from 1903 to 1923 when it was bought by Walter P. Chrysler.

1914 Dodge.

obviously impossible to re-pave the surface on the eve of the race. A drivers' strike seemed equally unlikely in view of the high value of the prizes involved (this was a feature of Indianapolis right from the beginning). Fisher therefore offered the drivers a compromise. Instead of many races culminating in a 250-mile final, there would be just one race — 500 miles in one race. The compromise was immediately accepted.

Indianapolis, apart from the technical significance of its races over fifty years, has been for American car enthusiasts a spectacle without equal, both on and in the vicinity of the track.

Much is more folklore than motoring, but an incident in 1912, the second year of the race, illustrates the attitude of drivers and public.

One of the competitors, Dave Evans, skidded at high speed against a protecting wall in front of the grandstand. His machine shot into the air and another car passed clean under it without being touched. Evans fell heavily but at once jumped to his feet and waved his clasped hands above his head like a boxer, receiving a huge ovation from the crowd. Immediately afterwards he fell unconscious to the ground. He was seriously injured and was a long time in hospital. Indianapolis was like that even then.

with Macadam; there was also a cloud of red, abrasive dust which penetrated even under the cars' bonnets. These difficulties virtually led to the introduction of the 500-mile race, a formula rare in America in those days when races were usually over 100 or 200 miles. The drivers, worried about the dust, gave Fisher an ultimatum — either he changed the surface or they would not compete.

This was clearly unrealistic. On the one hand, it was

Fast, elegant and in harmony with its surroundings. A 1916 Perry.

A 1908 Adams.

A 1908 Unic 12/14 H.P. It was built by
Georges Richard after he separated from
Brasier. The name derives from his policy
of building only one type of car. Unic now
forms part of Simca.

The 1913 edition was won by a European, Jules Goux, in a 7½-litre Panhard. When leading early on, he had to stop at the pits because of tyre trouble and restarted in thirteenth place. He then drove a reckless race and, notwithstanding the efforts of his competitors, took the lead again and held it to the end.

Seeing the verve with which Goux drove there were many who held that the race was won not only by the qualities of the car and its driver, but also by the French champagne which flowed freely in the excited pits and which Goux was seen to sample at every stop. Goux returned to France not only with the usual mountain of dollars but also with a young American wife.

Repeat performance

Goux's coup was repeated with interest in the 1914 "500 mile" by four Frenchmen. The only American in the race in a position to oppose the Europeans was the veteran Barney Oldfield, who could achieve only fifth place in a Stutz. The race was won by René Thomas in a Delage after an exciting contest with the other three. Duray gained second place — surprisingly, as his Peugeot was a three-litre normally used in touring car races. Guyot in the second Delage was third and Goux, unable to repeat his previous year's victory because of more tyre trouble, was fourth.

Naturally the performance that most struck the public was that of the "little" Peugeot, which had maintained the formidable average of over 82 m.p.h., only slightly below that of the winner.

Although not possible in Europe, motor racing continued in America in 1915 and 1916. Both the 500-mile races of those years were won by European cars. The first was won by a Mercedes driven by De Palma, which gave him some revenge for the occasion in 1912 when his machine, also a Mercedes, broke down near the finishing line.

On that occasion De Palma and his mechanic pushed their heavy car for a mile towards the finishing line before being overtaken by the other cars. In 1916 the Indianapolis 500-mile was won by an Italian, Dario Resta, in a Peugeot.

This was the last racing activity in the U.S. before that country was plunged into war, and the story of the motor car may be considered to have now completed its first cycle.

Beginning with the early pioneers, there had been gradual technical evolution and the laying of the foundations of large scale production. At a surprising pace, the motor car had passed from being an expensive possession for a privileged élite to being a tool essential for everyday living.

End of an era

The races in Europe and the U.S. provided spectacle and competition, the occasions for sporting rivalry and the meeting-place for those in the car industry concerned with technical improvements of all kinds. In little more than a decade, it had become an entertainment for a wide cross-section of the public.

The war called a halt to this; the car itself was called to the battlefronts of Europe. It was to return in civilian life to play an ever-increasingly important role both as a method of transport and as the subject of a participant and spectator sport.

Sir John Briscoe's 1911 Delage.

front view of a 1921 ROLLS-ROYCE "SILVER GHOST"

engine - six cylinders
bore and stroke - 4½" x 4¾"
capacity - 7428 c.c.
output - 48.6 H.P.
ignition - dual magneto and battery
clutch - fabric cone
gear change - 4 speeds plus reverse
weight - 5040 lb.

The Daimler Sovereign is a high quality car that embodies years of experience. Below — the 1906 side valve Daimler with chain drive and 35 H.P.

CHAPTER EIGHTEEN

AMERICA FORGES AHEAD

The first World War had a relatively marginal effect on industry in the U.S., while that of Europe was to suffer the effects of the war for many years. The opportunity to experiment and test led to developments, industrial and technical, which assured the United States a prominent position after the war.

Radical differences

The years immediately before the war had seen an interesting change in the American industrial picture. In addition to Ford and Buick (the latter being the most important part of General Motors), a third large manufacturer came to the fore. Overland was an old company whose fortunes, after some difficult years, began to pick up when John Willys, already president of American Motor Car Sales, joined the company. In 1907 he became president of Overland and made a number of improvements to production, possible because of a private agreement he had with the Pope Company of Toledo, Ohio. A short time later the company changed its name to Willys-Overland and moved to Toledo.
In 1908 4,000 vehicles were produced, and five years later Willys-Overland, with 37,000 vehicles, was in sec-

ond place between Ford (107,000) and Buick (28,000). The commercial policy of these three largest American companies differed radically one from another, though

Checking the petrol level.

A view of the assembly line of Dodge Brothers.

perhaps it would be better to say that Ford represented a unique case and it is therefore difficult to make comparisons.

In 1913 the price of a Ford T in the four-seat "torpedo" version was only 360 dollars and there was even a two-seater "roadster" at 345 dollars. The cheapest product by a competitor was an Overland at 780 dollars.

Offer refused

An industrial concern as important as General Motors could not accept the position indefinitely, especially since they had been pushed into third place by a relatively small company such as Willys-Overland.

The first attempt to improve the situation was of a financial nature — the offer by Durant to Ford to form a huge car manufacturing complex. The offer was refused by Ford; this marked the beginning of Durant's decline, and shortly afterwards he was replaced by Charles W. Nash, his former colleague and last president of Buick.

A 1904 Siddeley.

It was Nash who was to engineer General Motors' recovery. Between 1912, when he became president, and 1916 when he left to form his own company by buying Thomas Jeffery's plant, he instituted a number of reforms.

Above all, he incorporated in General Motors a group of companies manufacturing components and accessories, already amalgamated as the United Motors Corporation. He also decided to launch the maximum possible sales attack on Ford, using as the spearhead one of his companies, Chevrolet, which so far had been relatively neglected.

1905 Buick model "C". This car had a flat twin engine. The catalogue says "Price 1200 dollars, 22 H.P. guaranteed . . . . . a car that overcomes any hill. Two forward speeds and reverse. Simple but built to last!".

The Chevrolet production from 1912 to 1920. That of 1916 is the famous "490"

The acquisition of the Chevrolet company by General Motors in Durant's time improved the standing of the name, and General Motors built over 2,000 of its first model under that name, acquiring a loyal clientele.

The famous '490'

Nash did some market research among customers to determine which features they liked best. He found these were overhead valves, the solid chassis and the three-speed gear-box with central gear lever — all points which were considered better than Ford's solutions. Nash therefore ordered his designer to produce a new model incorporating these features. Thus in 1914 was born the "Baby Grand", with a number of features which anticipated the cars of the 20's.

The "Baby Grand" was only the beginning of General Motors' enhancing of the Chevrolet brand name. The

"490" was to have a tremendous success with the American public, to which it was offered at a price relatively near that of the Ford — 490 dollars for the "torpedo". To this basic price it was necessary to add 60 dollars for the lighting system, then considered an extra.

With Chevrolet thus launched on a mass market (which was to exceed Ford in later years) Nash was free to create a degree of specialisation in the other companies such as Buick, which had enjoyed notable success in earlier years. For this name he sought an impression of medium-priced luxury, with high-quality interior and a six-cylinder engine (though a four was optional).

In an ascending order of luxury came the other General Motors makes — Oakland (six cylinders), Oldsmobile (six cylinders or V8) and Cadillac (V8).

When Nash became president of General Motors it left vacant the presidency of Buick. This was given to Walter P. Chrysler — another exceptional man — whose

The Rover 20 H.P. that won the 1907 T. T.

1917 Kissel 6 cylinder. Kissel production, which went on until 1931, was known for its "European styling".

272

name was to be perpetuated by a great motor company. As technical director of the American Locomotive Company, Chrysler had joined Buick in 1911. Even though he was to become senior vice-president of General Motors, his most important work came later.

He joined first Willys-Overland in 1920 to save it from imminent failure, showing remarkable commercial qualities. Some years later he was to use these qualities to some effect in saving another company, Maxwell-Chalmers, with which he began an association on a personal basis in 1924. This association was to result a short time later in the birth of the Chrysler Corporation.

Numbers fall

In addition to the three great manufacturers, an immense number of smaller ones were working. In 1915 there were 170. In the space of a few years, however, these were to be reduced to about 10; this was inevitable as other manufacturers adopted Ford's mass-production techniques to stay in a market where craftsman production, and consequent high price, were less and less in demand.

In 1914 548,000 motor vehicles were built in the United

1918 Nash "681".

1914 15 H.P. Napier with 2,684 c.c. 4 cylinder engine.

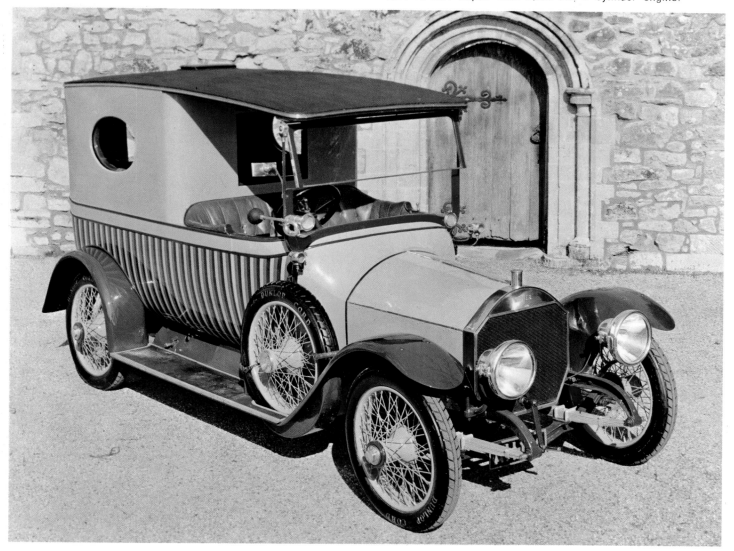

1919 Essex roadster.

1912 Oakland "Colonial Coupé". This was considered outstandingly beautiful at the time. The coupé body was interchangeable with the roadster.

States; of these 412,000 were produced by the ten largest companies. Thus, though the closing of so many companies was distressing, it was economically inevitable. This was shown by the fact that even what would be considered relatively large companies were having to accept offers from the giants in order to avoid a slow and miserable decline.

It might seem a paradox that in such a position other companies, such as Nash and Chrysler, could be created. In reality, though, the prospects were bleak only for those who — by dint of personality or out-of-date factories — were unable to adapt themselves to the times. Another reason, which finally was the determining factor for many companies, was the rapid change in the general concept of the motor car when a vast extension of the motorway network permitted higher performances.

Some cars had maximum speeds of around 40 m.p.h., which was acceptable in 1914 but was no longer so by

1913 Renault type AX two-seater tourer.
1,205 c.c. twin. Top speed 40 m.p.h.

1918. To meet these demands the manufacturer had to re-design not only the engine but the whole car, including suspension, steering and brakes.

A particular role was played by the company set up in 1914 by the brothers John and Horace Dodge, who had been associated with the Ford Motor Company and subscribed one-tenth of the capital, being responsible for the engines of Henry's cars. Their acceptance of Ford's offer, severely criticised at the time by their friends, paid them — when they severed their connection with Ford in 1919 — something like 25 million dollars against the 20,000 of their original investment.

Copied by competitors

Even before then, the dividends they received had enabled them to set up their own factory equipped with the finest machinery. It permitted them to design a "car of the future" in collaboration with their chief designer, Flanders, and a company in Philadelphia called Gowen Budd, which specialised in the welding of steel sheet. The success of the new Dodge, built from 1914 onwards, was great. By 1915 production was 4,500 and two years later it had been doubled, largely owing to the

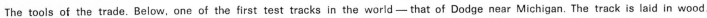

The tools of the trade. Below, one of the first test tracks in the world — that of Dodge near Michigan. The track is laid in wood.

1908 Stears model 45/90. Six cylinders, 90 H.P. Below a 1909 Chalmers.

Ricotti's torpedo and an American "Dream car". More than 50 years separates them.

PIONEERS OF AERODYNAMICS

In the early days of motoring, designers were usually concerned with the straightforward problems of function. The problem of aerodynamics received little consideration. It was only in the 30's that the first tentative attempts were made to adapt coachwork to penetrate the air. Yet this is one of the ways, and by no means the most difficult, of obtaining the increase of performance and speed for which designers have always been looking.

There were nevertheless, a few isolated efforts in earlier times to built aerodynamic cars. First was that of Jenatzy, the Belgian ex-coachbuilder who became a racing driver. In modifying his Jeantaud electric vehicle, the "Jamais Contente", he took full account of aerodynamic problems and made it in the form of a marine torpedo. In doing so, however, he disregarded the comfort of the driver who had to insert himself in the most uncomfortable position for his record attempts.

The "Jamais Contente", however, was not a motor car in the real sense of the term. A remarkable vehicle ordered by Count Marco Ricotti in 1913 from Alfa Romeo and the coachbuilder Castagna certainly was. This was bomb-shaped and could hold six people. This unusual car, with which Ricotti made a number of speed attempts, had a door and four windows in each side. The front of vehicle was formed mainly of a large curved windscreen.

Droplet of water

The engine was a 40-60 H.P., four cylinder 6,082 c.c. which gave the normal car a maximum speed of 78 m.p.h. Ricotti was able to achieve about 87 m.p.h. in his version. But, almost inevitably, the car was never put into production.

A somewhat better fate awaited the "Tropfenwagen" (droplet car) designed in Germany in 1921 by Rumpler, who took advantage of a mass of data derived from the practice with aeroplanes. His studies led him to the same conclusions as Ricotti: that the best shape was that of a drop of water falling freely in air, the front rounded and then tapering away to the tail.

But as Ricotti had to use an available chassis and so built a very large vehicle, Rumpler started from scratch and was able to modify many of the features of a normal car. The body conformation demanded the use of a layout in which the engine was immediately behind the passenger seats. This meant that there could be a short-drive shaft, but longer linkages on gear change and clutch were necessary.

One headlamp

To remain true to the concept of aerodynamic form, Rumpler designed a fully enclosed body which covered the wheels. For the same reason there was only one headlamp, in the centre of the nose, and the mudguards were reduced to horizontal fins.

The "Tropfenwagen" had a better commercial fate than Ricotti's car. Its construction went on for a number of years though in limited quantities, many of them being used as public vehicles.

Today the science of aerodynamics is one of the major concerns of the car designer. Ironically, the missile-like shape of the modern high-speed racing car is, in a sense, a return to the earliest days of the record-breakers.

lasting qualities exhibited by the earlier models. One compliment to the success of Dodge cars was paid by their competitors, who copied them, even to the appearance. Both of the Dodge brothers died relatively young, in 1920, but the company continued for a number of years until it was absorbed by Chrysler.

Another important secondary company was Studebaker. The brothers Clem and John Studebaker's organisation had lived through the first decade of the century without great difficulties and without striking achievements, building both electric and i.c. engine vehicles, until it merged in 1911 with the E.M.F. Company (Everitt, Metzger and Flanders). From that time they produced only petrol vehicles.

Gold-plated showpiece

The next year their first four-cylinder model was built — in those days the number of cylinders served to define the degree of luxury of the car — and it was a success. The brand image that Studebaker adopted in those years was that of robustness and long life, and to demonstrate this the company exhibited a gold-plated chassis in 1916. Another U.S. firm which grew quickly was Hudson, formed in 1909. After trying various formulae, it finally specialised in six-cylinder cars, which were large and strong but of reasonable price — something half-way between a "cheap" and a "luxury" model. The most famous of these cars was a celebrated 29 H.P.

A less happy fate awaited another company, Maxwell, set up by Jonathan D. Maxwell. After working with Ellwood Haynes on the latter's first motor car and building a number of twin-cylinder engines with Benjamin Briscoe, he set up on his own account to build cars with four-cylinder engines.

The failure of this venture caused him to withdraw finally from the motoring field in 1913, but not until he had made an important contribution to the motor car, as designer for Oldsmobile and other less important companies and as the inventor of a cooling system. The Maxwell was later revived by Flanders, along with the Chalmers.

'Orphan cars'

A typical American phenomenon of the years between 1915 and 1920 was represented by the "assembly companies", whose products were often known as "orphan cars". These were cars sold under a wide variety of names, to which their originators contributed some part of the bodywork, the radiator surround and the badge. They were built in some hundreds of small workshops all over the States, with components bought from specialist firms such as Continental, Hercules and Waukesha for engines, Borg and Beck for clutches and Timken for gearboxes and bearings.

At first they won a certain amount of public favour because of their low price and distinctive appearance.

Soon it began to be appreciated that such cars, which had no unity of design, might have faults such as an excellent gear change but a poor engine, or a transmission too weak for the rest of the car. The "orphans" gradually went out of existence.

Individually these companies had a short life, but as fast as one company died another was born and the public took some time to learn the value of the new one. The final coup de grace was given when the big manufacturers organised nationwide service, which the small companies were obviously unable to do. When these cars broke down they really became orphans; they were abandoned.

Another characteristic of the time was the introduction of the first luxury cars "Made in U.S.A.". Until the outbreak of the first World War, the upper income bracket of the American public had gone overseas for its vehicles. Neither Haynes, Locomobile nor Stoddard-Dayton, to name only three of the American luxury makes, succeeded in persuading the wealthy to buy a home-produced car. Those who could afford to do so continued to go to Europe for De Dion-Bouton, Mercedes, Fiat, Minerva, Delaunay-Belleville or Rolls. The outbreak of war changed matters as European cars became unavailable, and rich Americans were forced to buy American cars.

Among those who profited from this situation, at a time when the American gross national income was rising rapidly, the most successful was General Motors with Cadillac, which had been in the luxury market for a long time but with relatively little success.

In 1914, as the supply of European cars dried up, Cadillac was able to produce the V8 engine, underlining its indirect European ancestry. This was the beginning of a new production policy which led to 12- and even 16-cylinder engines.

The V8, however, remained the major Cadillac engine and formed the base for the commercial development of

1914 Renault taxi. This was one of the famous "Taxis of the Marne" requisitioned by General Gallieni on 5 September, 1914, to rush troops to the front.

1913 Opel racer which would exceed 105 m.p.h.

the company. This is shown by the fact that it sold — at prices of over 3,500 dollars — 47,000 cars from the end of 1917.

Parallel rows

Not only Cadillac benefited, however, by the changed situation in the luxury market. In 1915 Packard launched a "Twin-Six", a large 12-cylinder car whose engine, in addition to its high output, was very flexible and able to go from three to 38 m.p.h. in 12 seconds in top gear. It took its name from the fact that its 12 cylinders were arranged in two parallel rows of six, each being derived more or less from the old six-cylinder engine. There were differences, however, and the length of this new 6,800 cc V-12 engine was less than that of the previous six. The "Twin-Six" was an immediate success and over 35,000 were built, 10,600 of them in the first year.

Inevitably, the V-12 had imitators. National, Pathfinder, Austin-U.S.A., Hal, Haynes and Kissel all built engines of this type. One of these, the Hal, had a curious device which permitted one bank of cylinders to be cut out when appropriate, in order to save petrol.

A survey of this ten years of American car production would not be complete without mention of two manufacturers of sports cars which were to win an enormous popularity among the American public, and especially among the young. These were the Stutz and the Mercer. The first carried the name of Henry C. Stutz, an inventor who headed first the Ideal Motor Company and then the Stutz Motor Car Company, both in Indianapolis. Stutz produced successive series of his "Bearcat", which was a technical anomaly for the period, as its engine had only four cylinders and side valves which had been given up by most manufacturers. All the same, these cars were lively, mainly because chassis and body were reduced to the minimum. The most expensive model was a six-cylinder coupe.

The Mercers were technically even less forward-looking and their life was brief. Nevertheless, they had some years of success, particularly because of their showing in the 1912 and 1913 Indianapolis 500-mile races, when they took second and third places respectively. The Mercers were built in Trenton, New Jersey, and designed by James Moose, an able engineer who came from Simplex, another well-known name in the sporting field.

'Souping up' engines

Many other American sports car companies first saw the light of day in this period. The so-called "orphans" were strong in this field, though many cars used in races were "souped-up" versions of standard production. The first car to become popular for this treatment was the Ford "T".

Because of its basic solidity and its resistance to mechanical breakdown, the car could be adapted for racing after much changing of the bodywork, often only the chassis

Only lifting the bonnet would indicate that this is a steam car, a 1911 Stanley tourer. Below a Gardner-Serpollet of 1906.

remaining. One of the best-known modifiers of the "T" was Louis Chevrolet in the second period of his motoring career.

Towards the end of the first decade a third generation of American sporting cars appeared, clearly inspired by the European cars which until 1916 were winning at Indianapolis. The most important feature was the adoption of overhead camshafts, a mechanism so far spurned by American constructors.

Hybrid cars

In certain cases the inspiration from Europe was taken to the point of direct copying. Such was the case of Premier, which built at Indianapolis copies of the 1914 Peugeot Grand Prix 4½-litre. In 1919 Goux raced, in fact, in a hybrid machine, part Premier, part Peugeot. The brothers Duesenberg quickly distinguished themselves among the list of imitators and in later years some of the most admired American cars were to bear their name. Their first was a racing car in 1920, closely copied from the Delage.

The part-experimental activity of these smaller companies, often guilty of imitation but also initiating a design revolution in American motor car manufacture, was interrupted in 1929 with the first indications of the world slump in that year.

front view of a 1935 HISPANO-SUIZA "KS"

engine - front mounted 6 cylinder
bore and stroke - 100 × 100 mm.
capacity - 5184 c.c.
ignition - distributor and 2 plugs per cylinder
clutch - single plate
gearchange - 3 speeds plus reverse
brakes - servo on all four wheels
chassis weight - 2750 lb.

A typical example of standard components modified for competition. The Fiat-Abarth 2,000 which develops 230 H.P. Below — The Aston-Martin "Razor Blade" which also had its engine modified.

CHAPTER NINETEEN

PEACE BRINGS ITS PROBLEMS

The resumption of production by European car manufacturers at the end of the first World War was rapid in view of the tremendous difficulties which had to be overcome. The problems included lack of raw materials, disorganisation of transport, the necessity to rebuild ruined factories — and shortage of money. In such conditions, small companies often have advantages over large ones. This accounts for the fact that so many new companies were formed in Europe at that time; most, however, were not destined to exist for long.

In general, European cars between 1918 and 1920 were considerably different from those of the immediate pre-war years. Those manufacturers who had intended to pick up production where they had left off were quicklv made to feel the change in public taste.

Both bodies and chassis were lighter. All separation between driver and passengers had disappeared. The first attempts to simplify the hood mechanism were made, so that one person was able to raise or lower it, as was already possible across the Atlantic. So far as the mechanical components were concerned, the final disappearance of chain transmission and the cautious introduction of four-wheel brakes were the most important.

France once again took the lead in the quality of cars

1911 Opel 6/16 H.P. in which Ford influence is seen. 4 cylinder engine, magneto ignition. Below a 1909 Mercedes 45 H.P.

produced — but was not so predominant as in the years before 1914 — and a new name appeared there, Citroën. His personality was to influence the whole French motoring world, and indeed, that of Europe.

André Citroën was the descendant of a family originating in Holland. As a young engineer from the Ecole Polytechnique, he had set up a small factory before 1914 to make a particular type of double-v gears whose patents he had bought in Poland. These gears (from which the company's sign is taken) enabled considerable power to be transmitted in silence, and were not superseded till the advent of double helical gearing.

He agreed with the brothers Emile and Louis Mors to manage their famous factory and to reorganise production, which was still much on a craftsman basis. His great industrial advance, however, came with the war when he proposed to the government a system of mass production of shells. His proposals were accepted and, building a new factory at Javel, he extricated the French army from a grave crisis.

It was the problem of reconverting the Javel factory that took Citroën back into the motor car field, after a short period making articles in mild steel.

Citroën was converted to the principles of Ford and

was determined to produce on a large scale. He therefore decided to concentrate on the production of one model only. So he sold the design of a second, a luxury car with a Knight sleeve-valve engine of 3½ litres, to his friend Gabriel Voisin, who made it the basis of his future 18 H.P.

The car chosen by Citroën was a robust 1½-litre four-seater designed by Jules Salomon, who had previously designed for Zebre. The car was as light and spacious as he could make it, with a pressed steel body and easy maintenance features. Top speed was 40 m.p.h.

The first appearance of the 10 H.P. "torpedo", or open tourer, was in 1919. It was immediately improved by the addition of four-wheel brakes and a fourth gear. The pressed steel wheels were made by Michelin. In order to attack a wide market and go quickly into full production, the model "A" was launched at the fantastically low price of 7,950 francs. This was quickly raised first to 12,500 and then 15,000 francs, thereby upsetting those customers who had been originally attracted by the lower price. In spite of this, the car was a great commercial success and by 1926, when production of the "A" ceased, it had reached 500 a day.

Citroën's example and his great success in the 20's was to have a marked influence on the big French and European manufacturers, as he was the first to introduce mass production of cars in Europe.

Influenced by Model 'T'

Before this development, motor shows had begun again in 1919, and a number of new and interesting models were launched in France. Renault, who had also played an important part in war production making tanks and aero-engines, presented a new car. This was a four-cylinder 10 H.P. clearly inspired by the Ford "T", with which he replaced the glorious 9 H.P. of "Taxis of the Marne" fame.

In addition, a range of pre-1914 cars was produced, including the huge nine-litre 40 H.P. Peugeot's range of production was also wide, from the luxurious 25 H.P. down to a cyclecar, the curious "Quadrilette", with two seats in tandem and 760 c.c. engine. Surprisingly, this car was to have considerable success when the seats were re-arranged side by side.

Panhard, in 1919, adopted Knight sleeve-valve engines for all their models with the exception of one. Besides

Reputed to be the second oldest Bugatti in the world. Built in 1911, it can still reach over 35 m.p.h.

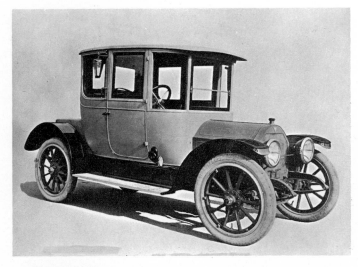

American car production, unlike European, expanded rapidly during the war. Above, top to bottom — Two Hudsons respectively of 1913 and 1917. Below — The company's range in 1920.

revamping the old models, one brand new car was introduced — a four-cylinder 16 H.P. whose engine, when doubled, was to form the basis of the famous 8-in-line 35 H.P.

Alongside these big companies were medium and small ones which were working hard to impose their new models on the market — Hotchkiss, Delahaye, Brasier, Bollée and many others. Apart from Citroën, new manufacturers included Farman, Voisin and Bellanger.

Mainstream makes

In England and Scotland during 1919 and 1920 there were as many as 90 motor car builders, the majority of them making decidedly "austerity" cars after the artificial boom times of war. There were, nevertheless, serious attempts at quantity production to meet the U. S. challenge, and these attempts were in some cases successful. By 1924, there were over 100 manufacturers.

Parallel to the introduction of new mass-production and luxury cars, there was also a boom in cyclecars. Almost everywhere in Europe, the tax authorities began to bear heavily on car owners, usually on a basis of cylinder capacity and therefore of performance. Thus hundreds of cyclecar manufacturers mushroomed in those years, and even some of the big makers entered the field in case it might have proved to be a lasting phenomenon. These immediate post-war years have gone down in motoring history as the years of the cyclecar, but it would be wrong to judge the industry by the standards of those spindly, unreliable machines (among which the Morgan was about the only device that deserves to be remembered, and this was more of a light car with three

Continuity of style. The upper car was built in 1911 and the lower in 1921. One might think that they were of the same year. That of 1921 is the Renault type JM with 2,812 c.c. 4 cylinder engine.

One of the first cars built by Voisin, an 8 H.P. "sports". Below a 1922 Maxwell "charabanc".

wheels than were the virtual motor bicycles with four). The G.N. was more car than cyclecar, too.

The era should properly be assessed on the mainstream makes such as the Austin, Morris, Riley, Clyno, Sunbeam, Talbot, Wolseley, Humber, Hillman and Standard. Of these the fastest progress was made by the first two, and although Austin was slow to get going, he was making 100 cars a week by 1920, concentrating on a "mid-Atlantic" 20 H.P. and then adding a 12 H.P.

It was Morris who produced the real sensation of the period. The "bullnose" Morris Oxford and Cowley cars had been in production before the war, but in the early post-war years William Morris captured the low-price market so effectively that even as admirable a car as the almost competitive Clyno did not survive for many years.

Success stories were also being recorded by such firms as Rover, Hillman, Humber, Standard, Riley and Jowett, whilst considerable numbers of cars were being made by A.B.C., A.C., Angus-Sanderson, Bean, Cubitt, Palladium, Ruston-Hornsby and Star.

There were several makes of slightly better quality, and produced in lesser numbers, including Talbot, Sunbeam, Wolseley, Alvis, Armstrong-Siddeley and Crossley. Some of these included thoroughbred sporting cars in their ranges. But the true "sportsters" of the age were the

The "T" in commercial use — a 1912 lorry. Below the Peugeot "Quadrilette", built in 1920. 4 cylinder engine, 3 speeds and reverse, multiplate metal clutch.

Bentley and the Vauxhall — the kings of today's vintage machinery.

The three-litre Bentley made its bow at the 1919 London Show and was an instant success. Production may have seemed ludicrously low at two or three a week, though even today some of the great G.T. cars are produced in single figures per week. Bentleys went on to dominate the road race scene soon after.

The Vauxhall 30/98 existed as a prototype even in 1914, and small numbers were made during the war, between great batches of 25 H.P. military cars. Production was stepped up in 1919 and this side-valve E-type would do over 85 m.p.h. In later OE form, it was capable of 100 m.p.h., yet was docile when required.

Choice of monarchs

Among the out-and-out luxury cars were Rolls-Royce, Daimler, Lanchester, Leyland and — how many people remember — Guy. The classic Rolls-Royce Silver Ghost, virtually a 1906 machine but now with a self-starter, travelled on imperturbably into the early 20's. Daimler was the choice of monarchs and presidents, and its six-cylinder engine gave it a smooth and sophisticated performance. The great Lanchester Forty was another favourite of Royalty. The Leyland of today can claim

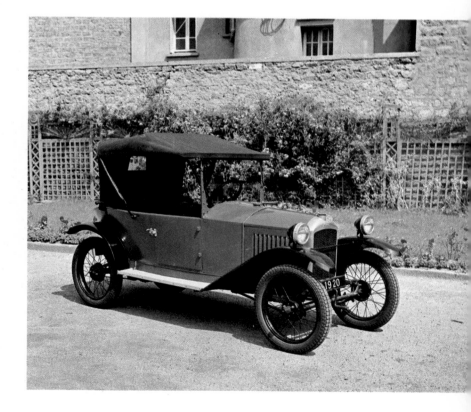

A Fiat "tipo 2", with floral fitments, in production from 1912 to 1920. Below a Fiat 501 tourer under load.

paternity of numerous makes of car, but this is a recent phenomenon; the Leyland 8 of the 20's was a magnificent car but at £3,000 it was dearer than a Rolls, and not more than a score were made. The Guy was more realistic, and was almost unique in being a Vee eight. Smaller models were also made.

Other names of the period are Arrol-Aster, Arrol-Johnston, Storey, Argyll, Belsize, Beardmore, H.E., Horstmann, Deemster, Hampton, Swift, Albert, Straker-Squire, Enfield-Allday and Sheffield Simplex.

In Italy Fiat was predominant in the 20's, not only because of its size but also because it was the only company in the country to follow an up-to-date production policy. This was based on a simple and robust product, capable of attracting a large market and of being manufactured on a mass scale. The car was the Fiat "501", designed by Carlo Cavalli, which was similar in some ways to the Citroën "A"

Though the "501" was only one of three models on which Fiat relied, the others being the "505" and the

"510" both introduced in 1910, it was the first European car built by modern techniques.

Its 1,460 c.c. engine developed 23 H.P. at 2,600 r.p.m. and there was later to be a supercharged version, the "501 S", which could reach 58 m.p.h. Other technical improvements of interest were a new cylinder head design, reduced dimensions of the engine, clutch and gearbox assembly and better carburation.

Production of the "501" ceased in 1926, by which time 45,000 had been built. For a good part of its production life, it was built in the new factory at Lingotto, near Turin, which came into use in 1923.

Lancia production immediately after the war was concentrated on the "Kappa", a face-lift of the 1913 "Theta", which had been one of the first cars with an electrical system built in rather than being treated as an accessory. Only the chassis was modified, and the engine remained the same four-cylinder five-litre. A new engine, a 12-cylinder o.h.v. 7.8-litre which developed 150 H.P., had been designed for the Kappa, but then Lancia decided he could not afford it.

Still elegant

Lancia's new production was to be seen, however, in the following years, first with the "DiKappa", a sporting version of the Kappa, and then with the "TriKappa", which used the chassis of the DiKappa but with a new V8 engine of 4,600 c.c. Top speed was over 80 m.p.h. Production totalled 850.

Other Italian manufacturers' new models included Bianchi with the "S.15", Ansaldo's tourer "4 c" with an 1,800 c.c. engine and a later sporting version, and models by SCAT and SPA.

In Germany the immediate post-war models were of little interest. The older companies such as Benz and

Opel produced austere four- and six-cylinder models, and Mercedes reproduced their old elegant models.

Against the trend in Europe, 1919 marked the disappearance in Belgium of companies well-established before the war and at that year's Brussels Salon there were only the "three M's" (Miesse, Metallurgique and Minerva), and the Excelsior (with an interesting front suspension). In Holland Spyker built a six-cylinder very similar to the current Delaunay-Belleville in France.

In Spain a number of companies were formed, notably Hispano-Suiza in Barcelona, which built sporting and luxury cars. These included an eight-cylinder car which was nearly 23 feet long, shown at the Paris Salon in 1921.

A survey of Europe at this time might close with Czechoslovakia, where Skoda built Hispano-Suiza under lic-

The Lancia 8 cylinder "Trikappa". Above a spartan-looking 1911 Alfa 24 H.P. 4 cylinder, 4,084 c.c. engine giving 42 H.P.

Two Ceirano racing prototypes built in 1922.

An A. V. Monocar of 1921, a typical example of the craze for building individual "specials", particularly popular in Great Britain where races were run for this type of car.

ence and there were other manufacturers such as Praga and Tatra; Switzerland with the Martini, Maximag, Saurer and the Piccard-Pictet; and Austria with three active manufacturers, Austro-Daimler, Gräf and Stift and Steyr.

Among the great luxury vehicles among European cars, the Hispano-Suiza "32 H.P.", which was presented at the Paris Salon in 1919, probably incorporated the biggest technical innovations. They came from the brain of Marc Birkigt, the engineer from Switzerland whose nationality gave rise to the name of a company which united Spanish finance and Swiss technology.

This car had double ignition (coil and magneto), an aviation-type twin-choke carburettor, four-wheel servo-operated brakes and superb suspension. Its many less obvious technical qualities included a crankshaft carved out of a single billet of special steel, which weighed 433 lbs. before machining.

Isotta-Fraschini, too, were successful in the 20's. They introduced their model "8" in two versions, "A" and "B". The Isotta-Fraschini was an imposing car, longer and heavier than either the Hispano-Suiza or the Rolls-Royce, but its 80 H.P. engine could not match the performance of the former and barely that of the latter, whose Silver Ghost had been born in 1906 and was to remain in production until 1924. The Isotta had the advantage of eight cylinders against the six of its competitors, but it was not as silent as the Rolls.

The used car show at Crystal Palace in 1921. Below a 1920 Picard-Pictet.

The tragedy of the Isotta-Fraschini, an excellent car, was that it was launched at the same time as the Hispano-Suiza — which was in almost every respect its better — while the Silver Ghost and the later Phantoms had an aura of their own which not even the Hispano-Suiza could quite match.

There were inevitably other "luxury" cars, including the most expensive of all, the Farman, which had a special appeal in the world of film stars, with the somewhat ambiguous slogan "A car drives, a Farman slides". This company was, however, to leave motoring to concentrate on aeroplane production.

Another was Voisin, who, like Rolls-Royce, Hispano-Suiza, Isotta-Fraschini and Farman, used experience gained in the aero-engine field. His "18" had considerable success, above all because of the silence of its Knight sleeve-valve engine. Delage, too, was producing luxury cars at this time.

Wartime ideas

So far as the sporting side is concerned, after the Armistice the first exploit of note was the speed record set up by de Palma at Ormond Beach in 1919 in a 12-cylinder Packard at just over 150 m.p.h. A short time later the first post-war Indianapolis "500" was held. A strong American entry — including Duesenberg, Frontenac and Packard — was joined by a Peugeot, four specially built Ballots, which had just started car manufacture, and the machine which Goux built from a pre-war Peugeot, making up the deficiencies with Premier parts.

The genuine Peugeot driven by the American Howard Wilcox again won, but it was to be the last European victory for many years. The Peugeot-Premier finished a surprising third. For various minor reasons none of the Ballots finished the race but they were obviously advanced machines destined for success. They had been designed by Henry, formerly of Peugeot, and had his engines' typical characteristics such as twin o.h.c. and four valves per cylinder, to which were married ideas from aircraft production such as aluminium pistons and twin-choke carburettors.

By 1919 the big U.S. companies were using publicity photographs showing women at the wheel. This acknowledgement of the influence of the woman driver was much slower to reach European manufacturers.

Winner goes backward

Another French success was seen in the only other race of international interest held in 1919, the Targa Florio. Run in terrible weather, it was won by André Boillot in a 2½-litre Peugeot. The fastest lap was put up by Antonio Ascari in his first important race.

Boillot won in spite of a spectacular incident. Arriving at the finish at high speed he saw the road ahead blocked by spectators. To avoid an accident he braked, spinning around and crossing the line backwards. At the crowd's insistence an official made Boillot turn his car round and cross the line the right way — just as the other cars came thundering up.

front view of a 1937 PACKARD "SUPER-EIGHT"

engine · front mounted vertical 8 cylinder
bore and stroke · 81 × 127 mm.
capacity · 5261 c.c.
output · 125 H.P. at 3200 r.p.m.
ignition · coil and distributor
clutch · single dry plate
gearchange · 3 speeds plus reverse
weight · 4600 lb.

Austin, from its establishment, was geared to producing a "car for everyone". Above, a 1967 Austin Mini in rural setting, and below a 1922 Austin Seven, with 747 c.c. engine, four cylinders, three speeds plus reverse and four-wheel brakes.

CHAPTER TWENTY
YEARS OF THE CHARLESTON

The years between 1920 and 1925 are among the most important in motoring history. It was in that period that, aided by a favourable economic climate in most countries, manufacturers finally moved from experiment to settled technique for car building. The age produced a breed of cars with the qualities of technical common sense, simplicity, robustness and excellent all-round performance; they have righly been given the name "vintage cars". The period for this includes cars built from 1919 to 1930.

Time of evolution

It was the time of first maturity of the motor car, though the time of frivolity for many who drove them — the Charleston Years. Most of the car's essential features had been defined and brought to a high degree of efficiency and the "Vintage Years", so far as touring cars were concerned at any rate — it was different in the field of racing cars — were to be years of rational evolution rather than revolution. It was in these years that European and American cars were to diverge in types of vehicles produced. Choice on the other side of the Atlantic, which was served by large-scale production, was

limited. In Europe, on the other hand, a wide variety of types of vehicle was produced, yet nearly all with the qualities that have made them "vintage".

The vintage car was quite different from its Edwardian predecessor. The chassis was lighter but rigid and, for all but the start of the 20's four wheels were braked. Engines were smaller and revved at higher speeds following the introduction of aluminium pistons after wartime aero-engine experience. Racing engines went as

high as 4,500 r.p.m., compared with 2,500 r.p.m. before 1914. Gearboxes were now often integrated with the engine, and ignition was electric. Carburation was efficient and free from trouble. The steering was positive, if frequently rather heavy.

So far as bodywork was concerned, the motor car had now finally disregarded its horse-drawn ancestry. Design of the car had a logic of its own. Styling was horizontal rather than perpendicular, and the bonnet line was carried through the scuttle and along the body. Saloon cars no longer had to accommodate passengers' vast headgear and were consequently lower and better proportioned. Exceptions could be found to these generalisations, of course. The Rolls Royce Silver Ghost for instance, never had four-wheel brakes as standard and the later Vauxhall 30/98 had unsuccessful ones, but both of these were essentially Edwardian cars whose excellent qualities enabled them to live in the vintage era.

With regard to production in the years 1920 to 1925, in France Citroën was the innovator as far as line-production was concerned. It replaced the 10 H.P. model "A" with a more powerful version known as the "B. 2", and enlarged its market by launching a successful taxi version.

Clover leaf

In 1922 Citroën presented what was to become one of the best known French cars of the period the 5 H.P. Type "C", in one form known as the "clover-leaf" from its seating plan of two in front and one behind. Unmistakable with its paintwork in lemon-yellow, the 5 H.P. was one of the first cars to be driven by women in any number. It had an 855 c.c. engine which developed 11 b.h.p. and top speed was around 42 m.p.h. Like the "B. 2" it was produced in coupé and drophead

Above, a 1926 Citroën taxi. On the left a Peugeot "163" tourer with four-cylinder engine capable of 37 m.p.h.

"torpedo" versions. This car was also manufactured in Germany under licence by Opel.

Citroën also produced other less important vehicles such as the "Caddy", a sporting version of the "B. 2" with unusual lines somewhat similar to the Labourdette "Skiff". It was not particularly successful. A certain number of tracked vehicles were also produced — the first for civilian use — and memorable journeys were made. They included the first trans-Africa trial, crossing of the Sahara, and cruises across Asia. Renault, too, entered the field of cross-country vehicles but preferred to use six wheels instead of tracks.

In 1920 Peugeot was the second largest French manufacturer after Citroën, but its production consisted of largely outdated models.

1922 SPA "23 S".

Radiator replaced

Renault had been relegated to third place, not because of any shortcomings in its products but because the company had concentrated on "vertical" integration, producing in its own factories a high proportion of all the components used in its cars. Renault was also very active in manufacturing tractors, railway engines, tanks and aero-engines. The Renault range was headed by the huge 40 H.P. which would do 87 m.p.h. and cost the enormous sum of 60,000 francs. Due to the competition from Citroën a strong and economical 6 H.P. was introduced in 1922 with a 950 c.c. engine. This car reappeared two years later as a four-seater, the "N N", which on the track at Miramas covered 10,000 miles at an average of almost 50 m.p.h. About this time the famous coal scuttle radiator was replaced by a rectangular radiator with a grill at the centre that was at first round and then diamond shaped.

Among less important but technically interesting cars

The 5 H. P. Citroën "bateau".

A reunion of venerable cars at a Bentley Drivers' Club meeting.

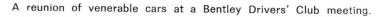

The 1923 Vauxhall 23/60.

produced in France was the Irat two litre with many advanced features such as forced feed lubrication and an American Delco distributor; the sports cars built by Bignan and by Sizaire with overhead camshafts and advanced suspension; and the Omega-Six, a light six cylinder car. So far as Panhard-Levassor and Delahaye were concerned, they continued with their traditional models, concentrating on the 10 H.P. market.

The Austin Seven

On the other side of the Channel, the most important event was the introduction of the famous Austin Seven which was to have, not only in Great Britain but all

Chevrolet equipped a few experimental chassis with air-cooled engines, but it was not until 1960 that the company produced an air-cooled engine for commercial sale.

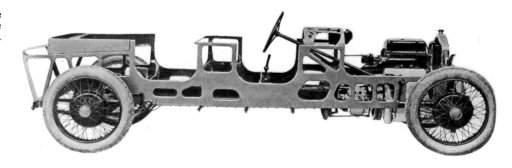

The "monocoque" construction of the Lancia "Lambda" which was one of the manufacturer's many revolutionary ideas.

over Europe, an importance comparable to that of the Ford "T" in America. It was, in fact, the first small car built in Europe which was available, if not to everyone, at least to a much larger public than hitherto. It had something of the appearance of a cyclecar, but there the similarity ended. It was made of the best materials and it was robust and well designed. The engine was famous for its long life and was in production right up to the 60's in one form or another — a little side valve four cylinder of 747 c.c. with a three speed gearbox. It had four wheel brakes at a time when the Rolls Royce Silver Ghost did not, unusual in 1922 when it was launched. Over 100,000 were built.

Another successful English car, but larger, was the famous 1½ litre Morris Cowley built by William Morris, who had designed and put into production in 1912 the Oxford with an 8.9 H.P. White and Poppe engine. After the war the Oxford was produced with a Hotchkiss engine and the cheaper version, the Cowley, was introduced. These "bullnose" cars, so-called because of the shape

1923 Renault 3-4 seater, type KJ 1 with 951 c.c., 3 speeds plus reverse and 47 m.p.h.

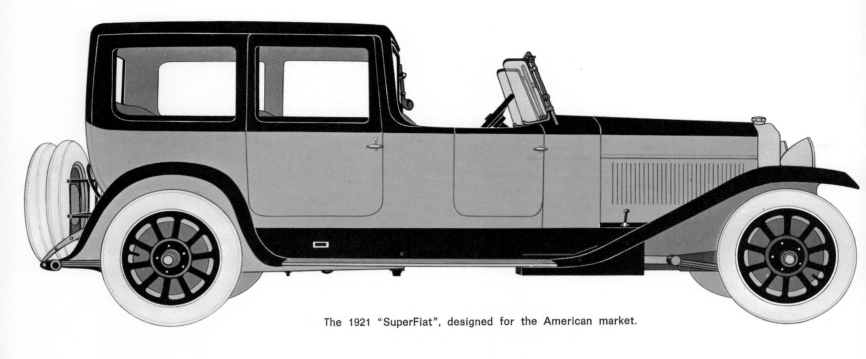

The 1921 "SuperFiat", designed for the American market.

The Fiat "509", the first Italian "utility" car and the first car sold in Italy on hire purchase.

of their radiators were a great success. A series of price reductions in 1922, combined with their sturdiness and reliability, and an excellent gearbox, earned Morris a respect and affection that was similar to that inspired by the Ford "T" in America.

In the luxury class, Rolls Royce decided in 1924 to stop production of the Silver Ghost after 18 years of life. Since October, 1922, it had ceased to be their only model as the 20 H.P. or "Ladies' Rolls", had been introduced on that date, with a three litre six cylinder engine. In 1924 a four speed gearbox and four wheel brakes were fitted.

From Ghost to Phantom

The most significant event for Rolls Royce in the period to 1925, however, was the substitution of the New Phantom or Phantom I for the Ghost. This, in effect, consisted of an improved version of the Ghost chassis but with an entirely new engine. Isotta Fraschini had introduced the eight cylinder "A". This car, with the tremendous eight litre 45 H.P. of Hispano-Suiza, were challenges that could no longer be ignored. A new Rolls Royce chassis was also being developed but this was not to appear until 1929 as the Phantom II.

The new engine retained some of the characteristics of the Ghost, being an in-line six cylinder in two blocks of three, but had a capacity of 7,668 c.c.

Bentley for his part had begun production of the three litre in 1921 but it was not until 1926 that production reached significant quantities. Daimler, ever faithful to the double sleeve-valve, brought out a 12 cylinder version, the double six.

Hire purchase introduced

Italian industry also made considerable technical progress in the period. Fiat presented, in 1921, the luxurious

1923 Alfa P.1, 6 cylinder, 1,990 c.c. engine which produced 80 H.P. at 4800 r.p.m.

"SuperFiat" as a prestige car, particularly for the American market, but it had little success. It was a very long car with a V-12 engine. It had overhead valves and a hydraulic brake servo system. This was the first Italian car to be fitted with a Delco distributor. The body work was horizontal and modern looking in style. In 1922 the Fiat "519" was introduced but was not a commercial success. It was a six cylinder 4,766 c.c. o.h.v. The most important Fiat model of the period was the "509" introduced in 1924 and 1925. It was the first Italian car for the mass market. This car was a great success, partly because Fiat introduced hire-

purchase for the first time. It was sold in four versions with a 990 c.c. engine, torpedo, spider, cabriolet and saloon, and its relatively low price at last took motoring from the exclusive sphere of the rich in Italy.

Lancia, too, introduced in 1922 a memorable model, the Lambda, which exhibited two revolutionary technical characteristics — independent front suspension and "monocoque", or load-bearing body construction. The i.f.s. consisted of vertical springs controlled by hydraulic shock absorbers.

The bodywork was designed to eliminate a problem that was occupying the attention of manufacturers every-

1926 Morris Cowley.

The Oxford, Morris' first pre-1914 saloon, which was continued with great success after the war.

305

THE COUNT AND HIS "CHITTIY"

A boys' book written by Ian Fleming, author of the James Bond books, tells the story of a fantastic motor car capable, among other things, of flying. The car was called Chitty Chitty Bang Bang, which has now given its name to a film. This name, usually abbreviated to Chitty, was also that of three real cars built at the beginning of the 20's. These, too, were extraordinary, and belonged to a singular constructor and driver called Count Louis Zborowski.

Zborowski, known affectionately as "Zbo", was the son of Eliot Zborowski, a keen motoring enthusiast who was killed in 1902 in one of the early motor races. "Zbo" had inherited some remarkable qualities as an "inventor" of motor cars and his first Chitty first saw the light of day in March, 1921.

His aero-engine car had a six-cylinder engine with the far from negligible capacity of 21 litres and followed his usual formula of putting a powerful aero-engine in a skimpy chassis. The car is reported to have consisted of a Maybach engine in a 1913 Mercedes "75" chassis. It would produce over 300 b.h.p. at 1,500 r.p.m. Each cylinder had four overhead valves.

It competed at Brooklands against other monsters such as the V12 Sunbeam and the Wolseley Viper, being frequently defeated and finally destroyed in an accident, when it went off the banking at the track.

Chitty II was similar in general conception to the first but, with better weight distribution, it lasted somewhat longer. This car, which was a Benz, was used in a trial in Africa and, of course, raced at Brooklands.

Chitty III was a relatively smaller car with an engine of a mere 14,700 c.c. and the usual Mercedes chassis. Like its predecessors, this car had brakes on two wheels only, but this time they were on the front. Zborowski built a fourth car in 1923 which, for some reason, was not called the "Chitty IV" but Higham Special, after the place where it was built.

50-litre spectacle

This was the largest car ever to race at Brooklands, having a 27-litre engine. It was raced against Mephistopheles, which was a reconstruction of Eldridge's Fiat. This latter giant had spectacularly blown up the previous May when racing against a Chitty, also wrecked before the end of the race. The reconstructed Fiat had a 21.7-litre Fiat engine and still exists.

The sight and sound of nearly 50-litres in two engines thumping around the circuit — though the "Higham Special" at 100 m.p.h. was revving only at 1,200 r.p.m. — was an impressive spectacle. With the disappearance of these monsters, racing became safer but undoubtedly less colourful.

Zborowski intended to build a fifth car to the same formula. Before he could do so he was killed in the 1924 Monza Grand Prix, when driving a Mercedes.

where; this was the movement between body and chassis caused by the rough roads. One of the solutions tried was the use of flexible coachwork, such as that of Weymann in wood and leathercloth. Lancia simply got rid of the chassis, hanging the mechanical components on a semi integral structure in pressed steel. This lowered the car's centre of gravity, enhancing stability but producing style problems, especially as it was a new type of construction. Thus the first series Lambdas had a long horizontal look that was to be characteristic of later series.

The engine of the "Lambda" was derived directly from the "TriKappa", a 2,120 c.c. narrow V. 4, a type of engine layout which Lancia was to use frequently and still uses today in the Fulvia. It produced 49 b.h.p. at 2,350 r.p.m. and gave the car a top speed of 72 m.p.h. The immediate post-war years were also when Alfa

Romeo made its mark, as the company was now called after Nicola Romeo had joined the old Alfa (Anonima Lombardia Fabbrica Automobile) which was itself the successor to the Italian branch of Darracq. Production was concentrated on sports cars; the first was the assembly in 1919 of the pieces of the "Grand Prix 1914", which had been hidden for the duration of the war in a medicine factory.

Monza winner

The most important of the Alfa Romeo cars was the "20-30 ES Sport" which could reach 80 m.p.h. It was also produced in a touring version. There was also a three litre six cylinder, the "RL" which could achieve 70 m.p.h. in its touring version and 80 m.p.h. as a

Above — Salamano in a Fiat "805" in the European G. P. at Monza in 1923, in which he and Nazzaro took 1st and 2nd places. Right — two perfect models of an "804" and an "805".

The chassis of the Alfa 20-30 ES (1921 to 1923) six cylinder, 4-250 engine giving 67 H.P. at 2,600 r.p.m.

Two of the surviving three Charon Laycocks. Both cars were built in 1921.

sports car, in which was produced in various series until 1924, and there was an "RM" derived from the previous model.

At the same time Alfa Romeo was preparing the first fabulous racing cars — the "P. 1" of 1923, with the two-litre six-cylinder twin o.h.c. engine, and the 1924 "P. 2" with a supercharged two-litre engine. Designed by Vittorio Jano, the latter was to gain many victories for Alfa Romeo down to 1930, including the 1925 Monza Grand Prix, the first world championship.

Among the lesser but very old Italian companies of the time, one of the most active was the SPA. In seeking to attract a new clientele after the immediate post-war difficulties, SPA quickly launched four models, the "23", the "23. S", the "24" and the "24. S". They satisfied neither market, not being luxurious enough to attract the rich and too expensive for mass appeal.

Porsche design

German industry was known best in the earlier years for its racing cars, for which most of the credit belongs to Ferdinand Porsche, he had just joined Daimler and at

Count Masetti winning the 12th Targo Florio in his Fiat S.57/14B after a long duel with Sailer in a Mercedes. It was the first time that German cars and drivers raced in Italy after the first World War.

once designed a two litre which performed brilliantly in the Targa Florio. Shortly afterwards, in 1924, Daimler and Benz merged into one company.

One of the sensational racing results of this time was the victory of an American car, Jimmy Murphy's Duesenberg, in the 1921 Grand Prix de l'Automobile Club de France at Le Mans. There was particularly keen rivalry between the Duesenberg and the four Ballots, both types being three litre eight cylinders. It was to remain the only U. S. victory, however, and the follow-

ing year at Strasbourg the main competition was once again among European manufacturers. The reduction of the formula to two litres led to an effort to reduce weight resulting in several of the cars being particularly dangerous. This cost the life of an up-and-coming young Italian driver, Biagio Nazzaro, nephew of the legendary Felice. The latter won the race (15 years after his first victory in 1907) a few minutes after his nephew died when thrown on the track after an over-fragile rear axle broke. The winning car was a Fiat "804" with a six cylinder

Count Louis Zborowski at the wheel of an Aston-Martin in the 1922 French Grand Prix.

A type 172 BC 5VC Peugeot cabriolet with four cylinders, three speeds and multi-plate clutch.

engine, which averaged about 80 m.p.h. — a figure which was unthinkable only a few months before for a two litre. The quality of this Fiat was confirmed later in the year when Bordino won in a supercharged version the first Italian Grand Prix at the newly opened circuit at Monza.

Revenge for Fiat

The 1923 French Grand Prix was held at Tours and was particularly interesting, because of the wide variety of cars taking part. Fiat entered a supercharged eight cylinder two litre. Delage had a 12 cylinder and Bugatti, whose cars had been having growing success in competition, appeared with three original if somewhat unstable models. Sunbeam had a supercharged six cylinder, clearly inspired by the 1922 Fiat "804 s" and designed by Bertarione, who had joined them from Fiat. It was one of these which won, driven by Henry Segrave, a future world land speed record holder.

Fiat, defeated in France, had its revenge at Monza where its cars could not be beaten either by the Benz "Tropfenwagen" designed by Porsche, or by the "P. 1" Alfa Romeo. The winning driver was Salamano.

1923 Hotsman.

310

1967 DAIMLER "V8"

engine - V8 cylinders
capacity - 2548 c.c.
output - 140 b.h.p. at 5800 r.p.m.
gears - 4-speed plus reverse
brakes - servo discs
weight - 2968 lbs.

From the start of motoring, spasmodic attempts were made to design bodies offering lower wind resistance. Only in recent years has the study become widespread and scientific. Above is an Alfa Romeo 2600 SZ, and below a 1909 Vauxhall "KN".

CHAPTER TWENTY ONE

LE MANS SHOWS THE WAY

"Le Vingt Quatre Heures du Mans", the Le Mans 24 hours, the most celebrated of all long-distance races, arose almost by chance among three enthusiastic drivers. The journalist Faroux, Coquille, the French manager of Rudge-Whitworth, and Durand, secretary of L'Automobile Club de l'Ouest, decided to create a competition which would be a test of robustness and staying power of the cars involved. To this end they arranged to bring back into service, at their own expense, the old Sarthe circuit at Le Mans and to prepare some tough rules for the cars using it. They did not expect to attract much public interest, at least for the first year, but in the

The Bugatti, with its specially designed body, at the 1923 French Grand Prix.

The first "all steel" Citroën.

Baron Manuel de Teffet at the wheel of a 1923 Alfa RL.

event they were pleasantly surprised. At 4 p.m. on 26 May, 1923, when the competitors set off, thousands of spectators were lining the circuit.

All the cars except three were "torpedoes" (open tourers) with sports engines, but strictly standard production models. The three exceptions were closed cars. In spite of the heavy rain, 30 cars finished. There was no winner because the organisers, perhaps from lack of confidence in their enterprise, had stipulated no precise regulations to decide a winner. However, the greatest distance, 1380 miles, was covered by the Chenard-Walker, driven by Lagache and Léonard, at an average speed of 57½ m.p.h.; the fastest lap, at almost 67 m.p.h. was that of Duff and Clement's three-litre Bentley.

Manufacturers' interest

Right from the first meeting the Le Mans 24 Hours showed itself to be worthwhile, and attracted much interest from manufacturers who quickly saw its publicity value. In 1924 another "24 Hour" was held at Spa in Belgium, a clear imitation of the French race.

By that year Americans had beaten off the European invaders at that other great long-distance race, the "Indianapolis 500". In 1920 the "Indy" was won by a

Monroe built in the U.S. by Louis Chevrolet and driven by his brother Gaston, the engine being a copy of the Peugeot. The next year the victory was completely American because the driver was Tommy Milton and the car, a Frontenac, was entirely designed by Chevrolet; second and third places were taken respectively by a Duesenberg and another Frontenac, instead of by Ballots as in the previous year. Meanwhile Gaston Chevrolet had been killed in a speedway crash when driving a Monroe-Frontenac.

Racing Model 'T's

In 1922 Jimmy Murphy won in a car built by himself, a victory he repeated the following year in an H.C.S. (Miller). The European entry in this race was heavy, partly because of the presence of Count Zborowski, the Bugattis (Ettore Bugatti was just beginning the most brilliant period of his career) and the "120 H.P." Mercedes supercharged. The driver of one of these, Lautenschlager, dropped out of the race when his car hit a wall.

The 1924 race was won by a Duesenberg, but one of the points of interest was the entry of three model "T" Fords, modified by and bearing the name of Barber-Warnock. Henry Ford himself had encouraged the entry

1923 Rolls-Royce "20". Below a Chenard & Walker at Le Mans in 1929.

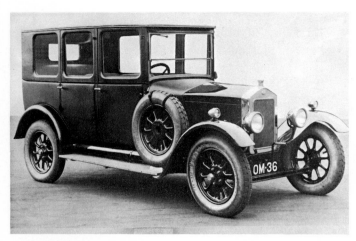
1924 Wolseley 11/22 H.P.

1921 Studebaker "Big Sedan".

after the brilliant performance of one which had been entered the previous year. In these races, the name of Harry A. Miller, ex-carburettor specialist, was always prominent, with cars bearing his own name or those of Durant or H.C.S.

He was also to build in 1923 the first modern racing car, with front-wheel drive, having an advanced brake layout working on the differential. From this car, the Murphy, there was to be developed more or less directly a long line of f.w.d. vehicles culminating in the famous Cords, which are now prized by collectors.

Balloon tyres

About half-way through the 20's, at the same time that large scale production was being introduced by the large European manufacturers, radical technical developments were taking place on the car itself. One of these was the introduction of the low-pressure tyre, after a number of unsuccessful attempts since the beginning of the century.

This was in part due to the way such tyres exaggerated the effects of uneven roads on the steering wheel, an effect known as "shimmy". When these problems had been mainly overcome by modifying the suspension and steering box, balloon tyres quickly became universal. Apart from being more comfortable, these tyres were safer; the effect of a burst was less drastic than when the pressure was seven or eight atmospheres.

A great step forward was the adoption by most manufacturers, after 20 years of hesitation, of four-wheel brakes. The same period also saw the first tentative ap-

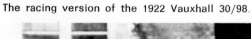
The racing version of the 1922 Vauxhall 30/98.

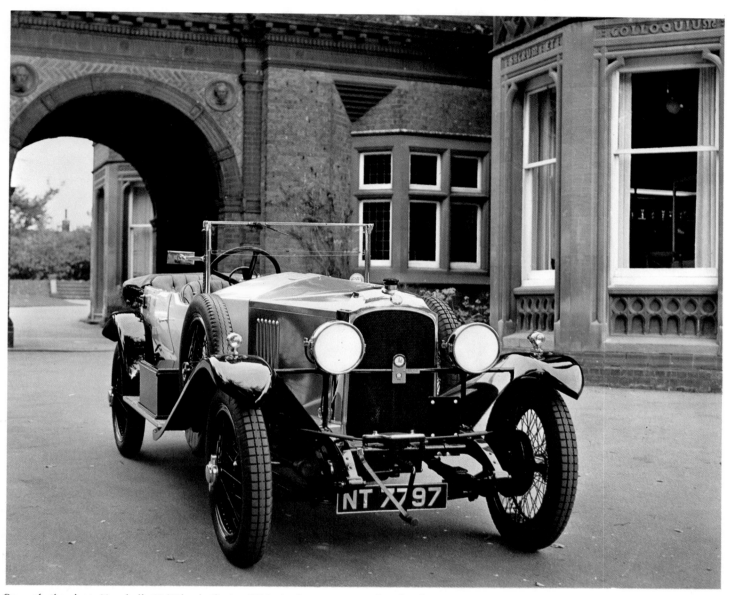

One of the last Vauxhall 30/98's built in 1926. It is uncertain why the figures 30/98 were used; they were given to the car by an unknown engineer.

Steel bodies

One important development, this time of a technological nature, was the adoption of the "all steel" body. This consisted of a structure of welded steel panels fastened to the chassis, resulting in a box structure considerably stronger than was possible with composite construction. Citroën were the pioneers, using this system in agreement with the Budd Manufacturing Company of America, on later editions of the "B. 2".

The introduction was not without difficulties. The chassis was too light and did not stand up well to the stresses placed on it by the rigid superstructure; at nearly every bounce, for instance, the doors would fly

plications of brake servo mechanisms, built on a wide variety of principles and at the time limited to luxury cars. Some years later hydraulic braking was to be introduced.

open. The chassis was reinforced, and later a new model, the "B. 12", appeared in 1925-6.

Finally, even the noise from a motor car in motion began to decrease. There were a number of reasons. Devices stopped the interminable squeak of the springs by means of pressure-greasing and gaiters; crankshafts were better balanced; gears were more precise. New oils and pressure instead of merely splash lubrication played an important part.

Most of these changes were introduced gradually by manufacturers on models already in production, and 1925 to 1928 were mainly years of re-design and technical improvement for most companies.

One car with several unusual features, however, was the Citroën "B. 12" referred to already. Apart from the new all-steel body, it had an angular body at a time when others were beginning to soften the line. This partly explains the limited success of the model.

Another "great" car of the period was the twin overhead camshaft "6C 1500" Alfa Romeo, designed by Jano to

1928 Alfa-Romeo 6 C 1,500 SS.

1928 Simca Violet with air-cooled twin engine.

1930 Austin 747 c.c. special.

an unusual formula — six cylinders as in luxury cars, but with a capacity of only 1½ litres. It was the only car built by the Milan company that directly exploited their racing car experience.

The new car was presented at the motor show in Milan in 1925 but did not enter into production till 1927. It was at once a great success and was produced in various versions until 1931. Power ranged from 44 H.P. in the "normal" version to 54 and 60 in the twin overhead camshaft "sport" and up to 84 H.P. in the last series, which were supercharged and could reach 97 m.p.h. The "6C 1500" had many racing successes, particularly in the open two-seater and tourer versions built by the coachbuilder Zagato.

Closing up

Across the Atlantic Walter Percy Chrysler was intent on starting manufacture on his own account with a car that had some unusual features. At the time there had been a decisive change in taste. The public was tired of the "torpedo", the open tourer, and had opted for the "sedan", or closed saloon. A relatively small company, Essex, were largely responsible for this revolution, having attracted attention with a four-cylinder car of modest size but comfortable and well-proportioned. Even the largest companies had to review their production programmes quickly and introduce "sedans". The tourer was abandoned, and a new form of open car was to appear, the cabriolet or "roadster".

The only one not having to react immediately to the change in the market was Ford, well-entrenched with a model for which there was no price competition. But even at the moment when the giant of Detroit was recording an industrial triumph (20 June, 1925 - 9000 cars built in 24 hours) the first signs of the rapid decline of the "T" were apparent. The Lizzie was given face-lifts such as wire-spoked wheels, lowered bodywork and coloured paintwork, but in May, 1927, the last "Lizzie", No. 15,007,003, came off the assembly line.

A 1924 Peugeot and a 1925 Ford "T" "Lizzie".

The first Chrysler. Below the 1922 Nash model "46".

A close-up look at the 6,597 c.c. engine of a 1922 Hispano-Suiza

Her closest rival, the "490 Chevvie" was having ever-increasing success. It was the car which William P. Knudsen, the president of General Motors, had made the principal weapon in his attack. The establishment of the third big American company was rapid. Walter Chrysler, the car "company doctor" first with Willys-Overland and then with Maxwell-Chalmers, conceived between 1923 and 1924 the idea of launching under his own name a car which was to be very different from its competitors. One of its main features was a high-compression six-cylinder engine, with an improved performance made possible by the recent advances in the quality of petrol then available.

Hotel exhibition

The birth of the "Six" was not easy. The organisers of the New York motor show would not give Chrysler a stand so he exhibited the car in the Waldorf-Astoria. The public was favourably impressed by the elegant body, the interior finish, and the car's silence (the engine had seven main bearings and flexible mountings). The "Six" was an immediate success, a success then possible only in America; 106,803 were sold in the first years of its introduction at the competitive price of 1526 dollars.

This impressive launch of the "Six", also known as the "70", led to Chrysler quickly becoming third in size after General Motors and Ford. The company set up branches in Europe and absorbed Dodge.

Other aspects of the American scene in the 20's were the diffusion in the luxury field of eight-cylinder in-line engines, the brief appearance of a luxury make, the Wills-Sainte Claire, and the last efforts by the supporters of the steam car.

The "straight eight" engine was popularised by Ballot's racing success with a similar engine in Europe. Whereas in Europe production of such engines remained small (Fonck, Isotta-Fraschini, Leyland), in America considerable numbers were produced to the eve of the second World War, beginning in 1923 when Packard introduced an engine of this type and gave up the over-complicated 12-cylindered "Twin Six".

The Wills-Sainte Claire was a large and extremely silent car, admired and desired both in America and Europe. The engine was a V-8 overhead camshaft. The company was founded in 1920 by Harold C. Wills, who had worked with Ford since 1903 but who was dissatisfied with the standstill policy on production at Detroit. He decided to do in America what Marc Birkigt was doing in Europe with Hispano-Suiza.

The early success of the Wills-Sainte Claire was helped by publicity from a series of coast-to-coast drives with the new car and a Packard doing the run alternately. Wills' time for the first in 1925 was 102 hours. The last run was by a Rickenbacker which had inserted itself into the private duel, and beat them both with a time

A 1925 3 litre Bentley.

The 1925 3,993 c.c. Sunbeam "Tiger".

of 72½ hours. Wills-Sainte Claire shut down in 1926, beaten by its inability to compete with the big companies.

Steam has its day

The Indian summer of the "steamers" was due to the initiative and skill of an unfailing supporter of the steam car, Abner Doble. He began to build luxurious cars of this type in a small workshop in California. When Doble finally had to close down, only 28 of these vehicles had

been built — but one of them had achieved 125 m.p.h. In the European sporting events, 1924 was the year in which "Mephistopheles" gained the world speed record at Arpajon near Paris. (This record was the first event of world interest held on the new French circuit inaugurated on the occasion of the 1924 Paris Salon. The circuit was established after the French magazine "Automobile" held a referendum among the major world motoring personalities, resulting in a strong feeling in favour of a new circuit near the French capital).

The Fiat "Mephistopheles" of 1924 was very different

1924 Essex "roadster special".

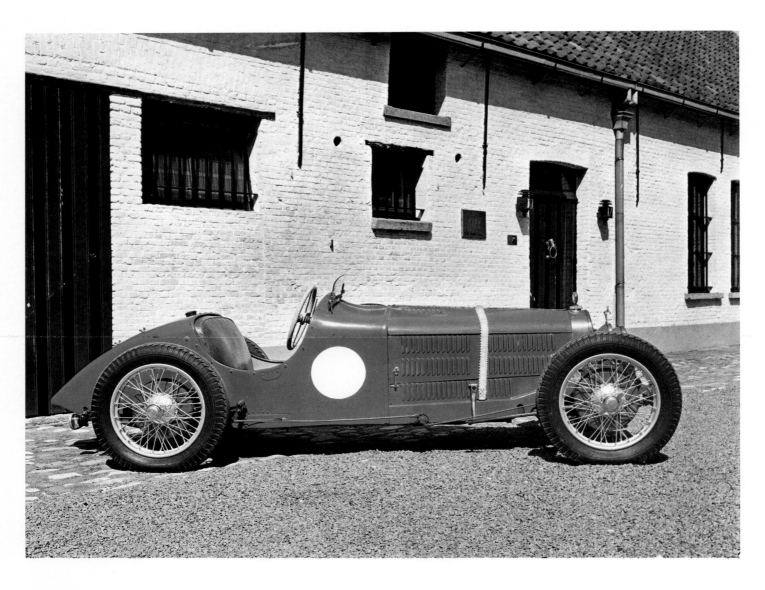

A 1920 Lombard and the Bugatti team at the 1924 French G. P.

A single-seater 40 H.P. built by Renault specifically for performance records. In July, 1926, it broke the 24-hour record at Montlhéry by covering 2,587 miles at over 107 m.p.h. It had a nine-litre engine.

from that which is reputed to have recorded 120 m.p.h. at Brooklands in 1907. The chassis was much the same, but lengthened. In 1921 it had lost two of its four cylinders in the course of a race — they literally came off — and Ernest Eldridge fitted a Fiat 22-litre aero-engine, the six-cylinder "A 12 bis" which produced 300 b.h.p. at 1600 r.p.m.

It was to accept this engine that the chassis was made longer, and a new radiator of nine-gallon capacity installed. The car weighed two tons. After testing at Brooklands, "Mephistopheles" was taken to Montlhéry and on 12 June, 1924, reached the spectacular speed of 234.986 k.p.h. over the flying kilometre (about 146 m.p.h.).

Secrecy and triumph

The 1924 Grand Prix of the Automobile Club de France was held on the circuit near Lyons where it had been held ten years previously, though the track had been considerably modified in the meantime. It was in this race that the Alfa Romeo P. 2 made its first triumphal appearance in an international event.

Jano had previously run it in a race at Cremona where it had astounded the opposition (it had been built in great secrecy) by winning at almost 100 m.p.h. in the hands of a new racing star, Antonio Ascari. Ascari also drove in the French Grand Prix, when victory went to his team colleague Giuseppe Campari at an average of 71 m.p.h., a high speed in view of the circuit's famous S-bends and "devil's elbows".

Many of the cars in the race were supercharged, though second and third places went to two aspirated Delages. Another point of interest of this race was the first appearance of the new sleek and elegant "Type 35" Bugattis which embodied the best of Molsheim's design capabilities. In the 1924 race they did not have the speed to defeat their rivals, but from that year on they were to exhibit qualities of reliability and road-holding which were to enable them to win many races in future. The Bugattis also became the favoured car of the sporting enthusiast.

The P. 2 repeated its success at Monza in the Italian Grand Prix, this time driven by Ascari. It was here that Count Louis Zborowski, of Chitty Chitty Bang Bang fame, was killed in his Mercedes.

This was the last year of the two-litre formula, which

1927 Talbot Darracq G.P.

was then changed to 1½ litres and the minimum weight raised 50 kilograms. This was an effort by the authorities, who had become alarmed by the high speeds already possible, to reduce the danger to drivers.

The 1925 Grand Prix was run at Montlhéry for the first time. Also for the first time, the regulation requiring a mechanic to be carried in the car was abolished. This gave rise to the introduction of "pits", where the mechanic and his tools were now accommodated.

Victory went easily to the new supercharged Delage driven by Benoist. The Alfa Romeo team retired from the race as a mark of mourning for Ascari, who was killed when his P. 2 overturned after hitting a wall. The Delage victory was especially significant as it showed how a vastly complicated engine like the 12-cylinder, which revved up to 7,000 r.p.m., could run to the limit for hundreds of miles without stopping. This was a test of reliability that would have been considered impossible a short time previously.

GYROSCOPIC CARS

In dealing with the motor car it is difficult, if not impossible, to produce an idea which has not already been achieved or at least tried. There have, for example, been cars with only two wheels, however strange this may seem. The idea arose from consideration of the friction between tyres and road, which absorbed a good part of the power produced by the engine, and it seemed obvious that to reduce four wheels to two would also reduce this loss of power.

Russian first

One of the first to be attracted to this idea was the Russian engineer Schilowsky who, after much study, modified a Wolseley to his ideas. He had first to provide for the stability of his vehicle — the rotation of the wheels in this heavy six-seater tourer having insufficient gyroscopic effect in themselves, unlike those of a bicycle or motorcycle. He did this by fitting a heavy gyroscope low down, driven by the engine and connected to it. The car was ready in 1910 and performed "reasonably well" according to contemporary reports, but quickly disappeared.

Much more soundly based were the theoretical studies of an American, James Scripps Booth. Aware of Schilowsky's experiment, he produced a more advanced design, again using a gyroscope, but with two auxiliary lateral wheels which were retracted when the car was in motion. Scripps Booth needed a powerful engine to

drive the gyroscope as well as the wheels, but it had also to be compact to make room for the gyroscope. He had difficulty finding such an engine and finally went to Europe, where De Dion had just produced his famous V8 to power his luxury models.

After a long consideration of the De Dion engine, Scripps Booth returned to America where he built a modified version. Output was raised to 45 H.P. and the engine was installed it in an aluminium chassis.

This strange vehicle, the "Bi-Autogo", worked well but apart from limitations in its use — it was certainly not suitable for use on congested roads — it was never put into production.

Having spent 25,000 dollars on it, the inventor was then out of funds and eventually gave his "Bi-Autogo" to the technical institute at Cranbrook in Michigan, where he lived.

Common characteristics

He was, however, pleased with his engine and set up a small factory producing luxury cars fitted with it, but with four wheels. Here again the outcome was unsuccessful and in 1913 he sold his rights to General Motors. In the same year C. F. Kettering designed for Cadillac (part of General Motors since 1909) a luxury car using a V8 engine directly derived from that of Scripps Booth. In this way the Cadillac engine descended directly from that of De Dion, as their common characteristics of power, flexibility and silence showed.

1967 LANCIA FULVIA COUPÉ

engine - front mounted 4 cylinder
capacity - 1216 c.c.
output - 80 H.P. (DIN)
gearchange - 4 speeds plus reverse
brakes - discs
transmission - front wheel drive

The station wagon was born in America to meet the demand of customers who needed a private goods/passenger vehicle. The value of such a car was appreciated much sooner in the U.S. than in Europe. Below, a 1958 Buick and above, the Citroën ID 19.

CHAPTER TWENTY TWO
EUROPE TURNS TO THE WEST

The principal characteristics of the touring car in the years around 1926 may be summed up as follows: a more rounded appearance, which was a step towards aero-dynamic styling, high bonnets with low windscreens, prominent rear luggage platform with space for one or two spare wheels and pressed steel wheels. Wire wheels were almost entirely limited to sports cars.

Travelling to China

From the technical point of view the major evolution was to come later, towards the end of the decade, when European cars adopted features recently introduced in America such as higher compression ratios — 7 to 1 became common — and higher engine revs, frequently reaching 3,500 r.p.m.
One of the more interesting cars of the period was the Citroën "B 14", a more powerful version of the "B 12". After initial difficulties due to reducing the weight of the chassis, the "B 14" became popular in France and was

Citroën B 14.

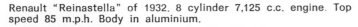

Renault "Reinastella" of 1932. 8 cylinder 7,125 c.c. engine. Top speed 85 m.p.h. Body in aluminium.

produced also as a van, the first with an enclosed driving position. This car also figured in the early introduction of the motor car to China when 1,200 were supplied to Nanking.

Later Citroën launched the "C 4" and the "C 6", large cars in the American style with respectively four and six cylinders for which the Javel factory introduced two unusual elements for Europe — two-tone coach-work and an engine mounted on flexible supports, both ideas inaugurated years before in America by Chrysler.

Renault launched a wide range of new models, finally abandoning the famed coal scuttle bonnet: the "Reinastella", a large stately vehicle of 41 fiscal horsepower which replaced the famous "40 H.P." with a capacity reduced from 9,125 to 7,125 c.c.; the "Monastella" and the "Vivastella", two six-cylinder luxury cars; and the "Monasix", an elegant 1½-litre six-cylinder.

Opel becomes American

Peugeot, too, at last succumbed to the fashion for six cylinders, with the "12 Six". The new make of Lucien Rosengart, an ex-colleague of Citroën and formerly managing director of Peugeot, came out with a "4 H.P.", which was the Austin Seven built under licence and

with coil ignition. This was a great success. There were also several minor French makes at this time, among which were numbered Hotchkiss, which returned to the six-cylinder formula with a three-litre, Sizaire with a double sleeve-valve engined car with i.f.s., and a number of supercharged sports cars such as Godefroy and Levêque, CIME and Chapuis-Dornier. There was also a sensational prototype by the Bucciali brothers, with front-wheel drive and electric brakes.

In Germany there was a revival of Opel after it had been bought by General Motors, and a number of new

four- and six-cylinder models were introduced. Mercedes redesigned the appearance of its car, using more modern finishes, and, under the guidance of Hans Nibel, it also returned to racing with Rudolf Caracciola at the wheel of a big supercharged SSK.

Finally, two German versions of the ubiquitous Austin Seven were built — the little Hanomag, and the "Dixie" produced by BMW (Bayerische Motorenwerke).

In Italy Fiat replaced the out-of-date "501" by the "503" which kept the same capacity (1,460 c.c.) but increased the output from 21 to 27 H.P. It had a new

Above a 1931 Opel 6 cylinder. Below the 1928 Mercedes-Benz SSK, supercharged.

Above a Fiat "520". Below the first B.M.W., built in 1928.

"turbulence" cylinder head — introduced by Ricardo in England — to improve burning of the petrol and air mixture. Later Fiat added another luxurious model, the six-cylinder "520"; from this car two larger versions were evolved — the "521" and the "525" — to add to the already wide range.

Lancia, with the long series of Lambdas drawing to a close, inaugurated the "Dilambda", a long car with a four-cylinder V8 engine capable of 75 m.p.h. when introduced and over 80 m.p.h. later on. Alfa Romeo in 1929 launched the glorious "6C 1750", a development of the previous 1½-litre model that for many years was to be the pride — or the dream — of so many motoring

A 1932 Fiat "Balilla", which was for Italians what the Ford "T" had been for Americans.

1929 Bugatti. Below two Bugattis in the Burgoyne four-hour race. Chiron is in second place.

enthusiasts all over the world. It was built in tourer, G.T. and sports forms, and later versions were supercharged.

In England Riley introduced in 1926 the important and long-lived sporty 1,100 c.c. "Nine". Its triumph was marred by the death of Parry Thomas, who designed the Brooklands version and who was killed in a record attempt in "Babs", the chain-driven Leyland, on Pendine Sands.

In the U.S. the Ford "A" had finally replaced the "T", and though its performance was up-to-date it clearly showed its ancestry. This new Ford four-cylinder had hardly begun to win back its own market when the celebrated Chevrolet "Six" was introduced — more modern-looking, lively and silent.

With this car General Motors became the largest motor company in America, on the eve of the 1929 world economic crisis.

In the light car field the Studebaker Corporation had success in Europe as well as in America with the "Erskine Six", named after the company's president — who committed suicide during the crisis — while Chrysler with the Plymouth brand name returned to the four-cylinder formula. Among the bigger cars Cadillac introduced a model with an unusual device — an all-synchromesh gearbox.

1929 Duesenberg "J" — an American high quality car.

Bugatti supreme

In the sporting field the second half of the 20's is filled with memorable achievements, of glorious ends and brilliant beginnings. Almost all the races of 1926, based on the new 1½-litre formula, were won by Bugatti, who was almost without competition. Most other man-

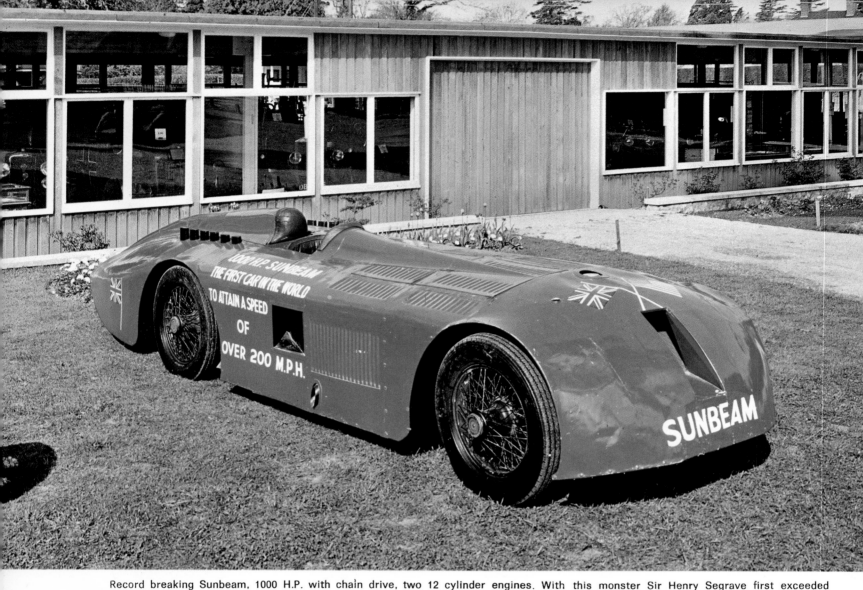

Record breaking Sunbeam, 1000 H.P. with chain drive, two 12 cylinder engines. With this monster Sir Henry Segrave first exceeded 200 m.p.h.

The "Golden Arrow" built in 1929 to the designs of Capt. J. S. Irving. Its engine was a Schneider Trophy type Napier Lion 12 cylinder aero-engine which gave 930 H.P. With this car Segrave raised his own record to 230 m.p.h.

A splendid American special and a famous woman. The car is a "Terraplane" special and beside it is Amelia Earhart, the first woman to "solo" the Atlantic in 1932.

ufacturers had withdrawn rather than face the huge expense of re-design involved in a change of formula. These Bugatti successes culminated with wins at Monza (Sapiba-Charavel) and in the French Grand Prix at Miremas with Jules Goux, and served to create an atmosphere of fanatical support for the cars among their many supporters. To be the owner of a Bugatti at that time was indeed the pride of a privileged few in Europe. It was just after this that eight of the most fabulous cars ever built were produced at Molsheim — the Bugatti Royales. Made to the highest standards of craftsmanship, the big cars — the engine was 12,760 c.c. and produced 300 b.h.p. at 1700 r.p.m. — had many unusual features, including wheel spokes attached to the brake drums.

In 1927 the world championship, won the previous year by Bugatti, went to Delage, who in the meantime had developed the 1½-litre formula to the limit of its then possibilities, getting an output of 170 b.p.h. with a supercharger (in 1965, 1½-litre non-supercharged Formula I cars were producing over 220 b.p.h.). The victories were at Montlhéry with Benoist and again at Monza, as well as in the Grands Prix of England and Spain.

The year 1928 opened with an unusual endurance trial between the French industrialist Charles Weymann and F. E. Moskovics, manager of Stutz, at Indianapolis. The race took on the aspect of French v. American industry, with the respective sides being represented by a relatively well-worn Hispano-Suiza six-cylinder and a Stutz eight-cylinder. The Hispano-Suiza won when the Stutz engine gave up after 19 hours.

For three years, beginning with 1928, Grands Prix were run to a "formule libre" with weight limits of 550 and 750 kilograms. As has occurred whenever the "formule libre" has been in force, interest in Grand Prix racing declined. In spite of this, many of the famous drivers of the future years made their first appearances at this time, including Chiron, Nuvolari, Divo, Varzi, Bordino, Ferrari, Arcangeli, Materassi, Etancelin and Brilli-Peri. Many of the victories went to the various forms of the

The Ford V8-40, 65 H.P. at 3,400 r.p.m., top speed about 75 m.p.h.

1934 MG "K 3 Magnette".

"Type 35" Bugatti, as was the case in the Grand Prix of 1928 won by Williams at Comminges, and the Italian Grand Prix at Monza won by Chiron. This Monza had one of the worst accidents in the history of motor racing, when Materassi ran into the crowd in a Talbot, and 22 spectators were killed.

In 1929, the year of the great U.S. slump which had effects all over the world — including European motoring — British motor production became for the first time the largest in Europe (235,000 vehicles in the year against 230,000 in France).

Also in 1929 Ford set up its new subsidiary at Dagenham, and Renault built a new factory on the island of Séguin in the Seine.

A little later there was a second wave of endurance trials in Africa, culminating in a desert crossing by a Peugeot "201" and a van. A Citroën caravan, using half-tracked vehicles to cross Asia, had exciting adventures in the Pamir and China; it ended tragically with the sucessive deaths of the two leaders, Haardt and Point.

In England the beginning of the 30's marked the end of two famous and glorious names as separate entities — Bentley, which was absorbed by Rolls-Royce, and Lanchester, which became part of the Daimler company. Some years earlier Vauxhall had been bought by General Motors.

On the other side of the Atlantic a new company of mixed nationality was formed, Durant-Mathis, by the ex-head of General Motors and the French manufacturer Emile Mathis. This company, from its factory in Lansing, produced an interesting small coupe called the "PY", quickly christened "wonder car" by the Americans, who were amazed at its small size.

American super-cars

The most important launchings of 1930-1931, however, were the American "super-cars". They were a reaction against the crisis just overcome, when film stars and millionaires once again began to put their wealth on show. These cars included a 16-cylinder Cadillac, designed in secret by Charles Kettering in 1926 and launched in 1930; the "160 H.P." Auburn; a redesigned front-wheel Packard "Twin Six"; and 12-cylinder Pierce-Arrows and Lincolns. The last two had hydraulic tappets to ensure silence.

All these cars, however, remained one level below the fabulous Duesenberg "J", designed after the young industrialist Erret Lobban Cord had taken over leadership of the company. This car was the undoubted star of American cars until it was replaced by the even more

The 12-cylinder Pierce-Arrow of 1929 made tentative steps towards incorporating headlamps in the mudguards.

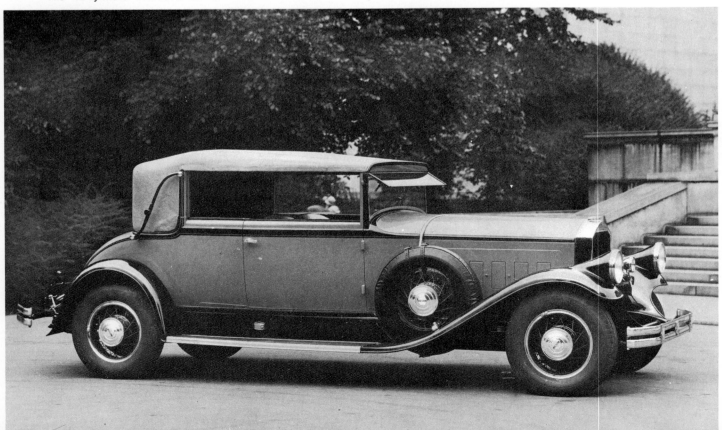

striking supercharged 325 b.h.p. "SJ" in 1932, a car which cost Fred Duesenberg his life in an accident.

With regard to racing, 1930 was again dominated by Bugatti, even though Alfa Romeo re-entered the field with a redesign of the "P. 2" — modifications which mainly concerned the suspension and the body, which was now cut short to accommodate the spare wheel. Maserati, however, were making progress, having begun to build their own racing cars in 1926 after years of tuning and modifying Isotta-Fraschinis. The French Grand Prix was won by Etancelin, with Sir Henry Birkin's sedate but potent Bentley four-seater tourer in second place. Monza, however, was won by Varzi in the new eight-cylinder two-litre Maserati.

In 1931 the monumental Mercedes "SSKL", the outcome of a number of successful predecessors, with its long bonnet and its chassis bored for lightness, made its first impact in the German Grand Prix, driven by

1928 supercharged 4½ litre Bentley.

1929 Alfa-Romeo 1,750 SS.

1932 Maserati 2,000.

Caracciola. At Le Mans, however, it was beaten by Howe and Birkin's Alfa Romeo. The "SSKL" was only one of the new cars in the battle being fought in Europe.

Bugatti abandoned the aging "Type 35", redesigned the engine to 2,300 c.c. and 160 b.h.p. and fitted it in the new "Type 51". Jano at Alfa Romeo had also designed the new "8C 2300". The year's victories were divided among the manufacturers. Alfa Romeo won the Targa Florio and the European Grand Prix at Monza with Nuvolari driving, and Bugatti the French Grand Prix with Chiron and Varzi.

The years after 1930 saw a wave of new ideas in touring cars after the relative inertia of the preceding years. In France Citroën redesigned the "C 4" and the "C 6", improving the engines' flexible mountings. In Italy a great new car was born, one that was to be widely distributed — the Fiat "508". In "Balilla", or sports form, it was produced only in small numbers.

The Mercedes SSKL 6 cylinder 7,100 c.c. engine giving 225 b.h.p. at 3,200 r.p.m.

Launched as the first Italian popular car, the small three-speed "508" saloon and touring versions were shown at the Milan Salon in 1932. The cars had a 995 c.c. engine and could reach just over 50 m.p.h. Consumption was 30 to 34 m.p.g. A second version was launched in 1934 with more rounded bodywork and a built-in boot. The car was famous for the robustness and longevity of its engine, as was to be its successor, the renowned Fiat "1100".

At almost the same time a second important car in Italian motoring history was launched, the Lancia "Augusta", a sleek 1194 c.c. saloon, with the usual narrow V layout of the engine. It had two American characteristics redesigned for European use — a "free-wheel" which enabled the engine to idle while the car was running, and the front suspension and steering joints lubricated by engine oil.

In England Hillman gave up building large vehicles and began production of the Minx, which has persisted in various forms right up to the present. On a different basis entirely, success was achieved by M. G. (Morris Garages) which had built sports cars from its foundation by Cecil Kimber in 1923. In 1932, after the "M" and "J" type Midgets, the 1100 c.c. K. 3 Magnette was introduced. This was to be very successful in road racing, driven by Nuvolari and others.

In France Peugeot redesigned the "201" in 1931 and fitted independent front suspension, which was later applied to a redesigned 1½-litre "301". Renault increased its vast range of cars with a relatively cheap large eight-cylinder sporting car, the "Nervasport".

Citroën, having extensively modernised the Javel factory, had to forego the expense of designing new models and instead sought publicity by means of unusual endurance runs with Rosalie I, Rosalie II and Rosalie III ("Petite Rosalie"), which were based on the C 6 and the 8.

Between 15 March and 27 June 1933 Rosalie III covered 300,000 kilometres (about 186,000 miles) on the track at Montlhéry at an average of 58 m.p.h., breaking 106 world and 193 international records. The offer of a substantial sum to any car that could do better was not taken up.

Designed for lorry

Also in France, Delahaye's engineering director, Weiffenbach, built the Superluxe, which he developed into the "135" that was to become one of the finest sports cars in the world, by fitting a six-cylinder engine originally designed for a lorry into a Pegase chassis designed for Amilcar! The brothers Angelo and Paul-Albert Bucciali built a series of prototype front-wheel drive cars which, though anticipating a layout which was to become widespread, had little success.

Across the Atlantic Ford was playing a series of commercial aces. First of all, in 1932, he launched a redesign of the "A", called the "B". Two months later this car was offered with an optional V8 engine with excellent characteristics — 65 b.h.p. at 3,400 r.p.m. giving 75 m.p.h. in the saloon and over 80 in the roadster. Its success was immediate.

Within a year the V8, which cost only 505 dollars against the 495 of the four-cylinder, had sold to the tune of 300,000 cars. Then Ford changed everything, replacing the "B" with the "V8-40", with more modern lines, of which three million were built in three years.

In racing in Europe in 1932, there was very keen rivalry between Alfa Romeo, Bugatti and Maserati. Alfa had prepared a new racing car, the "type B" or "P3", by combining the old Monza with a 12-cylinder "Type 3" which had made a brief appearance the year before. This car had twin superchargers and produced 215 b.h.p.

A red Fiat beside a 1922 Delfosse.

at 5,600 r.p.m., giving a top speed of over 140 m.p.h. The season opened with a Nuvolari win at Monaco in the Monza (the "P 3" did not appear until the Italian Grand Prix). Caracciola, temporarily in an Alfa, won at Nürburgring but Nuvolari won the Targa Florio and then, in the "P 3", the Italian Grand Prix at Monza and the French Grand Prix at Rheims.

In 1936 the Scuderia Enzo Ferrari was born. The former driver and mechanic took over the Alfa Romeo racing cars, the company having officially withdrawn from racing. The "P 3", however, was not available to him and he had to modify the old Monza, increasing capacity to 2,650 c.c. and fitting a single-seater body in his well-equipped workshop in Modena. Varzi won the first victory at Monaco (the race which included the famous finish of Nuvolari, pushing his smouldering car) and then Campari won the French Grand Prix at Montlhéry in the new 2,900 c.c. Maserati. After this, Nuvolari left Ferrari and joined Maserati, taking these cars to victory in race after race that season, apart from the Ulster T.T. which he won in an M. G.

This caused Ferrari to press Alfa Romeo for the "P 3", which he finally acquired. With these cars — in the hands of Fagioli and Campari — he won the races at Pescara and Monza. Campari died the same day at Monza in a subsequent race.

Era of aerodynamics

At this point the era of aerodynamics arrived. Manufacturers made the first serious steps in considering the problems of penetration of the air, although tentative efforts had been made much earlier. The techniques were usually limited to streamlining the mudguards, re-designing the radiator grille and removing the more obvious angles and projections. One car was particularly notable, the Chrysler's Airflow. Chrysler quickly dropped it, however, and with good reason because it was not a particularly handsome car.

Streamlining has little effect on performance and fuel consumption at average speeds and usually involves

Montlhéry 1934. Achille Varzi at the wheel of a "P 3", follows Fagioli in a Mercedes.

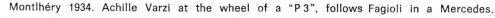

The famous "P 3", a 1932 Alfa Romeo "Grand Prix" Type B. An eight-cylinder 2,654 c.c. engine with two compressors.

significant sacrifice of useable space. However, the move in the 1930's towards cleaning up body lines was entirely justified on safety grounds and could produce aesthetic advantages.

'Little mouse' is born

Both Peugeot and Fiat in Europe made progress in this field, the former with the "402" of 1935 and the second with a new six-cylinder called the "1500", which had very smooth lines and was well accepted.

The same styling principles were applied a year later to the first Italian utility car, the Fiat "1500" which was known as "Topolino", or "little mouse", to millions of Italians. This car was remarkable, apart from its aerodynamic lines, for its solution to the problem of making room for two people and their luggage in such a little car. Among other features, the engine was cantilevered out in front. The Topolino had a 570 c.c. engine which produced 13 b.h.p. Third gear was synchronized.

The birth of the "500" also saw the birth of a new French company, "Simca" (Société Industrielle de Mécanique et Carrosserie Automobile) created by H. T. Pigozzi to build Fiat cars under licence, the first of which was the "500", renamed the Cinq. About the same time another new company, Matford, was formed in Strasburg by Emile Mathis to build Ford cars in Europe; production began of a medium-size V8.

Among French cars of the time the Citroën "7" was of considerable importance. This, with its successor, the "11", was to have the longest production run of any car, exceeding both the Rolls-Royce Silver Ghost and the Ford "T".

In 1934 Citroën was in a crisis, despite the publicity from the "Petite Rosalie" model in the previous year. Competition was keen and the company was short of money. It was clear that an outstanding new car was essential, but there was no capital available to design

one. In a corner of the Javel factory was a prototype so unusual and so advanced, however, that the company had hesitated to launch it. The crisis, however, called for desperate measures. It was hastily put into production and launched as the "7".

This was no ordinary car — the protoytpe even had automatic transmission — and was received enthusiastically, possibly even too enthusiastically considering its many teething troubles and defects. These were eliminated in late models of the "7" and in the "11", which was derived directly from it. The models were popularly known by their main attribute, "Front Wheel Drive". In 1934 it was courageous to launch a f.w.d. car for mass sale and production, though the car had many advantages. The absence of a propeller shaft enabled the body to be lower and more spacious. The engine had overhead valves; the pistons and con-rods were in light alloy; and brakes were hydraulic. The whole car was light, under 2,000 lbs. The engine of the first "7" was only 1,298 c.c. but this was raised later to 1,624 c.c. and then to 1,911, for both the "7" and "11".

Front-wheel drive

The "Front-Wheel Drive" had a profound influence on Citroën. It not only determined production policy for many years to come but its very success made new capital more than ever necessary, leading to the entry of Michelin into the company.

In Germany Ferdinand Porsche had already begun, following Nazi instructions, to design the "people's car" which was to see the light of day many years later. The country had a boom in production and replaced France as second among European car manufacturing nations.

In England the Jaguar was introduced, being produced by S. S. This was itself a development of a small Coventry company, Swallow Sidecars, which had previously produced sporting cars based on Standard components.

1967 FIAT DINO COUPÉ

engine · front mounted V6
capacity · 1987 c.c.
output · 166 H.P. (SAE)
gearchange · 5 speeds plus reverse
brakes · servo discs
weight · 2810 lb.

The Simca 1000 GLS, off the beaten track but with a welcome passenger, is a colourful descendant of the 1936 model shown below.

CHAPTER TWENTY THREE

BATTLE FOR MASS MARKET

The shadows of the political and economic crisis that was to lead the nations into the second World War were already apparent when that most elevated of companies, Rolls-Royce, abandoned the formula it had faithfully followed for almost 30 years and substituted the six-in-line engine of the Phantom II with the 12-cylindered one of the Phantom III. The background of the "double R" plaque was changed from red to black as a sign of mourning for the death in 1933 of the man who preferred to call himself "mechanic", Sir Henry Royce.

In the motor shows of 1936 another great 12-cylinder car was seen for the first time, the Bentley-designed Lagonda V12.

Russians go into production

At the same time the world became aware of a new motor industry, that of Russia. This had started in 1927, but on a small scale, only 1,702 vehicles being built in that year. From 1936, however, vehicles were mass-produced following the opening of the Molotov factory in Gorki, which produced the Zis, clearly inspired by the then current Buicks and Fords, and the opening

Peugeot 201 C type N 2 L. 4 cylinder 1,122 c.c. side valve engine.

of the Stalin works in Moscow where U. S.-type luxury cars were made.

Before war broke out, European manufacturers were engaged in a battle for the mass market, which gave rise to a wide variety of models with engines of one-litre capacity or a little more.

In Italy, Fiat produced the Nuova Balilla or "508 C", which was really a modified version of the 1934 "four-speed" car. A year after its introduction, the name was changed to "1100", and gave rise to a series of cars of importance to Italy, and to Europe in general, to the present day. The new o.h.v. engine had a longevity and reliability that made it famous.

In France the same role was played by the Simca "Huit" (still a version of the Fiat), by the Renault "Juva-quatre" inspired by the new Opel "Kadett", the German representative of the single-litre capacity, and by the Peugeot "202" which was derived from the "402" and from

1936 Opel Kadett: 4 cylinder 1,100 c.c. 23 H.P. engine, 3 speeds plus reverse, hydraulic brakes, speed 60 m.p.h.

the "302" (a 10 H.P. which appeared in 1936). Grégoire, the arch-disciple of front-wheel drive, had built his Compound in collaboration with Amilcar-Hotchkiss. In these years before the outbreak of the second World War, cars were built mainly in response to the needs and moods of the moment and were not destined to reappear after the war. Examples were the Renault "Suprastella", a redesign of an earlier eight-cylinder; the English Daimler of the same formula, which marked the abandonment of double-sleeve valve engines; Standard models, of which the "Flying" versions were particularly in demand; and the splendid Mercedes of the "540" series with eight-cylinder engines, and the huge eight-litre of the same make, as used by the top Nazis. Bugatti produced a number of variants of the "Type 57", the most powerful of which produced 260 b.h.p. Alfa Romeo introduced two new versions of the "6 C" series with 1900 c.c. and 2300 c.c. engines respectively. With Europe plunging into war, 1939 also marked another manufacturing boom in the American car industry.
The output figures themselves — over three million vehicles in a year — are impressive. But the most interesting technical event was the introduction by Cadillac on a commercial scale of automatic transmission, the Hydramatic. Chrysler introduced the hydraulic clutch. Both were examples of development that were to influence American post-war manufacturing policies. It was also in the late 30's that American styling, heavy with chrome, was finally divorced from European.

The Germans return

In the six years before the second World War, the sporting scene in Europe and elsewhere was remarkable both for racing, where the formulae permitting large engines led to tremendous outputs, and for successive land speed records. Over a short period speeds of more than 350 m.p.h. were recorded.
In 1934 the most important races were again dominated by Italy, firstly with the Alfa Romeo "P 3", which Ferrari had enlarged to 2900 c.c., and the "old" Mase-

The 1933 FIAT "522 S" derived from the 1927 "520".

The first Oldsmobile with automatic transmission, in 1940.

The handsome Talbot "105" of 1930.

Peugeot 401 D, type A 8 S built in 1934-1935. 4 cylinder 1,720 c.c.

Trossi at the wheel of the car which he designed with Augusto Monaco. It had front wheel drive and a radial engine.

rati of the same capacity. Against these, the new 3300 c.c. Bugatti "Type 59" had not enough speed. Already on the horizon was the German return to racing in strength, with Mercedes and the new Auto-Union, a company formed by the amalgamation of Audi, D.L.W., Horch, and Wanderer. This amalgamation and the return of Mercedes to racing under Hans Nibel was due to Hitler. Mindful of building Nazi prestige, he offered a huge prize to the German company that achieved the greatest number of victories in the next year's racing.

One outcome was the birth of Ferdinand Porsche's extraordinary "P-Wagen", a V16 designed for Auto-Union with a 4400 c.c. engine. On its first outing Stuck achieved 122 m.p.h. on the Avus circuit near Berlin. Varzi, Chiron, Guy Moll, von Stuck, Trossi (who had once built his own front-wheel drive, radial-engined racing car) were the names most frequently heard in racing circles in 1934. The Alfa-Ferrari victories began at Monte Carlo with Moll, continued at Alessandria and Tripoli with Varzi and again with Moll at the Avus. Auto-Union made its first and unsuccessful debut here. After Von Brauchitsch's success at Barcelona, Alfa carried on with Chiron, Varzi and Trossi at Montlhéry. Only in the German Grand Prix was Auto-Union victorious, with von Stuck.

1934 Auto-Union "P-Wagen" in the French G. P. of that year, one of its first appearances. Momberger is driving.

Renault "Juvaquatre" with 1,003 c.c. 4 cylinder engine. The first monocoque Renault.

The season ended tragically at Pescara when Guy Moll was killed; in the same race Caracciola lost a wheel and Chiron's car caught fire.

In the same year, 1934, Eyston and Denly in a Hotchkiss put up the 48-hour record to 153.470 k.p.h. at Montlhéry. Then it was raised by four Renault drivers in a "Nervasport" to 167.445 k.p.h., and again by the Delahaye team in a "135" six-cylinder to 177 k.p.h. (about 110 m.p.h.).

In Great Britain, Raymond Mays was having great success; he was to become the leading driver for the new car, E.R.A. (English Racing Automobiles, financed by Humphrey Cook). So were Lord Howe, Malcolm Campbell, John Cobb, Kaye Don, George Eyston, Reg Parnell and Dick Seaman. Among others there was the performance of Cobb in winning the Brooklands "500 miles" at 123 m.p.h. in a 23-litre Napier-Railton.

In 1935, German supremacy began to establish itself on the continent. Caracciola in a Mercedes won the Grands Prix of Monaco, Belgium, France and Spain while von Stuck in the Auto-Union won at Monza. Surprisingly, only at the Nürburgring in Germany did Alfa Romeo win, with Nuvolari.

For 1936, Alfa Romeo had prepared only two new engines, an eight-cylinder 3800 c.c. and a 12-cylinder 4400 c.c., while Mercedes had produced a completely

Amateur signwriters were quickly at work on the eight-cylinder 4,852 c.c. Renault "Nervasport", which on 5 April, 1934, broke the world 48-hour record, together with another nine records for distances between 4,000 and 5,0000 miles at Montlhéry.

The American 8 cylinder supercharged Auburn. 4,585 c.c. engine with three speeds, hydraulic brakes. Below the Napier Railton.

1936 Jaguar "100". The car could be supplied with a 2½ or a 3½ litre engine; the latter developing 100 H.P.

new car, not fully developed due to the death of the designer Nibel. Auto-Union, like Mercedes, were achieving outputs around 500 b.h.p.; it was the beginning of a power race which culminated with Auto-Union reaching 650 b.h.p. in 1937.

The first race, in Monaco, was notable for a multi-car crash at the notorious chicane, involving Chiron, Farina, Trossi, Tadini and von Brauchitsch, in which no-one was seriously hurt, and for spectacular spins by Rosemayer and Fagioli. It ended in a victory for Caracciola in a Mercedes.

After Auto-Union had won at Nürburgring, where the young Rosemayer earned himself the title of the "King of the Mists" for his command of the fog-cloaked circuit, they went on to win convincingly the 1936 German Grand Prix in Berlin. Rosemayer was again in first place and three other cars in the first six. Mercedes was thoroughly defeated (four out of five cars retired) and then withdrew from the field, leaving only the Italians to fight Porsche's monsters. The French had given up the 750 kg formula for their Grand Prix, maintaining it for cars derived from production models.

In 1937 Italian and French cars were absent from the circuits and German domination was complete. Of the

Mario Tadini at the wheel of the Alfa Romeo 1900 during the 1937 Susa-Moncenisio.

1936 Mercedes 540 K Cabriolet.

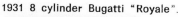

1931 8 cylinder Bugatti "Royale".

12 Grand Prix, seven were won by Mercedes (four by Caracciola) and five by Auto-Union (four by the equally successful Rosemayer). Ferrari disbanded his Alfa team and began to set himself up as a constructor in his own right. In 1939 he introduced three models, the "815 Sport", the "125", and the "159". Alfa Romeo prepared to return to direct participation in racing.

Grand Prix confusion

In 1938 the Grand Prix formula seemed to be designed specially to create confusion among designers and team managers. In addition to a relationship between capacity and weight and different weight rules if a compressor were fitted or not, there were different cylinder capacity limits according to the fitting of the compressors.

The manufacturers decided on three-litres supercharged and 4½-litres without compressor. Mercedes and Auto-Union quickly took a technical lead with outputs around 400 b.h.p. This was due partly to their experiments with fuel, which was not restricted.

In addition to the eight-cylinder "308" prototype which produced 300 b.h.p., Alfa Romeo produced a 12-cylinder 320 b.h.p. and a 16-cylinder 350 b.h.p., from which was to be developed the celebrated "Alfetta" after the war. Maserati had a 32-valve, eight-cylinder supercharged model, which was to have great success at Indianapolis between 1939 and 1950.

The season began with the sensational defeat of Caracciola at Pau by Dreyfus in a Delahaye, and "maestro" Nuvolari was in a spectacular accident with his car in pieces and flames. But then again the familiar series of German victories began. Von Brauchitsch won the Grand Prix de Rheims, Seaman won at Nürburgring in a Mercedes and Auto-Union, with Nuvolari, won at Monza. In the meantime, Rosemayer had been killed racing against Caracciola while trying to set up pure speed records for three-litre cars on the Frankfurt-Darmstadt autobahn; Caracciola reached nearly 270 m.p.h.

Mechanical breakdowns

For the last season's racing before the war began, the Germans were again ready with new cars, with outputs of 483 b.h.p. at 7800 r.p.m. for the Mercedes (which used petrol for engine cooling as well, thus giving rise to a consumption of 2½ miles per gallon) and 485 b.h.p. for the "183" Auto-Union.

These outputs were achieved by the use of new two-stage compressors. Maserati were not far behind however with 450 b.h.p. Of the more important races, which were won once again by the Germans, the most exciting was at Rheims in the French Grand Prix where, against all expectations, the whole Mercedes team retired one by one with mechanical breakdowns after Lang had smashed the record in practice. Muller won in an Auto-Union after Nuvolari had led for most of the race. In the meantime, on the other side of the Atlantic the Vanderbilt Cup had been revived with a win for Nuvolari.

Speed in the desert

The era of straight speed racing had begun on desert at Bonneville and at Salt Lake City, the only place where the huge cars could run; Daytona and Pendine were abandoned. In 1921 Abbott D. Jenkins had raced the Salt Lake City to Wendover express, and in 1933 and 1934 had set up records of 2,845 and 3,070 miles in 24 hours at averages around 118 and 128 m.p.h. The next year Cobb, in his huge Napier-Railton put up the 24-hour record to an average of 135 m.p.h. at Bonneville.

Then Gulotta beat Cobb's average by a small margin in a Duesenberg only for Eyston, Denly and Staniland (in the Rolls-Royce aero-engined "Speed of the Wind") to put the record up to 141 m.p.h. It was to be five years later, in 1940 when the rest of the world was too busy to care, before Jenkins could raise the 24-hour record to 162 m.p.h. in his Marmon Meteor III; this

Above
a 1933 1,496 c.c. Frazer-Nash,
a 1938 B.M.W.,
and below a 1935 1,087 c.c. Lagonda "Rapier"

The Citroën "11" was produced in varying versions for nearly 20 years from the 30's. It followed the famed Citroën "7", which was the first car with front-wheel drive to go into mass production. The "7" incorporated a vast range of other technical innovations. Thirty years later Citroën was the first European company to fit automatic transmission as standard. The interior of the "DS 21" is shown here — minus clutch pedal.

The famous E.R.A.s Remus and Romulus. In 1935 Romulus was bought by Prince Chula of Siam, who gave it to his cousin Prince Bira, a keen motorist. In Romulus, the latter won the 1936 Prince Rainier's Cup and the J.C.C. International Trophy.

was based on the Duesenberg but had a Curtis 750 H.P. aero-engine. Jenkins went on to average almost 150 m.p.h. for 48 hours.

In 1938, Cobb returned to Bonneville in his Railton to set up the world land speed record at 350 m.p.h., a speed that seemed fantastic but which was immediately beaten by Eyston in his 3000 H.P. Thunderbolt at 357 m.p.h. The last word before the war, however, went to Cobb in 1939 with 369 m.p.h.

When Europe was engulfed in war, racing came to an abrupt end. Civilian cars were garaged for the duration, or destroyed or commandeered in those countries that were occupied. Petrol was rationed. In nearly every country attempts were made to use fuel other than petrol for propelling vehicles, such as electricity, town gas, producer gas, methane and butane. Hundreds of thousands of bulky cylinders and gas bags appeared on cars. Even the electric car had a re-birth, especially in France, where in 1941 Peugeot designed small coupes; this was the VLV with two seats and a 1½ H.P. electric

1940 Alfa-Romeo 12 C 512 with a 12 cylinder 1,490 c.c. engine.

A 1937 Panhard "Dynamic". Below the 1937 Railton.

motor. Grégoire collaborated with the French C.G.E. to design a car which in 1943 was observed by the Automobile Club de France to go from Paris to Tours without recharging.

The first day of peace in 1945 found the world exhausted, damaged and hungry but with a tremendous will to get moving. The Allied armies had used huge columns of transport of all kinds, and when the war was finished this helped the revival. Europe became mechanised with war-surplus vehicles. Tens of thousands of jeeps peacefully invaded the countryside and cities, often battered but working marvellously.

For many civilians in the post-war period, the repair and maintenance of the Allied occupation forces' vehicles gave valuable mechanical experience to many thousands who had never worked on a motor car before.

From the ruins that covered Europe, the great car factories began to rise again; old machinery was put to work again, repaired, re-constructed perhaps but once again producing. From hidden warehouses machines and material appeared. The assembly lines were rebuilt and the production of the first post-war models began, usually identical to those of the immediate pre-war period. Europe was again on the move.

1968 ROVER 3500

engine · V8 cylinders
capacity · 3528 c.c.
output · 184 b.h.p. at 5200 r.p.m.
gears · automatic transmission, plus reverse
brakes · servo discs
weight · 2862 lbs.

The tracked Snowcat used by Sir Vivian Fuchs in his 1957 transantarctic expedition is powered by a 5,300 c.c. Chrysler V8 engine. Below is a Renault "special purpose" vehicle of the 20's.

CHAPTER TWENTY FOUR
THE POST-WAR BOOM

The story of European car manufacturing in the early post-war years is one of painful effort and fierce battles to get back on its feet in one way or another. In France, Ford at Poissy, Peugeot at Sochaux, Bugatti in Molsheim were either destroyed or badly damaged. But Simca was almost intact, while at Citroën only the records had been destroyed. Renault was struck by a second shock — nationalisation, following accusations of war-time collaboration against its head, Louis Renault, who had died in mysterious circumstances a little earlier in prison at Fresnes.

For the people at last

Somewhat less serious was the position of the British manufacturers, despite damage from bombing and "V" weapons, but with plant and machinery worn out. War had seriously damaged the Italian industry with the Fiat factory at Lingotto almost destroyed. Fiat therefore began the construction of a new factory at Mirefiore. Lancia and Alfa Romeo began to recover.

In Germany tremendous efforts were made to put factories into working order in some way. The job was particularly difficult for Daimler-Benz in Stuttgart and Opel in Russelsheim, but less so for Ford in Cologne and

Volkswagen in Wolfsburg, where fairly quickly the large scale production was begun of the "people's car" which Hitler had promised so many years before. Things were different for B.M.W. in Eisenach and Auto-Union

in Zwickau under Soviet occupation; these were to appear again later with new names and products.

In the U.S. the changeover from war to peace was rapid, and there was an increase in the number of cars on the roads from 24 million in 1945 to 61 million in 1955. Huge sums were spent on renewing plant and equipment, though the 1946 models produced were for the most part similar to those of 1940. A new manufacturer entered the field — Kaiser-Frazer, created by Henry J. Kaiser of "Liberty ships" fame, and Joe Frazer, who came from Willys-Graham. They introduced a new car, the "Special", at first with front-wheel drive, but later with the classic layout.

The Isetta, produced by B.M.W. with 250 c.c. engine in Germany, was a success in the 1950's. But in Italy, where it was designed, it found little favour. Above a 1947 Kaiser "Special".

Returning to Europe, among the more interesting early post-war cars was the Renault 4 CV with a rear engine, the first product of the newly formed "Regie Nationale". This car, based on a design produced in secret during the war, had only 760 c.c., but was spacious and manoeuvrable.

At the same time, all over Europe, bubble cars and minicars made a brief appearance; these included the British Bond, Italian Isetta and German Heinkel. Also in Italy the tremendous boom in scooters started.

Racing restarts

So far as racing was concerned, it made its first timid re-appearance on the formula of 4½-litres unsupercharged or 1½-litres supercharged. Delahaye chose the former while the Italians chose the latter; Alfa counted on the "Alfetta", as its "158" eight-cylinder was called, originally designed for sports car racing. Maserati, too, had a 1½-litre supercharged model, while the most formidable of all, Ferrari, was preparing to enter the field in 1949.

Another figure who joined the battle was Amedeo Gordini, who built cars based on Simca components. A projected eight-cylinder CTA-Arsenal, supported by a group of industrialists and the French military, never appeared.

In the U. S., however, the racing formula remained that of 1938 to 1940 — 4½-litre without supercharger and three-litre with supercharger.

A Messerschmitt KR 200 of 1958 shows its aircraft cockpit characteristics Below, a Nobel 200 convertible. Such vehicles had either a single driving wheel or two close together in order to eliminate the differential and reduce cost.

The first post-war motor shows were held in 1946 and reflected the manufacturing position — most models were of pre-war design but a number of interesting prototypes were on show, even though they were not in production. Among them were the single-cylinder (it soon became a twin) Rovin in France and the little front-wheel drive Grégoire, which was sold to Kendall in England.

The indications of revival seen in 1946 began to be justified the following year, when the first post-war Geneva Show took place and the new Austins were outstanding among British cars. In the motor shows of 1947 there were numerous new prototypes but most production models were outdated. The most interesting

The Alfa-Romeo 1952 1,997 c.c. "Disco Volante" (Flying Saucer)

models were the Cemsa Caproni 110 c.c. with a flat-four engine and front-wheel drive, a new Grégoire two-litre, an advanced prototype by Dechaux with a transverse engine and front-wheel drive, a Bugatti 73C 1½-litre tourer, and Isotta-Fraschini's last fling, the "Monterosa", with an eight-cylinder 3400 c.c. engine and hydraulic gearchange, which never actually went into production. A few months later Peugeot launched the "203" with 1300 c.c., which was a great commercial success with its inclined o.h.v.s. and high engine speed of 5000 r.p.m.

In 1948 the important technical development across the Atlantic was the introduction of the Dynaflow automatic transmission by Chrysler, which up to then had been using only semi-automatic. Together with General Motors' Hydramatic, the Dynaflow contributed to a massive shift in the American market to two-pedal motoring and Ford had to build a factory himself — Borg-Warner — to make automatic transmissions for his own cars. The same time saw the introduction of a completely new line of six- and eight-cylinder cars by Ford, the result of

Above a 1948 Cadillac. Below Indianapolis 1949 — one of the high-speed racers crashes into the protecting wall.

A sports car that does not appeal only to the young — the 1967 Fiat "124 Coupé", which reaches over 100 m.p.h.

the new dynamism brought to the company by Henry Ford II when he succeeded his grandfather as head of the company (his father, Edsel, had died in 1946). Among other features, the new long, sleek Fords had independent front suspension.

At General Motors the launch of the new Cadillacs and Oldsmobiles, with long tail fins and gaudy rear light clusters, signalled the introduction of new techniques. The use of high-compression engines designed by Kettering was to begin a dizzy "power output" race among American companies.

Manufacturers divide

But not only in America was 1948 a year of renewal. In Europe new cars were introduced which were to play an important role in succeeding years.

In England a division soon became apparent due to the specialisation by some manufacturers in small and medium cars and others in G.T. models. In the former category was the Morris Minor, redesigned by Alec Issigonis (future apostle of the transverse engine and Hydrolastic suspension), and the new Hillman Minx in scaled down U.S.-style, produced by Rootes Group. To

The unusual looking but practical Citroën "2CV".

1967 Hillman Superminx. Below the 1952 Austin A 30 2 door.

the G.T. group was added the first post-war Jaguar in the sports class, the extremely fast (125 m.p.h.) "XK 120".

In Germany Heinz Nordhoff, an ex-manager of Opel, became head of Volkswagen and, aided by the Allied occupation authorities, began the mass-production of the famous "beetle" that was to make the company the largest manufacturer in Europe within six years. The four-cylinder Borgward was born at this time from the first entirely new German company to be formed after the war.

French midget

The most sensational novelty from the technical point of view in the year was the introduction of the new version of the Panhard "Dyna 3CV" and the long-awaited economy Citroën "2CV". After the shock of its unusual appearance, the latter soon became popular on account of its remarkable robustness, spaciousness and excellent suspension and the way its 375 c.c. engine would slog along all day. (The 2CV had been ready in 1938, in prototype form).

In Italy the larger companies were not producing anything of great interest, but the fame of her coachbuilders was spreading throughout the world; among these masters of craftsmanship and design were Alemano, Bertone, Boneschi, Canta, Colli, Ellena, Fissore, Ghia, Moretti, Pininfarina, Savio, Scioneri, Touring-Superleggera, Vignale and Viotti. Their predominance was to persist for 15 years until serious problems of size forced some to change the basis of their production and others to disappear.

In the racing field, nearly all the big pre-war races started in 1948, though the French Grand Prix had been held the previous year on a new circuit near

1938 Buick experimental "Y".

LABORATORIES ON WHEELS

A car of the future has as much fascination for motorists as the veteran of the past. In the case of a car designed specifically for projection of ideas, it is impossible to talk of the "first" dream car. The reason is that there were two of them.

In 1938 General Motors asked Harley Earl and C. A. Chayne to design an experimental car, the "Y", for Buick, which supplied ideas that were built into their cars from 1942 onwards. At the end of the 40's the same two men were asked to design experimental vehicles for both Buick and Cadillac.

Both these cars incorporated many experimental suggestions which it was later considered useful to try and General Motors appropriately called them "laboratories on wheels". A condition of their design was that they had to have styling which would strike the public imagination and which would meet with the long-term forecasts of the companies' engineers.

Servo-assistance

These were the first two "dream cars" and were christened "Sabre" (Cadillac) and "XP-300" (Buick). For publicity, they were sent together to Europe and then toured the United States, where they attracted great interest.

The mechanical elements were common to both cars. Apart from the special three-litre V8 engine, the most striking feature at the time was the extensive use of

servo mechanism — for the windows, the aerial and the hood, which went up automatically when rain started to fall.

The bodies of the two cars, however, were different, though both had common elements of what might now be considered bizarre taste. The "Sabre" was a huge roadster, low and heavy-looking from the bulbous front to the long rear fins. The "XP-300" was smoother but on the same general lines. The body was built in light alloys with much decoration.

Both had panoramic windscreens with negative inclination, an idea which had safety as well as styling advantages and which was soon reproduced on various Cadillac production models. Some models, in particular the Eldorado, used other ideas taken from the two prototypes. So far as the feasability of many of the ideas incorporated in the "dream cars" of Earl and Chayne, they can be said to have kept their wheels firmly on the ground.

1951 "XP-300"

1967 Volkswagen "Beetle". The shape is substantially that of Ferdinand Porsche's first design. Below 1951 Fiat 1,500 with Siata body.

Lyons; it was won by Chiron in a Talbot. The Italian Grand Prix at Monza in 1947 and the European Grand Prix at Spa were won by the "Alfetta" with Trossi and Wimille the respective drivers.

The year 1948 was a period of considerable technical development, of rivalry between not only manufacturers and countries but also between supercharged and unblown cars.

In the 1948 races, again dominated by the 1500 c.c. "Alfetta", the name of the French driver Wimille stands out as the winner at Rheims and Monza, while his team-mate, Trossi, won at Berne in the European Grand Prix. Varzi was tragically killed in this race. At the same time the two-litre "166" Ferrari was beginning to make an impression.

Jaguar takes record

Jaguar was upholding British prestige with new models and excellent racing results, as were Austin-Healey, Allard, M. G. and Bristol. One of Jaguar's successes, which led to its considerable expansion, was the Mk VII saloon, using the XK 120 engine, which succeeded the attractive Mk V. In this year Jaguar had made history by covering the sports car flying mile at 132.6 m.p.h. in Belgium with the XK 120.

1954 Jaguar D type.

Across the Atlantic, General Motors launched a new series of V8 engines designed by Kettering, with o.h.v. and high compressions. The first two examples were the Oldsmobile "5-litre" and the "5½-litre" Cadillac. This represented a great step forward in America, giving substantial increases in specific output, and causing Chrysler — with a 180 b.h.p. engine having hydraulic tappets — and Studebaker to follow suit.

In 1949 Volkswagen reached its quota of production and was planning the improvements to be introduced to their "beetle" from 1951 onwards. That year the new Auto-Union-D.K.W. began work at Ingolstadt, launching a 700 c.c. vehicle powered by a flat twin-cylinder motor-cycle engine, leading to imitators such as Lloyd and Goliath.

In Sweden, Svenska Aero Plan introduced the Saab 92, and the Volvo "444" was launched. In the U.S.S.R., parallel with the large scale production of heavy vehicles, four touring cars were introduced, the Moskvitch, inspired by the Opel "Kadett"; the Pobjeda, a medium-sized saloon; the "Zum" six-cylinder inspired by Dodge, and the eight-cylinder "Zis 110" derived from the Packard. The 1949 racing year was dominated by the new Ferraris, after Alfa-Romeo had withdrawn their "Alfetta" as the deaths of Varzi, Wimille and Trossi in 1948 had robbed them of their drivers. Ferrari built three kinds of

Two 1959 Austin-Healey 3000's.

SAAB "96" 3 cylinder 2-stroke, 841 c.c. Top speed 80 m.p.h.

1961 Volga. 4 cylinder 2,445 c.c., 75 b.h.p. at 4,000 r.p.m.

cars — a 1500 c.c. supercharged racing car for Formula I, an unblown two-litre for Formula II and another model for sports car racing. With these he gained many victories, including the first post-war edition of the "Le Mans 24 hours". Gordini also had some successes, as did a young Argentinian driver called Juan Manuel Fangio.

Production peak

The middle year of the century was also the year of a production record. World production in 1950 totalled 10,017,000 vehicles, a figure which was not to be reached again until 1955. The figures for the major producing countries were U.S. 8,003,000; Great Britain 783,000; Canada 390,000; France 357,000; Germany 306,000; Italy 127,000.

In the technical field, short-stroke or "square" engines were more common and petrol injection was introduced by some German companies on competition models. On 9 March the first real gas-turbine engined car made its debut on the track at Silverstone: the Coventry-built Rover "Jet 1" which reached over 85 m.p.h. The chassis was that of a standard "75" into which was built a 100 H.P. jet engine, without heat exchanger, which

One of the rarest and most expensive post-war sports cars. The Spanish built 1953 Pegaso.

Classically red — the 1951 Ferrari Formula 1 "G. P." and the Maserati 250F of 1954. Both cars are in the Turin Motor Museum.

1952 B.R.M.

Juan Manuel Fangio in a Ferrari in the 1950 Monza G.P. Below, in the same race, Farina and Fangio at the famous Lesmo curve.

worked at around 50,000 r.p.m. Two years afterwards the car was developed to do 125 m.p.h.

The Rover gas turbine car was to have many imitations. In France, Turbomeca built some prototypes and Socema-Grégoire showed one at the 1952 Paris show. The year 1950 was also when the new two-litre Fregate of the "Régie Renault" was launched, the new factory at Flins, near Paris, being rapidly built and brought into use for its production.

Birth of the B.R.M.

The motor racing world saw the birth of a new Formula I car in 1950, this time in Great Britain. This was the B.R.M. (British Racing Motors) for which 160 British manufacturers agreed to co-operate to enable a Grand Prix car to be built which was capable of winning major races.

The initiative was due to Raymond Mays and Peter Berthon, designer of the old E.R.A. They produced an outstanding V 16-cylinder machine which had some success in the hands of Fangio, Parnell, Gonzales and Wharton. Indeed, the B.R.M. was developed to be the most powerful 1½-litre ever built, but it could not be called a truly successful car for a number of reasons. The two most important were probably its intricacy, which made it unreliable, and its flat power curve. These disadvantages were being eliminated when the

formula was changed. In 1953 B.R.M. was taken over by A.G.B. Owen, head of David Brown Ltd. which produced Aston-Martin and Lagonda cars, and by the 60's the B.R.M. was a very successful car indeed.

The outstanding characteristic of the 1950 racing season was the duel between Farina and Fangio. Farina won the European Grand Prix at Silverstone and that of Switzerland at Berne, while Fangio won the Grands Prix of Pau, Spa and Rheims. The Monaco race was notable for a nine-car crash in a race again won by Fangio.

Companies disappear

The following year marked the beginning of a second period of important industrial development in the motor car field which was to continue to the present. It was a period of greatly increased mechanisation, of automation, of unification of components and operations and of the development of ancillary industries.

All this required tremendous investment, and the disappearance of many manufacturers who were not able to tool up was inevitable. In some countries the small and medium companies disappeared completely; in Britain and Italy a number survived, due to their particular ability in specialist fields and to their customers' loyalty. All this was against a background of rapid expansion in the number of motor vehicles in the world. From just under 34 million immediately after the war, the total more than doubled by 1951 and was 102,655,000 by 1956.

In Europe the stream of truly new vehicles began to flow only in the period 1951 to 1955. In 1951 Simca introduced the "Neuf" which name was however quickly changed to the more interesting "Aronde"; in the same year the sports version of the "Dyna" Panhard was launched.

In 1952 most European countries were marking time, improving existing models. Total production was stationary. In Japan, however, the motor industry was beginning that phase of growth which was to make it the second largest in the world within 15 years.

In America the V8 engine continued to be the basic power unit of the industry. The 4.5-litre De Soto and the 5.2-litre Lincoln were introduced. Dodge launched the "little V8" with the "Redram" four-litre.

Formation of B.M.C.

At the end of 1950, the Morris and Austin companies in England combined to form the British Motor Corporation (B.M.C.) and launched a new small car, the Austin "A 30" and fitted its engine — an 800 c.c. side-valve — into the Morris Minor as well. Vauxhall launched the four-cylinder "Wyvern" and the six-cylinder "Velox" at moderate prices, while Ford of Dagenham continued with their existing range of cars.

The new models of 1952 included the "Grande Large" Simca, one of a number of variants on the "Aronde".

1948 Panhard "Dynavia".

1950 Pontiac.

1953 Vauxhall Velox.

1956 Sunbeam "Mk III".

The G. M. 1964 experimental gas turbine car "Firebird IV"

In America all the major companies were spending a great deal of money on promotional campaigns in order to maintain the buoyancy of the market. General Motors were giving sporting names to their cars (Chevrolet Corvette, Oldsmobile Starfire, Buick Wildcat, Cadillac Le Mans) and built an experimental gas turbine car, the "Firebird".

Ford launched the "Thunderbird" and Chrysler called in an Italian stylist. Three amalgamations took place in the United States — Kaiser with Willys, Nash with Hudson (to give rise to American Motors) and Studebaker with Packard.

European innovations

In 1953 Citroën fitted hydro-pneumatic suspension on their Fifteens which was to be more fully developed on the "D.S. 19". A few months later the French Ford company and Simca amalgamated and produced a hybrid vehicle, the "Vedette".

The next year Fiat built a gas turbine car which was capable of 150 m.p.h. In Germany Mercedes launched the "180 D", a version of their first diesel-engined private car, the "170 D", but of more modern appearance, and also the prestige sports cars, the 190 SL and the 300 SL. Many European manufacturers began to offer automatic transmission on some models.

The year 1955 was the beginning of a new cycle of design and production in Europe with the introduction, for example, of the rear-engined Fiat "600" and the little Fiat "500 C", which is still produced in slightly modified form. In France Peugeot increased the capacity of the "203" to 1½-litres and called it the "403", while Citroën introduced a new version of the Fifteen and Simca launched the "1300". In Germany, B.M.W. introduced two radically opposed cars — the fast eight-cylinder sports car, the "507", and the German version of the 300 c.c. super-utility "Isetta" that had been rejected by the Italian market.

In the U. S. the "output race" continued to the point were 400 H.P. engines were available.

An example of technical and styling co-operation. The Abarth 750 "Crocodile" with body by Pininfarina.

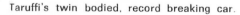

Taruffi's twin bodied, record breaking car.

1968 ZODIAC MARK IV

engine · front-mounted V6 cylinders
capacity · 2994 c.c.
brakes · servo discs
output · 144 b.h.p. at 4750 r.p.m.
gears · 4-speed plus reverse
weight · 2939 lbs.

Built for their markets — the huge 1967 Buick Electra and the Citroën Ami 6.

CHAPTER TWENTY FIVE
DESIGNING FOR THE FUTURE

History finishes where reporting begins; it is impossible to make valid judgments on contemporary events. In the case of a mechanical device such as the motor car it may seem that this might not hold true, but in fact it is so.

Technical progress on the motor car has reached the stage in recent years which means that mere creation and even commercial success are not enough to pass into history. In a record of the motor car it is necessary to single out those which have in themselves contributed something to progress. In the case of present production, or most of it, judgment becomes a matter of individual taste.

Electronics take a part

The direction which technical progress has been taking in recent years is a guide however to the lines it might follow in the future.

The greatest progress has been made not, as in previous years, in the adoption of new principles or previously unknown devices, but in the development of new production techniques and the use of new materials. So far as the former is concerned, the use of "transfer" machines, and automatic lathes (capable of performing a number of operations on thousands of components) and electron-

The 1950 Studebaker "Commander" convertible and the 1962 Studebaker "Avanti".

ic devices continually measuring tool wear and adjusting for it without human intervention, have led to greater engine silence, durability and strength. But such qualities were also present, it must be remembered, in the handbuilt Silver Ghost of 60 years ago, though at very much greater cost. Better raw materials have contributed to the same result.

Such advances have also permitted the use of much lighter components, thus improving performance in relation to power. Specific horsepower (output per litre of engine capacity) has also increased notably, with the use of new materials allowing much higher compression ratios, and the speed and acceleration of modern cars have increased greatly in the last few years.

Particular items of progress have been the increasing use of overhead camshafts driven by toothed plastic belts.

Studded tyres improved the notable road-holding of this Citroën DS, seen on an icy road in the Monte Carlo Rally.

The previous objection to their use was the cost of chains or gears and the noise of the operating gear. Valves have been developed, containing sodium and giving much better thermal performance. Doublechoke and multiple carburettors are increasingly common as is the use of petrol injection. Alternators are now replacing dynamos and electromagnetic fans are ensuring that engines are kept always at their optimum operating temperatures. Gearbox synchronisation, has improved. So have pressure lubrication systems.

Greasing points have been reduced to a minimum by grouping, or by the use of "sealed for life" joints. Routine maintenance has been much reduced.

Basic components of the car have been improved; the accessories have progressed. Iodine vapour lamps and asymmetric beams have made night driving easier. The use of laminated glass — safer than tempered — has increased safety. Major steps have been made in paint technology. Radial ply and tubeless tyres, with or without special treads, have also brought about improvements in the fields of safety and efficiency as has the widespread use of disc brakes.

The Autobianchi "Primula".

Two English sports cars for, literally, open country motoring are the M.G. Midget above and the Triumph Spitfire.

Plastic materials are now used by the motor car industry on a large scale. They have made changes, small in themselves, which in total have had considerable effect on noise, durability and cost.

Safety as a selling feature is now a major consideration in the design and manufacture of motor vehicles and plastic components are playing an important part here too.

Progress in lubricants

The tremendous advances in design of engines owe much to the progress made in the products that power them from the point of view of both performance and maintenance. Engines with high compression ratios would not have been possible unless petrol had been developed to suit them. Progress in the science of lubricants has been enormous, leading to reduced maintenance, increased mechanical life and increased efficiency of the high revving engines. Roads have been much improved, both in quality of surface and in vast extensions of motorway networks both in Europe and America.

Though the general lines of progress are common to all cars, there are divisions in motor engineering imposed by the type, price, size and use of vehicles, and by technical differences. Thus, in the small car field, there has been almost unanimous adoption of either the "all in front" or the "all behind" policy to reduce transmission size and weight and increase room inside the vehicle. Each of these formulae presented problems to be solved before they could be adopted. In the case of the "all in front" design, satisfactory constant velocity joints had to be designed and built cheaply on a large scale before the system could be used. For the "all behind" formula, suspensions had to be developed to reduce the weight distribution problems inherent in this type of layout; there were also problems with regard to engine heating. In the medium sized and high powered saloon, the classic formula of a front engine driving rear wheels still predominates, though there are some outstanding examples of front wheel drive. Nearly all racing cars are, however, rear-engined.

Machining in multiples

One of the characteristics of the present day is the range of types and models offered by the large scale manufacturers. This has been made possible, while still preserving most of the economic advantages of a small range of models, by using similar production operations such as machining in different multiples. The manufacture of six cylinder engines consists in effect of one and a half of an existing four cylinder engine.

In this way it is possible to produce four, six and V 8 engines cheaply from a basic design, and to fit these in a variety of kinds of bodywork in which many basic elements are common. Coupés and open sports cars often use a standard saloon engine with performance raised by increasing the compression ratio (a little more machining on the head or the fitting of different pistons), more carburettors, or a change in cam profile.

The use of cross-country vehicles is increasing, and although they are somewhat expensive, they are held within reasonable price limits by the use of many standard car components. Often they are specially built by small companies using basic units bought from large car manufacturers.

This, together with the production of high performance vehicles based on mass produced mechanical components, has been one of the ways of survival for many famous Italian coachbuilders. They had found themselves being priced out of the market by large companies that were themselves producing attractive "special looking" versions. To survive, coachbuilders have had to change radically their methods of production, setting up assembly lines for non-mechanical components and supplying the bodies produced to large manufacturers for the latter's special models.

Getting together

This is a particular aspect of a much more important tendency towards amalgamation going on, especially in Europe, as a necessity for survival in the face of the tremendous productive and economic power of the American giants. The alternative is elimination as has occurred with Studebaker-Packard in America. Among the more important of these amalgamations have been British Leyland in Great Britain (which has united the makes of B.M.H., Morris, Austin, Wolseley, Riley, M.G.

The Autobianchi "Stellina".

The Ghia-bodied Fiat N 500 "runabout" and the rear-engined Sunbeam Imp of 875 c.c.

Fiat 2300 saloon. Below the Abarth 750 sports — a small car with G.T. performance.

Austin-Healey, Jaguar etc., with Standard, Triumph, Rover, Daimler etc.) Citroën and Panhard in France — with an attempt at fusion by these two with Fiat being vetoed during 1968 — and Auto-Union, D.K.W., Mercedes and Volkswagen in Germany.

Ferrari design

Reviewing the recent production of some of the individual makers, in Italy Fiat has progressively increased both model range and total production.

Alfa Romeo is also expanding both in the sports car and saloon fields with their 1300, 1600, and 1750 c.c. Giulia models. Lancia has the highly successful Fulvia as its basic model while still producing the Flavia (both f.w.d.) and the attractive but somewhat dated Flaminia. Innocenti produce a variety of B.M.C. cars, particularly an Italian version of the Mini and of the Austin 1100 and 1300's.

In France Renault has consolidated its place with the introduction of a series of popular cars from the Dauphine to the "8" and the "4" to the "6" and "16", the latter in particular being particularly advanced. Citroën production is firmly based on the D.S. 19 and its derivatives, the I.D. 19, D.S. 21, whilst the "Dyane" and the

The ASA 1000 G.T. in the 59th Targa Florio. Below an example of international cooperation on styling — the Opel Kadett with Vignale body.

Ami 6 are both derived from the famous 2 CV. Peugeot has had tremendous success with its robust and good performance "404" and "204" saloons. Simca have been purchased by the American Chrysler and have based their attack on the successful 1000 c.c. car and now on the medium saloon market.

In Germany the lead in mass sales is now held by the two American owned companies, the Ford-Taunus and Opel (General Motors) the former by means of successive and enlarged editions of the f.w.d. 12M and the traditional 17M and the latter by the "Kadett" and "Rekord". Opel also make a larger car (the "Kapitan" or "Admiral" according to bodywork) which clearly betrays its transatlantic association. Volkswagen, after many years of leadership, have lost ground in spite of the introduction of the 1500, 1600 and most recently

The Volkswagen 1,600 TL.

1967 Skoda 1,000 MB de luxe. 998 c.c. four cylinder, rear engine.

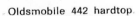

Oldsmobile 442 hardtop.

a two litre car. Mercedes have recently consolidated their position in the market for large prestige cars by means of a series of big saloons not differing much in appearance but technically progressive. Porsche and B.M.W. complete the range of German cars, the former with the high performance small saloons and the latter with a choice of medium sized precision-built models. In Great Britain Rolls-Royce and Bentley continue to produce vehicles of great luxury and refinement and Jaguar unfailingly astonish the world with a series of luxurious saloons and high performance cars at prices which are remarkably low.

A whole series of medium sized durable and attractive saloons are produced by the various members of British Leyland, which also produces two remarkable two litre cars, the Triumph and the Rover, the latter being outstanding for its high quality, modern appearance and interesting performance. The most outstanding product of this group and of the British motor industry in recent years has been the amazing Mini-Minor, child of Alec Issigonis's fertile brain.

American take-over

In this same period the Rootes Group has been absorbed by Chrysler and has thus become the third large British motor company to become American owned, the others being Ford and Vauxhall, subsidiary of General Motors. This survey of companies extends to Sweden where the Volvo and the Saab are produced, with a reputation for their robustness, and to Holland where that interesting little car, the DAF, is produced with an automatic belt-driven transmission. In Eastern Europe, Czechoslovakia produces the Skoda and the Tatra, and East Germany the Wartburg and Trabant. Russia produces a number of medium capacity cars similar to American cars of the 50's but is busy expanding small car production with the aid of foreign companies (Fiat and Renault).

On the other side of the Atlantic the divergence with Europe has remained, with the emphasis on large capacity, low stressed engines in large bodies, which are often heavy-looking and finished with much chrome. The brief flirtation with "compact" cars, intended as an economic measure to reduce European imports, is now almost a thing of the past.

Many U. S. sports cars of course, are of manageable proportions.

Japanese invasion

In this period a third large industry has been developing in Japan with the rapid expansion of the "old" companies and the creation of new ones. Daihatsu, Hino, Honda, Isuzu, Mazda, Mitsubishi, Nissan, Prince, Suzuki, Toyota are the names of the more important Japanese companies which in spite of duties and transport costs are beginning to invade overseas markets.

This Japanese production has long since left the field

of imitation and produces cars which are technically well advanced.

One major development of recent years, the Wankel engine, is dealt with separately in these pages. It has overcome its early production difficulties and is in series production by N.S.U. in Germany and under licence by Toyota in Japan.

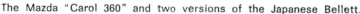

The Mazda "Carol 360" and two versions of the Japanese Bellett.

379

Sunbeam Hunter Saloon. 1,725 c.c. engine, 90 m.p.h.

The major American companies are still investigating the road use of gas turbines but there is no immediate signs of their adoption for normal purposes. Companies across the Atlantic are also conducting considerable research into electric cars for town use; most of the work in this field is concentrated on the battery, in order to increase its range and reduce its weight.

Precision and efficiency

Valuable experience in testing the varied innovations and improvements to different components of the motor car is provided by "prototype" racing. In this the cars are ostensibly cars built for the road — in that they have headlamps, closed bodywork and the general appearance of mass production models — but in practice are primarily racing machines.

So far as the traditional form of racing is concerned, the resurgence of Grand Prix races has resulted in cars becoming more and more divorced from normal production models — though they have been developed into marvellous instruments of precision and efficiency, reaching outputs of 150 b.h.p. per litre unsupercharged.

When it is recalled that the Renault "Grand Prix" model of 1906 produced 90 b.h.p. out of 13 litres, or seven b.h.p. per litre, an indication of the technical advance is dramatically illustrated.

Both achievements, though over 60 years apart, are tangible results of the continuing search for engineering perfection. The designer's invention and ingenuity, the manufacturer's craftsmanship and the driver's skill and courage on the race track have also materially contributed to the efficiency and comfort of the cars now on the roads of the world in millions.

The motor car has come of age. In a man's lifetime, it has moved from freak to luxury good, and now to a tool for everyday living.

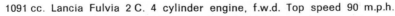

1091 cc. Lancia Fulvia 2 C. 4 cylinder engine, f.w.d. Top speed 90 m.p.h.

INDEX

ALPHABETICAL
INDEX
OF NAMES AND ILLUSTRATIONS

THE NUMBERS IN HEAVY TYPE REFER TO THE
PAGES   IN   WHICH   ILLUSTRATIONS   APPEAR

384

Ford Henry - 16, 39, 40, **42**, 65, **110**, 110, **111**, 111, 112, 115, 116, 143, 144, 145, 147, 148, 149, 157, 159, 160, 161, 164, 315, 331, **333**
Ford Motor Company - 140, 143, 144, 145, 160, 276
Forest - 83
Fossier - 47
Fournier Maurice - 16, 95, 100, 102, 104, 130, 131
"France Automobile" - 48
Franklin - 71, 253
Frazer Joe - 356
Frazer-Nash - **349**
Freeman - 77
Fench Grand Prix - **186**, 210, **211**
Frontenac - 296, 315
Front-wheel Drive - 338
Fuchs (Sir) Vivien - 355
Fry Vernon - 145

G

Gabriel - 132, 139, 165, 208, 214, **243**
Gardner-Serpollet - **282**
Garon - 44
Gemiani - 238
General Motor Company - **157**, 162, 212, 256, 270, 271, 272, 280, 320, 324, 329, 334, 359, 361, 363, **368**, 368, 378
Gepaa - 154
Gerard - 249
Ghia - 212, 360
Giffard Pierre - 47
Gillet Forest - 84
Girardot - 95, 104, 107
Giraud - 100, 102
Girling - 61, 169, **170**
Giusti - 62, 185
Gladiator-Pingault - 44
Glidden Charles - 112, 191, 192
G. N. - 290
Gobron - 83
Gobron-Brillié - 16, 56, 102, 185, 214
Godard - 195, 200
Godefroy & Levêque - 329
"Golden Arrow" - **332**
Goldschmidt - 65
Goldsworthy Gurney (Sir) - 9
Goliath - 363
Gonzales - 366
Goodyear Charls - 10
Gordini Amedeo - 356, 364
Gordon Bennett Cup race - 94, 99, 100, 107, 108, 118, **132**, 137, 165, **169**, 169, **170**, 180, 188, 205, 206, 216, 262
Gordon Bennett James - 94
Gordon David - 9
Goux Jules - **168**, 218, 243, 266, 282, 296, 333

Goudard Maurice - 226
Gowen Budd - 277
Gräf & Stift - 294
Grand Prix Automobile Club de France - 205, 237, 241, 309, 323
Gras - 136
Gray S. John - 145
"Green Monster" - 16
Grégoire - 352, 357, 358
Gribeauval (General) - 7
Griffiths Julius - 9
Griis - **100**
Grillon - **255**
Gross - 28
Guesdon - **56**
Guglielminetti - **206**
Guinnes (Sir) Algernon - 249
Guinness Lee K. - 16, **243**, 243, 249
Guizzardi Ettore - 200
Gulotta - 349
Gurney Nutting - **205**
Guy - 291, 292, 244
Guyot - 240, 243, 266

H

Haaga - 201
Haardt - 334
Hal - 281
Hammond E. T. - 75
Hampton - 292
Hancock Walter - 9
Hanomag - 329
Hanriot - 238, 239
Hansen - 200, 202
Hanthiot - 214
Harris W. T. - 39
Hautsch Johannes - 4
Hautvast - **243**
Haynes - 280, 281
Haynes Ellwood - 39, 40, 279
Haynes-Apperson - **84**
H. C. S. - 316
Heath - 165, 169, 253
Heinkel - 356
Heinze John - 149
Hémery - 16, 208, 214 ,238, 239, 253
Henry - 243, 296
Herkomer Cup - 240
Hercules - 279
Hero - 3
Hewetson Henry - 175
Hillman - 118, **163**, **178**, 178, 191, 290, 336, 359, **360**
Hino - 379
Hispano-Suiza - **214**, **224**, 240, **255**, 293, 294, 296, 320, 333
Homard - 44
Honda - 379
Hoover Herbert - 75
Horch D. L. W. - 344
Horstmann - 292
Hotchkiss - 207, 209, 288, 303, 329, 343
"Hot Rod" - **229**
Hotsman - **310**

Hovercraft - **78**, 78, **79**, 79
Howard Leslie - 209
Howe (Lord) - 345
Hudson - **239**, **262**, 279, **288**, 368
Hue - 200
Hugon - 28
Hugot - **49**
Humber - 60, 117, 118, 136, **162**, **200**, **255**, 290
Humber Company - 178
Humberette - 123, 178, **195**
Huntingdon F. A. - 39
Hurtu - 55
Hutton - 248
Huygens Christian - 12

K

Kaiser - 188, 201, **356**, 368
Kaiser Henry J. - 356
Kaiser-Frazer - 356
"Kaiserpreis" - 216
Keech-Ray - 16
Keeton - 254
Keller - 45
Kendall - 357
Kettering Charles - 246, 324, 334, 363
Kimber Cecil - 336
King Charles B. - 40, 71
King Edward VII - **160**, 176, 180, 188
King George V - **222**
King Victor Emanuel III - 188
Kissel - **272**, 281
Knappe - 201
Knight - 35, 222, 287
Knight Charles - 221
Knight J. H. - 175
Knipper - 254
Knox D'Arcy William - 24
Knudsen Paul William - 320
Koechlin - 89
Koehnin - 48
Koppel - 201

I

Ideal Motor Company - 281
International Motor Company 159, 160
International Rectifier Corporation - **45**
Irving J. S. - **332**
Irving-Napier - 16
Isetta - **356**, 368
Isotta Cesare - 42
Isotta-Fraschini - 42, 61, 65, 214, 240, 294, 296, 304, 320, 335, 338
Issigonis Alec - 359, 378
Itala - **108**, **137**, **186**, 195, **197**, 197, **198**, 198, 199, 214, 222, 238, 243
Italia - 119
Italian Grand Prix - 310

N

Nadig Charles - 40, 79
Nadig Henry - 40, 79
Nadig Lawrence - 40, 79
Nancy Tony - **229**
Napier - 16, 60, 101, 107, 112, 137,
 138, **169**, 179, 180, 191, 192,
 207, 216, 218, 238, 248, **273**,
 332
Napier J. S. - 248
Napier-Campbell - 16
Napier-Railton - 345, **346**, 349
Nash - 162, **273, 320,** 368
Nash W. Charles - 161, 170, 271,
 272
National Benzole Company Ltd. - 27
National - 56, 281
National Hot Rod Association - 228
Nazzaro Biagio - 309
Nazzaro Felice - 109, 119, 169, **186**,
 186, 208, 209, 210, 214, 216,
 218, **223**, 231, 238, 253
Newby C. A. - 263
Newcomen Thomas - 6
Newton (Sir) Isaac - 5, **6**, 6
Nibel Hans - 329, 344, 347
Nissan - 379
Nixon John C. - **62**
Nobel - **357**
Nordhoff Heinz - 360
"Nouvelle" - 41, 47
NSU - **167**, 167, 379
Nuffield (Lord) - 180
Nuvolari Tazio - 249, 333, 335, 336,
 337, 345, 349

O

Oakland - **121**, 272, **274**
"Obéissante" (l') - 12
"Oeuf de Pâques" - 108
Officine Meccaniche of Milan - 188
Ohio Company - 77
Oldfield Barney - 16, 115, 116, 266
"Old Pacific" - 75
Oldsmobile - **40**, 72, 73, **80, 112,**
 115, 116, **143**, 145, **158**, 160,
 205, 272, **343**, 359, 363, 368,
 378
Olds Motor Works - 164
Olds Ransom Eli - **40**, 72, 75, 116,
 159
O. M. - **137**, 188
Opel - **39**, 99, **102, 126, 163**, 214,
 232, 237, 238, **263, 281, 286**,
 293, **329**, 329, **342**, 349, 355,
 360, 377
Opel Adam - 65
Opel-Darracq - 146
Orio & Marchand - 63
OSI - **3**
Otav - 139
Otto Nikolaus August - 13, 14, **15**,
 19, 20, 28, 29
Otto Wilhelm - 14, 19, 34, 35
Oury - **100**, 100, **103**

Overland - 45, 269
Owen - 138, 367
Oxford (Morris) - **305**

P

Packard - 75, 77, 83, 145, 164, 169,
 281, 296, 320, 334, 368
Packard James Ward - 77
Palladium - 290
Palombella - 188
Panhard - 36, 99, 100, 101, **102**, 102,
 103, 104, 108, 109, 118, 130,
 139, 165, 194, 222, 287, 360,
 367, 367, 376
Panhard René - 31, 46
Panhard-Levassor - 31, **32**, 32, **33**,
 33, 34, **36**, 36, 42, 49, **52**, 55,
 57, 58, 60, 62, 93, 109, **130**,
 154, **164**, 164, 183, 194, **195**,
 207, 211, 253, 266, 302, **352**
Park - 44
Paris-Amsterdam race - **52**, 86, 93
Paris-Berlin race - 101
Paris-Bordeaux race - 44, 47, 99, **100**
Paris-Madrid race - 129, **130**, 131,
 137, **138**
Paris-Marseilles race - 41, 47, 48,
 52, 60
Paris-Rouen race - 35, 36, 45, 47
Paris-Toulouse-Paris race - 100
Paris-Vienna race - **103**, 103, 107,
 108, 129, 137
Parnell Reg - 345, 366
Parry M. David - 45
Parry Thomas J. G. - 16, 331
"Passe-Partout" - 109, 191
Pathfinder - 45, 281
Pecori Enrico - **34**, 40, 41
Peerless - 138
Pegaso - **364**
Pekin-Paris race - **11**, 11, 75, 195
Pennington E. - 39, 40, 175
Peraire G. - 35
Percy Lambert - 218
Périn - 31
Perrot Henry - 61, 227
Perry - **264**
"Petite Rosalie" - 338
Peugeot - 33, **36**, 36, 41, 42, 45, 47,
 52, 55, 58, **63, 74, 85, 88, 121**,
 138, 163, 170, 185, 218, 222,
 242, 243, 245, **261**, 266, 282,
 287, **291**, 296, **300**, 301, **310**,
 319, 328, 334, 336, 338, **342**,
 343, 351, 355, 358, 368, 377
Peugeot Léon - **48, 150, 168**
Peugeot-Daimler - **21**, 47, 48
Phoénix - 96
Pia - 31
Piccard-Pictet - 294, **295**
Pigozzi H. T. - 338
Piper Henri - 65
Pierce-Arrow - **334**, 334
Pierry - 208
Pignone-Hag - 154
Pininfarina - **119**, 360
Pinson - 101
"Pirate" - 115

Pirelli - 199
Pittsburgh Motor Vehicle Company
 - 76
Plantard - 35
Planté - 44
Plymouth - 331
Pobjeda - 363
Point - 334
Pons - 200
Pontiac - **367**
Ponts - 195
Pope A. Albert - 163, 164
Pope Manufacturing Company -
 76, 269
Pope-Toledo - 169, 170, 253
Popp V. - 35
Porsche - 310, 344, 347, 378
Porsche Ferdinand - 241, 308, 362
Porter - 133, 136
Pouchain - 44
Premier - 282
Prince - 379
Prince Henry of Prussia - 240
Prince of Sweden - 4
Prince of Wales - 59
Prince Philip - 212
Princess Margaret - 212
Prinetti & Stucchi - 62, 63, 93
Prosper-Lambert - 181
Protos - 201, **202,** 202
Pullinger Thomas Charles - 118

Q

Queen Alexandra - **161**
Queen Elena - 188

R

Rackhan H. Horace - 145
Raffalovich - 254, 255
Railton - 16, **352**
Rambler - 238
Raush - 169
"Rapide" - 41
Read Nathan - 8
"Red Devil" - 139
Red Flag Act - 9, 58, **60**, 71
"Régie Renault" - 366
Reithmann - 20
Renault - 42, **44, 48**, 55, 57, 85, 93,
 101, 101, 102, **103**, 104, **107**,
 108, **112, 118**, 118, 119, **126**,
 130, 132, **134, 150**, 154, 181,
 184, 207, 208, 209, 210, 212, **212**,
 212, 227, **230, 244, 250**, 253,
 254, 255, **275, 280**, 287, **289**,
 301, **303, 323, 328**, 336, 342,
 343, **346**, 355, 356, 376, 380
Renault Fernand - **131**, 132
Renault Frères - 183
Renault Louis - 42, 99, **100**, 100,
 104, 107, 130, 131, 132, 181,
 355
Renalt Marcel - 42, **44**, 99, **100**, 100,
 104, 108, 118, 130, 132, 136,
 181

PICTURE CREDITS

Abarth, Alfa Romeo, Ansafoto, Antony Nowarth, Aston Martin, Audie Photo, Austin, Austin-Healey, Autobianchi, Auto-Union, Bentley, Bizzarrini, BMW, British Petroleum, Brunaud, Civica Raccolta Bertarelli, Citroën, DAF, Daimler, Derek Livemore, De Tomaso, Eastern Press, Ediprint, ENI, Ewin Galloway, Farabola, Ferrari, Fiat, Ford, General Motors, Ken Phillip, Innocenti, ISO, Jaguar, Lamborghini, Lancia, Lotus, Maserati, Mercedes, MG, Montagu Motor Museum, Morris, National Benzole Company Ltd., News Blitz, NSU, Opel, Opera Mundi, Palnic, Peugeot, Photo Service, Porsche, Publifoto, Renault, Rochetaillée Motor Museum, Rolls Royce, Rome War Museum, Rover, Royal Automobile Club, Saab, Shell, Sibilia, Simca, Skoda, Soblisky, Sunbeam, The Telegraph, Triumph, Turin Motor Museum, Vauxhall, Volvo, Volkswagen, Votava.

This book was designed and produced by
EDIPRINT - Via Caboto 35 - 10129 Turin - Italy

———————

The book was printed by Stig - Turin - Italy

Paper supplied by Cartiera del Sole - Milan - Italy

Bound by Legatoria Industriale - Turin - Italy